RUILDING

MANAGING PEOPLE

IN

CONSTRUCTION

Dr Janet Druker MA is currently director of research in the Business School at the University of Greenwich, and is co-ordinator of the Flexibility in Employment Group. Her recent research has focused on employment and contractual relationships within the construction industry, and she is the author of a report published by the Small Business Research Trust early in 1996 on work status and self-employment in construction. In the 1980s she worked for the Union of Construction Allied Trades and Technicians, where she was head of research, and she has also worked for the University of Warwick. More recently she has been employed elsewhere in higher education. She is co-author of *Croner's Pay and Benefits Sourcebook*, *The Personnel Assistant's Handbook*, and the forthcoming *Croner's Employee Relations* looseleaf. She is a Fellow of the IPD.

Geoff White MA is currently head of the Management Studies Group at the University of Greenwich, and is a member of the Flexibility in Employment Group there. His research interests are reward management and public-sector industrial relations. He has worked on several IPD projects, including publications on competitive tendering and contract compliance in the public sector, and customer care. He was employed by Incomes Data Services for many years as head of their Public Sector Unit, and was later managing editor for research publications. He is co-author of *Croner's Pay and Benefits Sourcebook*. His MA, from the University of Warwick, is in industrial relations. He is a Fellow of the IPD and editor of the IPD's *Public Sector Review*.

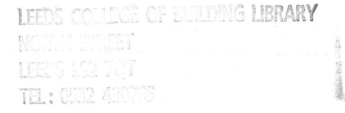

The Institute of Personnel and Development is the leading publisher of books and reports for personnel and training professionals and students and for all those concerned with the effective management and development of people at work. For full details of all our titles please telephone the Publishing Department on 0181 263 3387.

MANAGING PEOPLE
IN

CONSTRUCTION

JAN DRUKER
AND
GEOFF WHITE

INSTITUTE OF PERSONNEL AND DEVELOPMENT

Designed by Paperweight
Typeset by Action Typesetting, Gloucester
Printed in Great Britain by
The Cromwell Press, Wiltshire

British Library Cataloguing in Publication Data

A catalogue record for this book is available from the
British Library

ISBN 0-85292-642-1

INSTITUTE OF PERSONNEL
AND DEVELOPMENT

IPD House, Camp Road, London SW19 4UX
Tel: 0181 971 9000 Fax: 0181 263 3333
Registered office as above. Registered Charity No. 1038333
A company limited by guarantee. Registered in England No. 2931892

CONTENTS

ロ ロ ロ

ACKNOWLEDGEMENTS

There are many people who have assisted us in writing this book. Firstly thanks are due to the secretary and members of the Construction Group of Personnel Managers for their encouragement.

We would like also to extend personal thanks to the many people who have given us the benefit of their time and knowledge. In particular thanks are due to Martin Arnott (CITB), Allan Black (GMB), Peter Blackburn (Shepherd Construction), Michael Brown (CIOB), George Brumwell (UCATT), Betty Cairns (ECA), Andrea Cowling (Cowling Construction & Maintenance), Rob Cathcart (UCATT), David Chapman (FCEC), Richard Clayton (Spectrum Electrical Group), Karl Critchley (Tarmac Construction – Team 2000), Frank Duggan (Tarmac Construction), Richard Fitzgerald (Mowlem Training), John Foreman (Shepherd Construction), Claire Gummer (Biwater International Ltd), John Hanley (Mace Construction), Peter Harlow (CIOB), Roy Hay (Tarmac Construction – Team 2000), George Henderson (TGWU), Tony Hetherington (HSE), Chris Hudson (W.S. Atkins – Engineering and Management Divisions), Kathy Jackson (Drivers Jonas), Howard Jones (Amec Construction), Roger Leverson (Pearce Construction), Jane Lord (Tarmac plc), Iris Lyle (WAMT), Jackie Mollinson (self-employed carpenter), Steven Moon (BEC), John Murphy (Bovis), Chris Peek (W.S. Atkins – Engineering and Management Divisions), Ray Ryan (Mansell Construction), Peter Rimmer (HVCA), Lou Sampson (National Joint Council for the Engineering Construction Industry), Adrian Sprague (Kvaerner Construction), Mike Ward (Mowlem Construction), Graham Winch (Bartlett School of Architecture and Planning), and Ken Wright (Bovis).

Finally, thanks are due to Jane Cunningham of the University of Greenwich for help with learning resources, and to June Washer, also of the University of Greenwich, for administrative support. Special thanks are due to Matthew Reisz of the Institute of Personnel and Development for his support for this book.

CHAPTER 1

THE CONSTRUCTION INDUSTRY AND ITS PEOPLE

This chapter poses the question that provides a theme for the book: to what extent can the changing attitudes and practices which are associated with the term 'human resource management' be of interest and value to people who work within the construction industry? It sets the context for the discussion of the construction industry by identifying the importance of construction – in terms of output, and in terms of its size as an employer. The chapter assesses the implications of the volatility of construction activity for human resource planning, looks at changing practices in human resource management as a background for discussion of the construction firm, and considers the size of firms, the interdependent relationship of large and small firms, and associated changes in strategy and structure. It concludes with some comments on changing contracting practice and the importance of sub-contractors within the industry. Many of these issues will be familiar to readers who are already working in construction, but they are discussed here in order to identify the need for change in employment practices that is becoming more apparent within the industry.

We conclude with a case study of change in human resource management in Drivers Jonas.

Construction provides work for 7 per cent of all male employees, and for one in four of all self-employed people. In addition it generates employment in a range of activities in associated areas of manufacturing – for example, in building materials and plant. It is a key industry in terms of its size as an employer and, moreover, it is one that will not go away. Unlike some other industries which seem set to decline and never to be revived, construction will continue to be an important domestic employer in the year 2000 and beyond.

The construction industry is unusual in the demands it puts upon the people who work within it. The cyclical nature of investment means that it is insecure and unemployment is consistently higher than in other sectors. Employment is often project-based so that mobility from project to project is an inherent part of many jobs. Physical working conditions are harder than in other sectors, and the risks of accident or work-related problems are higher. Yet the degree of job control and the element of creativity may be higher too, with the added satisfaction of a visible and tangible result for the effort that is put in. Although a lot of emphasis is placed on financial benefits, rewards for the individual may be intrinsic as much as extrinsic. People are important to success in a very real sense. There is something in the nature of the work, in the product, in the recognition of the importance of individual skill to the success of a project, which can provide satisfaction and a pride in work undertaken – at a whole range of different levels within the industry.

The importance of the construction workforce is highlighted by the fact that the industry relies on skill and on the capacity to bring different skills together effectively. Each construction project relies on teamworking and co-operation. Whether it is a large site or a relatively small project, successful completion to time and to price requires co-ordination, initiative and independence from the workforce (Hillebrandt, 1990). The growing concern with quality as well as with productivity, coupled with the renewed quest for partnerships, both with suppliers and with clients, lends a new importance to the retention, development and reward of the construction workforce. Sub-contractors who are seeking closer links or more regular contacts with larger contractors are reliant on the specialist skills and knowledge which they can bring to a contract. There is a growing recognition that what the industry has to sell is bound up with specialist knowledge and expertise, and that organisations do not commend themselves to clients or to partners by a casual attitude to employment or to management.

The construction industry is defined as comprising new construction work, general construction and demolition work, the construction and repair of buildings, civil engineering, the installation of fixtures and fittings, and building completion work. Direct labour establishments of local authorities and

2

government departments are included (Revised 1980 Standard Industrial Classification, cited in *Housing and Construction Statistics, 1984–94*).

The industry embraces activity in new building projects and in rehabilitation and modernisation. It undertakes work for clients both in the public and in the private sector, providing buildings for industrial and commercial use, as well as to meet domestic need. Organisational structure and relationships are governed within the private sector by the competitive contractual process, which requires each project to be subjected to competitive tender, a process said to have become fiercer in recent years. The volume of activity within the public sector has shrunk as public industries have been privatised and the size of direct labour or direct service organisations has diminished.

The construction professions are well established: professional associations govern entrance and accreditation for individuals. Craft skills still play an important part in the overall construction process, and although their significance may have diminished in the face of initiatives to standardise work tasks, their importance has not been removed. Technological innovation has proved less readily applicable to the construction process than to other industries, and craft-based occupations are still widespread – although only a minority of the workforce could claim to have served a traditional apprenticeship as an entry route into employment. The industry is still perceived, according to some commentators, as a 'father-to-son' industry, boys following their fathers into a male-dominated preserve. The majority of entrants to the manual workforce acquire their skills through experience, sometimes with family support, rather than through formal training.

Construction activity

The level of new orders for construction work is dependent on the wider economy and on the choices available to the industry's clients – both in the public and the private sector. Inevitably, interest rates and the level of public expenditure play an important part, and although the level of demand was high towards the end of the 1980s, it never equalled that of the 1960s and early 1970s. In figure 1 we show the volume of new construction orders since the late 1950s, highlighting fluctuations in activity and the long-term decline in house-building.

Figure 1   *Volume of new construction orders by contractors: Great Britain, 1990 prices*

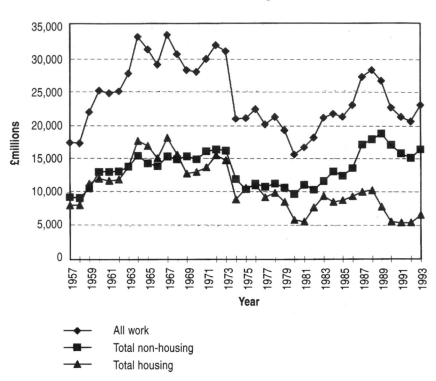

—◆— All work
—■— Total non-housing
—▲— Total housing

Source: Department of the Environment: *Digest of Data for the Construction Industry, 1995.*

Contractors, sub-contractors, suppliers, employees and the self-employed have had to adjust to fewer and more limited opportunities within the UK, and in the wake of insolvencies, redundancies and insecurity many people have left the industry, probably never to return. Some parts of the industry are particularly dependent on government expenditure – road building, for example, still relies to a large extent on government for its finance, despite intensive debate about the potential for private finance initiatives. The balance of activities within the industry will vary over time. Renovation and rehabilitation were important in the 1980s, as was activity in the commercial sector, but these areas, like others, were affected by the downturn of the early 1990s.

What is important is that this instability in activity limits the

4

capacity of contractors, sub-contractors and those who make their living within the industry, to plan and to co-ordinate their resources in the medium term. The concept of 'human resource planning' (discussed more fully in Chapter 3) is developed within the field of human resource management to enable enterprises to forecast the level and the nature of their activities over the months and years ahead, and to develop the balance of their human resources accordingly. Human resource planning requires the capacity to forecast skills needs and to respond through recruitment or through employee development to ensure that they are met. Even 'scenario planning' – a less precise and more flexible variant of human resource planning – is rendered difficult within construction, where firms both large and small are unwilling to bear the overhead costs of labour in a highly variable product market. Redundancies and downsizing have been recurrent themes for many construction firms. Uncertainty about future contracts has been compounded by cash-flow problems and a reduced capacity to sustain employment levels where workflow has diminished. Where organisations are successful in bidding for work, they often confront labour requirements after the event – with the inherent risk of skill shortages as a consequence.

Changes in human resource management

There has been a significant change in the language and the practice of management over the last decade. Ideas imported from the United States of America have seen a shift in the terminology of human resource management (HRM) to a clearer focus on the relationship between business requirements and employee behaviour (Guest, 1987). Competitive pressures have led to greater concern with quality and productivity and a new emphasis on the contribution that can be realised with more positive workforce attitudes. The central contention of these debates is that the new competitive environment requires a more strategic and concerted approach to personnel management – that, in the words of the 'Excellence' school (see for example Peter and Waterman, 1982; Peters and Austin, 1985), commitment from the workforce is more effective than compliance, and that people should no longer be treated as a 'cost' but as a company's greatest 'asset'.

Not all of this vision is actually realised, of course. Within the wider world of employment there have been many innovations

5

in the management of people. They have often begun with 'downsizing', 'outsourcing' and 're-engineering'. These phenomena have been widespread, but in many cases they have been only a prerequisite to other forms of change. Employers, whichever sector they are engaged in, having reduced their workforce size want to know that the employees who remain are contributing to the changing enterprise in the most effective way possible towards the realisation of business objectives. Total quality management, quality circles, empowerment, the development of the 'learning organisation' and other comparable initiatives, were introduced to achieve such objectives.

The coherence of a strategic approach to human resource management (HRM) and the extent of a new flexibility in employment practice has been questioned by academic researchers within the UK (Storey and Sisson, 1990; Guest, 1990), but there is no doubt that employment policies are changing. Storey (1992) conducted extensive research across a number of industries, including motor manufacture, engineering, food manufacture, the health sector, and local government. He concluded that there is no one standard formula for managing change, but pointed to a number of distinctive aspects of change which emerged in different sectors. The management of labour through collectivist structures has less prominence as collectivism gives way to individualism. There is also a greater stress on the initiative of line managers, and their potential enabling and empowering role.

Some of the themes that emerge in practice are shown in the box opposite.

HRM is seen as distinctive because of its holistic approach to management, such that personnel issues are given closer attention by line managers, who are expected to be more pro-active in approach to the way in which they manage people. Human resource management can be 'hard' – focusing on the cost or 'resource' dimension of human resource management; or it can be 'soft' – emphasising the importance of the 'human' input (Guest, 1989).

Within the practical approaches explored by Storey, the emphasis is placed on the integration of different themes, so that a changing approach to business objectives and culture may well be accompanied by more careful attention to recruitment and a new interest in performance management, with the possibility of greater opportunity for training. In some cases

Human resource planning, recruitment and deployment
Use of part-time, temporary and sub-contract labour
Variation in working hours – eg annual hours contracts
Diminished job boundaries – moves to multi-skilling
Reduced number of job grades
Emphasis on new forms of work organisation – eg Just in Time (JIT)
Teamworking and new roles for supervisors
Encouraging workforce to go 'beyond contract'
'Competence-based recruitment'

Employee development
'Competence-based' qualifications
Modular study/accreditation processes
Career break schemes
Psychometric testing – use of assessment centres
Increased use of consultant packages
Greater emphasis on management skills – role of manager as facilitator
Emphasis on individual responsibility to initiate development
Innovative forms of learning – eg open learning
Accommodation of new technology
Ensuring a customer focus in activities

Employee motivation
Culture change – the 'can do' organisation
Individualisation of reward – moves away from collective bargaining in some cases
Goal-setting through appraisal – emphasis on measurable targets
Introduction of variable pay, including performance-related, competence pay and profit-related pay
Reduced significance of incremental pay spines
Emphasis on communications – team briefings,
Devices to encourage 'employee involvement' – eg quality circles
Harmonisation of working conditions of different categories of staff

companies may match these initiatives with other changes. These may include accreditation as an Investors in People (IIP) company, the introduction of or with changes in arrangements for variable pay, and new forms of employee communication or teamworking.

Our case study of Drivers Jonas at the end of this chapter provides a practical example of human resource management initiatives within the construction sector.

Construction firms

Our consideration of change in the construction industry must begin with some attention to company size. The industry is notable for its mix of large and small firms (using 'large' and 'small' to denote numbers in employment). There are very few large firms and a high proportion of small firms, and the disparity between the two has become more marked in recent years, medium-sized firms declining in significance. For many years it was assumed that the size of organisations would grow, but by the 1980s it was clear that there was a diminution in the number of the largest firms – that is, those with 1,200 or more employees – from 39 in 1983 to 33 in 1993 (Department of the Environment, 1995: 124).

The largest firms are well-known, but they are often part of a huge empire which undertakes a mix of activities sometimes only partly related to construction. Companies such as Tarmac and Amec undertake a complex range of activities within their portfolio, including such areas as property development and quarrying as well as aspects of manufacturing. Yet many of the other activities support, or are in their turn supported by, the important construction processes. Balfour Beatty, for example, which engages in a range of civil engineering and construction work, is an important part of the BICC Group, which is notable for its cabling interests, whereas the P&O group, which owns management contractor Bovis, benefits from the high turnover of their subsidiary operation.

Mergers and acquisitions continue to be a concern, notably in the acquisition of Trafalgar House Construction Ltd by the Norwegian company Kvaerner in 1996, to create Kvaerner Construction Ltd. There has been some rationalisation within the larger contracting firms (for example, the exchange of housing and quarrying divisions between Wimpey and Tarmac towards the end of 1995), but there has been some diversification too. Facilities management, for example, has attracted the attention of some of the larger players in the industry and may seem to be a logical extension of the renovation, modernisation and repair which falls under the heading of construction activity.

Competition from European contractors, which was little known within the domestic UK market 10 years ago, cannot now be ignored: some of the major UK firms which experienced problems during the recession have been acquired by contractors from the mainland of Europe. Privatisation of the utilities offered an opportunity for European competitors to acquire a UK base, so that the major European players – such as Bouygues or the Société Générale des Eaux (SGE) from France, or Hochtief or Holzman from Germany – are now to be found in the UK, in the utilities or property sectors, in construction, or in a combination of these. Rules on public procurement have opened up contracts in the UK to competitors from the mainland, and the largest contracts (for example, the Channel Tunnel and the new Severn Bridge) have involved consortia which include contractors from there. Although this European intervention may have been weaker than some commentators anticipated in the late 1980s, there is nonetheless evidence of a more concentrated effort being made by non-UK interests – including some Japanese contractors, who have followed major clients into the UK. Construction is, now more than ever, a highly competitive business environment.

Family ownership and management in the construction industry has a long history because the capital requirements for starting up in the business were, traditionally, lower than in some other sectors. Many of the best-known firms pride themselves on their small beginnings. Taylor Woodrow, Wates, Mansell, Kyle Stewart, and many others began as family businesses, and in some construction firms family members still exert an important element of control or influence over major decisions. Family influence may mean that relationships within the firm are more continuous and more personal than in other organisations, but there can be a downside too, for in some cases there may be a more arbitrary or autocratic style of management. However, the family firm is less conspicuous today than in the past and, perhaps because of retirement or change of ownership, some of the companies which have been subject to family influence are making a transition in their management style, employing professional managers who are not family members, and seeking a culture change towards more open and perhaps less paternalistic approaches to management.

The number of large firms has declined and the position of medium-sized firms within the industry has been under pressure. Yet the number of smaller firms has grown, and small firms represent a very important part of the industry. In 1984 there were 169,999 firms in the industry, of which 71,386 (42 per cent of the total) were one-person operations and 81,614 employed between two and seven people. By 1994 there was a total of 194,657 firms, but 97,141 (nearly 50 per cent) were single-person businesses and 87,333 – that is, nearly 45 per cent of the total – employed between two and seven people. Overall, the number of businesses with seven or fewer employees within the industry rose to almost 95 per cent of the total by 1994, and in that year only 1.6 per cent of construction firms employed 25 people or more (*Housing and Construction Statistics, 1984–94*: 35).

Smaller firms may operate within a limited geographical area, serving local needs. These are genuine small entrepreneurs, undertaking work for their own clients. However, many of the smaller to medium-sized firms are in effect sub-contractors to main contractors – working either as specialist sub-contractors or as labour-only sub-contractors (LOSC) who take no responsibility for supplying materials.

If the growth in the number of small firms suggests that business opportunities improved over the decade 1984–94, so too did the threats. Smaller firms in construction have been operating in a hostile environment in which the sub-contracting process and the pressures of cash-flow problems have been acutely felt. Whereas 12.4 per cent of UK companies were involved in construction in 1993, 15.4 per cent of all insolvencies in that year were in construction – many of them small firms. The number of insolvencies rose dramatically from 1988, as Figure 2 demonstrates (*Housing and Construction Statistics, 1984–94*: 36).

Although the number of large firms is lower now, as a proportion of the whole, than it was at the beginning of the 1980s, the smaller players have not gained any advantages within the competitive race for contracts. If anything, it seems that some of the developments which were expected to benefit the smaller

Figure 2   Insolvencies and bankruptcies

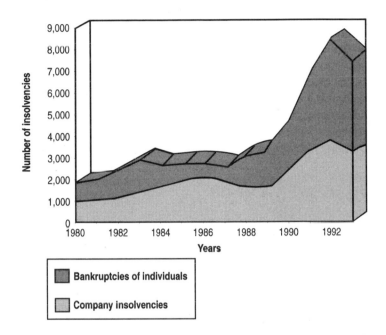

Source of data: Department of the Environment, *Digest of Data for the Construction Industry* (2nd ed.), 1995.

player have in fact confirmed the power and influence of larger contractors. Larger firms compete with the small or medium-sized firm by bidding for contracts of a lower value than in the past, because the number of large contracts has diminished. Although privatisation and compulsory competitive tendering were expected to benefit the smaller firm by generating opportunities to compete for work formerly done within the public sector, there are complaints that the work is packaged in such a way as to predispose the client to larger contractors – for example, by putting together a number of smaller contracts to make one large contract. Clients both in the public and in the private sector find that it is not cost-effective to manage a significant number of contracts, so they package them in such a way

11

that the number is reduced. There are local authorities and water authorities, for example, who have rationalised the management of commercial contractors by utilising fewer contracts which, inevitably, are larger in value, so inhibiting the capacity of the smaller firm to compete.

In fact, the share of work is tilted in favour of the larger contractors. The top 32 companies (that is, those with over 1,200 employees) claimed nearly 12 per cent of the volume of work done in 1994. Conversely, the single-person businesses – 50 per cent of the total number of businesses – did less than 10 per cent of the work in that year (*Housing and Construction Statistics*: 35, 37).

The role of the public sector

Local authorities have a number of duties which must be supported by construction activity. Traditionally, local authorities employed their own direct labour organisations to tackle the construction activities involved in the maintenance and improvement of properties for which they were responsible. The introduction of compulsory competitive tendering from the 1980s means that local authorities now differentiate between their roles as client and as provider of construction services. Contracts are awarded in open competition between the private sector and local authority direct service organisations, and there has been a significant reduction in public sector activity.

Because of financial pressures and the statutory obligation to tender for work, the public sector now employs fewer people in construction services than at any time in the last 20 years. The traditional contribution made by the public sector to training has been reduced, but the local authorities in particular still represent an important, though much smaller, component in construction activity.

Strategy and structure

'The only advantage that you can gain is in the quality of people on site.'

Personnel Director

The largest construction firms have sought to rationalise and to simplify structures during the 1990s, divesting themselves of activities which are not central to the business. They have tended to shed less profitable activities or those deemed not to be core. They are competing on cost, on market differentiation, and on the capacity to respond flexibly to client requirements – with an emphasis on repeat business for private sector clients.

Strategy and focus vary from firm to firm, but a major contractor typically operates in a number of product areas, grouped into major product divisions, which in their turn are subdivided into regions. Each product division has a significant degree of independence of the main business, subject to overall financial controls, and its regions may operate as strategic business units for all contracts below a certain level or value (although this pattern may be amended for contracts of higher value, or if a client is perceived to be particularly important for the company as a whole – for example, because of the regularity of contracts or the possibility of repeat contracts).

In the larger firms, management is typically devolved to strategic business units. It is the managers at this lower level who have the primary responsibility for winning contracts and for running them successfully to time and to cost. Planning, estimating, purchasing and project management are key to this process, and responsibilities for staffing may be delegated to regional level because staffing is seen as a downstream activity following on from decisions about cost. In smaller firms, managers take a wide range of responsibilities because firm size may not allow for functional specialisation.

In every case the award of a contract requires decisions on how the project is to be staffed. Control of the project and management of the construction process is a major issue, and one of the first considerations will be the selection of people and the creation of a team. Key issues in forming the team are those of quality and of product delivery to time and to customer satisfaction. Technical and management expertise are put into place on a scale that is appropriate for the project's value and complexity.

Contracts
A determining feature of relations in the construction sector is the short-term nature of each project – employment within the UK often being defined in accordance with project requirements. Contracts are awarded on the basis of competitive bidding, and although price is not necessarily the sole criterion, it may weigh heavily in the decision. One of the responses to risk and recession has been the more widespread use of sub-

contractors, allowing contractors to download responsibilities for the construction process onto sub-contractors. It is a process which reduces the in-house responsibility for management, and it allows contractors to benefit from the particular knowledge and expertise of specialist sub-contractors. On the other hand, in replacing an employment contract (with employees) with a commercial contract (with sub-contractors), it poses the dual requirement that sub-contractors be effectively managed, and that they, in their turn, manage their workforce in the most effective way (Ball, 1988).

New forms of contract (such as those for management contracting and construction management) which became more widespread from the 1980s had important implications for who was managing whom. Major contractors redefined their role as managers of the contract, devolving operational responsibilities to sub-contractors. Although these new forms of contract are by no means universal, it is clear that the range and volume of work which is sub-contracted has been extended, and that sub-contractors play an increasingly important part within the industry. The management of people is now the job of sub-contractors as much as main contractors, and there are few requirements or obligations placed on them by the contractors, other than with respect to health and safety.

The implications of the changing structure of the industry
The changing structure of the industry provides new opportunities for effective people management through a smaller organisational size and a more specialist workforce. Within most organisations it is likely that employment has by now been cut to such an extent that those who remain have key skills and expertise which are needed for the company's business. This would seem to provide a basis for the development of some of the 'softer' techniques of human resource management (Druker *et al*, 1996). In such a case some thought should be given to how such people – staff or operatives – can be retained, re-motivated and developed in the most effective way for the future.

Questions of 'people management' may in the past have seemed a luxury that the industry could not afford (Winch, 1994). Indeed, the construction industry seemed to pioneer some of the techniques associated with the 'harder' versions of human resource management, in the form of sub-contracting and outsourcing, precisely to avoid direct employment responsibilities. There are signs that, in some businesses, managers are rethinking their approach to the way in which people are managed and reconsidering the opportunities that can be generated by a more thoughtful and more integrated approach to human resource management. Preferred forms of contract highlight such changes – Private Finance Initiatives (PFI), for example, locate the contractor as the client of the construction process. This new approach brings a fresh interest in quality and a greater emphasis on getting things right first time.

Employees today are more educated and sophisticated than at any point in the past. It is the most effective of them who are likely to be lost to competitors if they are not provided with opportunities and rewards which ensure their retention. This is as true for key operatives as it is for the core groups of professional and managerial staffs. As skill shortages re-emerge, employers will need to review their practices and explore more innovative approaches to the reward and development of their in-house workforce.

In the chapters which follow we consider the range of issues which are central to such a review. We look at labour markets and at the question of self-employment within the industry, and offer a pathway through the problems of employment law and changing interpretation of taxation arrangements for self-employment. We consider questions of recruitment, selection, training and development. We look at the value for construction companies of accreditation through external bodies such as Investors in People. We explore the ways in which pay and benefits issues are handled, and consider too the management of employee relations and health and safety issues. And we conclude by shifting to the international plane, recognising the challenge and the problems of managing the expatriate workforce.

CASE-STUDY – Drivers Jonas

Drivers Jonas is the oldest firm of chartered surveyors in the UK. It was established in 1725 and advises on all aspects of commercial property. A partnership, it employs 230 people of whom about 170 are professional staff, including building surveyors and planners. The firm is committed to quality, both in terms of the people employed and the service offered.

Changes in human resource management were effected by means of a number of initiatives including employee development and Investors in People (IIP), with the aim of ensuring a stronger client focus for the firm.

Need for change

It was the recession which provided the motivation for change. In the late 1980s this firm, like almost every other in the property sector, was booming: there had been steady expansion throughout the 1980s. The recession hit Drivers Jonas at the end of the decade and was so long and so deep that it necessitated a major rethink. It was clear that only the most effective organisations would survive – and that, in order to be effective, the firm must be highly responsive to the demands of clients. As part of the process of change, Drivers Jonas focused intensively on the development of high-quality staff.

Training and development had been a commitment for some years, but from the early 1990s it became more focused on ensuring that it was valued by staff and that what was done was relevant to business needs. This in turn raised the question of staff involvement. At the end of 1992 all partners held a weekend workshop. They came out of that with three particular things they needed to do as a partnership: to motivate, to recognise, and to communicate more effectively with the staff.

The levers for change were provided through performance appraisal, through Investors in People (IIP), through improvements to communications, and via the introduction of profit-related pay.

Using appraisal

The process began with a review of the appraisal scheme which had been running for several years. It had taken a traditional form in the past, appraisers ticking boxes and retaining control over the process of performance review. The new appraisal scheme demanded greater staff involvement, requiring appraisees to set their own objectives within the framework of business goals. The substantial bonuses which had been a feature of the 1980s had ceased: there were no increases to pay over this period and no accompanying promise of improved pay rates or promotion opportunities.

A major staff benefit during this period derived from the new appraisal scheme which provided a mechanism whereby staff could take responsibility for their own career development, with training support from the firm to enable them to do so. The benefits were readily apparent to the staff involved. The initiative, which was launched early in 1993, followed redundancies and job cuts at the end of the previous year. The partners saw the new appraisal scheme as a means of recognising achievement, of procuring better and more open communication which would result in higher motivation. There were no claims that the process was perfect, but staff were asked for their support and involvement, and the resulting dialogue took the firm further than original plans had suggested.

One of these initiatives was a move towards quarterly rather than annual reviews of performance. People were setting goals and they needed to be kept under consideration. Although this involved time and effort, there was positive feedback from the people involved.

Because of the emphasis on training and development, the only budget which was not cut was the training budget – there was a belief that the company's future success lay in having the best trained and qualified staff. Training needs were identified at the corporate level as part of the business planning process. More specifically, individual employees were encouraged to set goals which were personally challenging and which required development at the individual level. Appraisees and the appraiser would agree goals and the associated training and development that was needed. It was not necessarily a question of formal or external training. Employee development could take the form of on-the-job coaching although it could equally be formal training. Overall, there was a more effective process for reconciling corporate and individual training needs with maximum scope for individual development.

Democratisation

This started to improve communications beyond the two staff meetings a year which had been a traditional feature of the company's communication policy. The management style had been caring and rather paternalistic in the past, but the competitive business climate necessitated a more innovative approach. As a partnership, the firm does not have to produce accounts, and in the 1980s business plans were not published. With a recognition of the need for change came an element of democratisation. Business plans were now published; people were given more financial information so that both the problems and the targets were clear. Staff were given a wider opportunity to bring in business, and in many cases were more demanding of themselves than their seniors in the company would have been. Marketing and sales skills as well as public relations assumed a new importance and an impetus which required full staff involvement.

From the point of view of individual staff members, the range and the pace of work intensified, with little immediate benefit in terms of pay or promotion prospects. What was clear, though, was that with unparalleled opportunities to train, they were more likely to remain in employment, and to become more skilled and effective than counterparts in other companies.

IIP

The move towards Investors in People followed naturally from these changes, for the company had already taken on many of the practices which would be expected by IIP – notably clarity in the establishment of business plans, effective procedures for employee appraisal, and a significant commitment to training and development. When the opportunity was presented, it seemed that a formal commitment to IIP involved a logical development of the initiatives already under way, particularly a review of the areas not yet given attention, primarily evaluation of the processes and outcomes which had been put in place. The firm's board gave approval to seeking IIP late in the Spring of 1993.

In September of the same year, an external review commented positively on the company's performance, suggesting that they were already 90 per cent of the way towards the IIP standard. The elements which required further attention were the provision of information given during induction and during the first three months of employment, and the process of evaluation. In December the company declared a formal commitment to achieving IIP. The next six months was spent putting in the additional processes needed to meet the standards – to link individual goals more tightly with business goals, and to make sure that training and development was genuinely needed and discourage employees from selecting courses just because they were available. The application for IIP recognition was made in July 1994. Assessment followed with outstandingly successful results, and by October 1994 the company had achieved IIP recognition.

Profit-related pay

IIP recognition was preceded by the introduction of profit-related pay. In the aftermath of the recession, things were looking more hopeful for the company. Profit-related pay was intended to reinforce the links between individual performance and company results, while providing a tax-efficient mechanism of giving people more money in their pockets. It was introduced as an addition, not as an alternative, to other forms of pay increase.

Profit-related pay is unusual in a partnership largely because there is no obligation on the partners to disclose profits. However, it is not unprecedented and, with support from external consultants, the company managed to achieve Inland Revenue approval for their scheme which was implemented in 1993.

Communications

Part of the preparation for IIP involved a review of, and improvements to, communications. The 'glossy' internal information sheet which had been published every two months was criticised as being too sanitised. People wanted something more relevant. The company changed to a monthly bulletin – less glossy and more immediate in terms of business information. The new bulletin still included social information about people in the organisation, but it also provided updates on business targets and new areas of work.

There had been significant rationalisation of organisational structure as part of the overall process of change. The move was from a pyramid structure to a flatter, delayered organisation structure – with one level of job titles removed. Within this new structure, more direct communication was initiated through team briefings, team leaders taking greater responsibility for communications.

The process of change

Drivers Jonas has moved from being a paternalistic but friendly firm to a more open, challenging and democratic organisation. The initiatives which were introduced – including changes to organisational size and structure, improved appraisal and development opportunities, and the introduction of IIP – were fundamentally inter-related, and corresponded to the partners' seeking greater involvement and commitment from their predominantly professional workforce.

The process of change has not been without its problems. Within Drivers Jonas, the staff work hard and they work long hours for no extra reward. Two years after the major changes were implemented there are few signs of a reduction in the pace of work. Employees' views are sought through upward feedback questionnaires and through face-to-face meetings with the managing partner. The employees say that it is a good firm to work for because training and development programmes are superb. But they also point out that it is a demanding firm in terms of quality and high standards, and that, viewed in the long term, there is a high level of pressure involved.

There are no final solutions to the problems of people management. Staff retention has the potential to become a problem in a tighter labour market unless skills acquisition is matched with a reward structure that fully recognises quality. Already senior managers recognise that they are vulnerable to losing the staff in whom they have made a significant investment. Efforts are in hand to reinstate the 'fun' element prevalent in the 1980s.

Yet the firm has emerged from a period of difficulty with a stronger staff base and a more client-focused approach.

The authors would like to thank Kathy Jackson and the management of Drivers Jonas for their help with this case study.

CHAPTER 2

LABOUR MARKETS – PLANNING AND FLEXIBILITY

Within this chapter we consider the different labour markets in the construction industry. The chapter begins by presenting an overview of the labour force and its composition and division by gender. It then highlights the different and overlapping labour markets, considering questions of human resource planning in relation to

❑ internal labour markets as they affect employment opportunities for administrative, professional managerial and clerical staffs, as well as for directly employed operatives

❑ external labour markets and the use of self-employed labour.

The chapter concludes with some guidance points on the use of self-employed labour, with particular reference to

❑ the question of taxation

❑ legal decisions.

Its purpose is to ensure that clear differences are made between people who are self-employed and those who are directly employed.

The construction industry is a major employer. There were 807,300 people employed within the industry as at March 1996, according to Labour Force Survey (LFS) figures (*Labour Market Trends*, July 1996). This figure includes those people who work in an operational capacity in local authority direct service organisations but it excludes the self-employed. Together with some 772,000 self-employed people in the industry in Great Britain it can be calculated that there is a total of some

21

1,579,300 individuals who make a living from construction activity – down from 1,832,000 in 1990. The numbers fluctuate in accordance with the level of activity in construction at any one time, for organisations within the UK tend to recruit and to shed labour in line with their immediate project-based needs.

A breakdown of employment to show the numbers of operatives and administrative, professional and managerial employees within the industry can be made using the Department of Environment's *Housing and Construction Statistics*[1]. The balance of employment is indicated in table 1. The workforce is divided between the public and private sectors, the public sector proportion playing a diminishing role. The industry is split between those who enter in a professional, managerial or technical capacity and those who make up the operative workforce – professional, managerial and administrative staffs constituting an increasing proportion of the employed workforce.

Table 1   Construction manpower (in thousands)

Year	Contractors: Operatives	APTC	Public authorities: Operatives	APTC	Other	All empl'd	Self-empl'd	All workforce
1985	556	213	169	84	64	1,086	470	1,556
1990	583	266	127	66	76	1,118	715	1,833
1995	350	200	88	39	70	747	613	1,360

APTC: Administrative, professional, technical and clerical staff
Source: Housing and Construction Statistics: 1983–93, and *1995* March quarter

The backgrounds, expertise and career expectations of the various groups which make up the construction workforce are very different, in terms of education and point of access to the industry, in terms of pay and benefits, and in terms of opportunities for training and continued professional development – points we return to in later chapters.

Professional, managerial and technical staffs tend nowadays to enter the industry from college or university. Company sponsorship and placement may be available while studying for a professional diploma or degree, or graduate traineeships may be found by those leaving university courses. Even quite small firms may have one or two such trainees, and there are more opportunities with larger firms. Graduate recruitment through the 'milk round' (touring the universities) is less common today than in the past.

Those entering the construction trades may have come in via modern apprenticeships or college training. They are, on the whole, less likely to have experienced formal training and more likely to acquire their skills in the process of doing the job.

Construction firms have, during the last decade, tended to operate in survival mode: cutting back on direct employment and retaining only those people who were visibly and actively engaged in current projects. Whereas other industries have seen a growth in interest in 'human resource management', and in association with it the question of human resource planning, there has within construction firms been a healthy scepticism about management 'fads' which may have conserved time and energies for survival.

However, construction firms and their employees could be losing out by failing to take advantage of practices which have become more commonplace in other industries.

What is human resource planning?
The oldfashioned term for the planning of human resource requirements was 'manpower planning', but the term 'human resource planning' (HRP) is more common today. This change in terminology does not just denote a change to reflect 'political correctness' – the new term suggests a more strategic and integrated approach to managing the employment requirements of an organisation.

The purpose of HRP is the design of 'schemes for the acquisition, development, management, organisation, and use of employees, so that, as with any other valued resource, they are deployed as effectively as possible to the achievement of organisation goals' (Torrington *et al*, 1991). Human resource planning is about the integration of all these activities so that they are mutually supportive and in line with the organisation's overall mission or philosophy. Whereas traditional manpower planning is about providing the right people with the right skills at the right time, HRP is about wider issues linked to the culture of the organisation – such as total quality management, performance management, customer care initiatives, and employment flexibility.

Human resource planning covers a number of areas of management activity:

❑ analysing and describing jobs and preparing person specifications

❑ assessing present and future employment needs

❑ forecasting labour supply and demand

❑ calculating labour turnover and wastage rates

❑ developing, operating and monitoring procedures for recruiting, selecting, promoting employees or terminating their employment

❑ ensuring employment law requirements are adhered to.

Internal labour markets

In the construction industry, human resource planning is relatively underdeveloped. Yet employment planning is crucial to the successful performance of the construction organisation. Four major issues characterise the approach of the industry to employment matters: casual labour, high labour turnover, inadequate selection processes and training, and the absence of specialist personnel managers and developed personnel systems (Ford et al, 1982). A study in 1978 noted that average levels of labour turnover in construction were roughly twice as high as the national average (EIU, 1978). The improvement of recruitment procedures and the adoption of routine personnel practices is key to improving performance in the industry.

Planning the professional and managerial workforce

Managerial, professional, technical and administrative employees constitute a significant part of the employed workforce – 36 per cent of all jobs in the private sector fall into one of these categories (200,000 out of 550,000 in April 1995, DOE figures). Staff numbers were cut significantly in the recession of the early 1990s, and although there was not a dramatic change in the number of private-sector APTC jobs over the period 1983–95, there are currently fewer such jobs in total because of the decline of the public sector. Employment for professional and related groups in the public authorities has seen a longer and more consistent downward trend, as we demonstrate in Figure 3. Budgetary constraints and the requirements of compulsory competitive tendering arrangements have taken their toll of the in-house provision of construction services.

Figure 3   Administrative, technical and clerical staffs employment

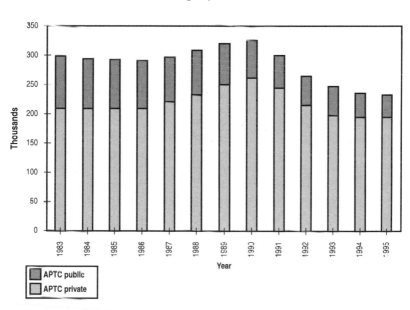

Source: Housing and Construction Statistics

Professional and technical employees include those who work as architects, builders, surveyors, estimators and engineers – occupations which typically require a university degree followed by a professional qualification. About one third of the employees within the APTC category might be in the area of clerical and sales staff. A further third will be managerial staff. And those employed as architects, surveyors and engineers would constitute less than 10 per cent of the total. This category of staff is key to the operations of all firms within the industry – both large and small – and employment opportunities for professionals and for managers exist across the range of firms, whatever their size. Recruitment is within a national labour market for the recognised professions and technical skills, and geographical mobility is an almost inevitable feature of the job for those whose work is primarily project-based.

Professional and managerial employees typically seek longer-term employment, with the expectation of remaining with one company for a period of at least several years (*Contract Journal*, 30 November 1995 survey).

Individual expectations for professionals at the point of entry into the industry encompass a notion of career progression – a concept which may be less reliable in application in the climate current in the 1990s than it has been in the past. In general it is still true that there are career lines for staff who can, with a combination of experience and enhancement of qualifications, seek progression internally within the organisation. Training and professional development have taken on an increasing importance for individuals in view of the lack of job security in recent years, so that younger employees may put a premium on training and development opportunities, particularly in the context of restrictions on pay increases. This may provide a mechanism for the retention of experienced employees.

White-collar occupations are not exempt from the high labour turnover associated with the industry. In the mid-1970s and early 1980s, civil engineering and building contractors' graduate retention rates were low. There was not only high mobility of such staff between construction firms but also a leakage of such graduates to other industries. The incidence of inter-firm mobility was relatively high compared to other industries (Young, 1991).

Research carried out in 1990 on the factors that affected the mobility of graduates in building and civil engineering found a number of trends. In their early professional life career-builders successively change jobs within an organisation, internal mobility being the main route to promotion. As a builder moves up the job hierarchy, promotion opportunities are reduced, especially in small and medium-sized companies, so that he or she begins to look beyond the current employer for career progression. Sometimes this relates to dissatisfaction with pay levels, or the degree of responsibility does not match reward and expectations. A comparatively high salary and prestigious company car are often the main attractions offered by other companies, and smaller firms simply cannot match the competitor offers. The research (Young, 1991) found that smaller firms are therefore resigned to a high turnover in managers. In comparison, the larger firms – operating in a number of product markets – are more able to accommodate their employees' aspirations. These companies can provide assignments overseas or in joint ventures as ways of retaining career momentum for junior and middle managers. Interestingly, compared to builders, civil engineers appeared to be more mobile across a career but were driven less by financial incentives. For civil engineers, personal growth and a sense of achievement appear more important factors in mobility than financial reward.

Companies need to replenish their stock of experienced staff, as well as recruit new entrants to the industry. In times of high economic activity in the industry, construction professionals and managers may move jobs frequently both to widen their experience and to increase their salary levels. In less buoyant periods companies may be reducing employment levels and movement, other than through redundancy, diminishes. Companies are usually keen to retain a core of experienced professionals and managers in order to compete for new contracts.

APTC employees have experienced considerable pressures and stresses in recent years, both because of the 'downsizing' tendency, which has been the most notable response to the recession, and because of the increased intensity of work which has accompanied staff reductions since the process of 'contracting-out' has added to or complicated the responsibilities of those whose job it is to manage sub-contractors and the sub-contracting process.

The experience of these groups has varied according to the nature of the occupation and the type of firm. The process of delayering is inevitably uncomfortable, and, for the individual, survival may not always be accompanied by a feeling of job security or confidence in his or her future within the firm.

Yet APTC employees are likely to represent an increased proportion of total employment in individual firms – largely because the process of 'contracting-out' has tended to encourage a disproportionate reduction in the numbers of directly employed operatives. Even in survival mode, construction firms may need to review the way in which this employment relationship is managed, not only to encourage the professional development (eg by study for membership of the Chartered Institute of Building) on which the organisation's reputation is made but also to ensure that, in a more positive employment climate, they do not lose the most effective and innovative members of their workforce.

Planning craft and operative requirements

According to one writer on human resource planning, 'The lack of appropriate data has resulted in very little research directed towards the development of labour supply forecasting models for the construction industry.' Much of the data available 'is unintelligible to companies, and instances abound of large projects being located in areas where there is insufficient labour to satisfy the demand generated' (Agapiou *et al*, 1995a).

The major method of dealing with skill shortages in the past has inevitably been to increase pay levels, leading to severe competition between firms and a consequent inflationary surge in labour costs. This leads in turn to a rise in construction prices and a downturn in demand which provides a temporary respite. Other methods of dealing with such shortages – such as the redesign of construction methods (eg new technology) or long-term planning of training needs – are relatively undeveloped (Agapiou *et al*, 1995a).

The Construction Industry Training Board (CITB) has its own computerised model which charts labour requirements against the prevailing economic factors and the projections for the industry's total workload. Statistical data on the supply of particular construction skills is more problematical to find. It is very difficult to assess how many trained craft workers are either unemployed or working outside the industry at any one time. Anecdotal accounts suggest that construction labour tends to materialise when demand picks up, as skill shortages on site push up pay levels and attract workers back into the industry. These workers may be either previously unemployed or those who have taken jobs in other industries. Despite this trend, there is also evidence of a general seepage of more mature employees out of the industry as older craft workers find more secure and perhaps less strenuous jobs as maintenance staff in private companies or in public sector direct service organisations. A further problem is that skills deteriorate when unused. In addition, many of these potential recruits from the ranks of the unemployed and other industries do not have the necessary skills for modern fast-track construction projects.

Apart from this general problem of the wastage of trained workers from the industry, current employment planning is complicated by demographic trends (fewer young people to recruit) and the increase in the numbers of young people staying on in education, leaving a substantial shortfall in recruits to the industry. This means that construction firms will have to seek alternative sources of labour (including upgrading existing operatives, attracting more women, more ethnic minorities, and more male adult retrainers), which in turn raises issues about the industry's public image as an employer. Skill shortages vary from region to region and organisations will need to be aware of the labour supply in their own locality, although there is also a tradition of labour mobility between regions.

Women in construction

One striking feature of labour force composition is the gender profile – despite some efforts by the Construction Industry Training Board, by professional and training institutions, by some employers and trade unionists, and by women's groups, the industry remains male-dominated from the boardroom through to the site. It is a fact taken for granted by most people in the industry on a day-to-day basis, yet it is surprising, for construction employers and their representatives regularly complain of skill shortages and of the quality of manpower available to them. Less than 17 per cent of the labour force is female, according to LFS data for March 1996, yet this figure disguises a still sharper differentiation in employment patterns, in that women work predominantly in clerical and administrative positions, with some representation at professional level but very little presence amongst manual workers.

The position seemed to be changing during the 1980s, when many local authorities operated positive employment policies through contracts compliance. However, the decline in employment opportunities in the public sector, the reduced size of many direct service organisations, and government restrictions on contracts compliance have all undermined such initiatives. Housing associations, like local authorities, have created some employment opportunities for women, but many tradeswomen find it easier to take up the opportunities of self-employment, particularly as jobbing builders, rather than to struggle to prove their skills and their capability on site (*Women and Manual Trades*, 1995).

In the past it may have been said that women lacked the physical stamina or strength to work in construction. But women who have worked on site often identify their difficulties in terms of the social relationships on site rather than complaining of the heavy work. The harassment and the isolation for the 'token' woman may be an impediment to remaining within the industry. In general, private-sector employers have not latched on to the advantages of expanding their recruitment networks to include women. They are therefore depriving themselves of the talents of those skilled tradeswomen who already work within the industry and of half of the population of school leavers every year. Skill shortages and the diminution in the number of 16-year-olds who leave full-time education and who are therefore available to enter the industry through traditional training routes should encourage them to take a more open view. Further advice on the potential for recruitment and training for women operatives is included in chapters dealing with these topics.

Strategies in skills supply

The key factors which attract recruits to the construction industry are the level of craft wages and the long-term prospects of the industry (Agapiou et al, 1995b). However, young people's (and, perhaps more significantly, their parents') perceptions of the industry are also important. If the industry's image is one of insecurity, low pay, low status, poor career prospects, and dirty and dangerous working conditions, it is not likely to attract potential employees.

Several training and recruitment strategies have been identified as necessary for the industry if it is to achieve a sufficient supply of skilled site labour in the future. These include (Agapiou et al, 1995a):

❑ upgrading the skills of the existing workforce through retraining of craft and operative workers

❑ creating a more positive public image for the industry to attract school-leavers

❑ recruiting more women and ethnic minority trainees

❑ attracting adult workers who have left construction back into the industry for retraining in modern skills

❑ recruiting the long-term unemployed and training them in modern skills

❑ recruiting migrant workers (although foreign migrants currently represent an insignificant proportion of the UK construction workforce – excluding Irish nationals).

The composition of the direct workforce in any particular firm depends fundamentally on the types of work which are regularly undertaken. A larger contractor with a varied workload may retain a mix of trades, whereas a specialist sub-contractor may concentrate on one area only.

The operative workforce has been a diminishing pool within individual firms in recent years, but perhaps for that reason, those who are still employed have a particular importance which could be more effectively acknowledged. Directly employed operatives may find opportunities for internal progression within their own organisation. There has been a tradition of upward mobility within the company – from tradesman through to chargehand and to foreman – and many senior managers say that they are looking out for good foremen for the future. Yet it may be that some of the traditional avenues of progression have been restricted as companies seek to recruit their junior managers from the ranks of graduates rather than from those who have been working as tradesmen. A review of the rewards and benefits of employment, as well as of opportunities for training and career progression, is a necessary part of the move for individual firms, from survival to consolidation.

The alternative to opportunities for internal progression within each company rests in the potential for mobility within an occupational labour market – a possibility which is open both to professionals and to skilled trades.

External labour markets and self-employment

The planning of craft and operative requirements in construction is normally part of the project-planning stage. Labour needs are normally estimated by the project-planning team. However, although labour requirements can be estimated, deficiencies in record-keeping may make the estimate of labour supply more difficult (Fryer, 1990).

Ultimately, construction firms are competing for skilled people – whether within national labour markets for such categories as professional managers, technical staffs and foremen, or in local or regional labour markets serving recruitment needs for chargehands, operatives, clerical workers and the sales workforce. The distinction between local and national labour markets is in reality rather blurred, particularly where high labour demand in one area is contrasted with slack in another. The boom in building activity in London during the late 1980s – at a time when work was less readily available in the north of England – saw active recruitment of operatives from the north of England to work on sites in London.

The industry thrives on networking – everybody knows somebody – and it is this capacity to know somebody which is so much a part of the process of problem-solving and getting things done. Whereas formal contractual relationships – for example, between contractors and sub-contractors – may often be characterised by conflict (Latham, 1994), informal networks, particularly those which are sustained at the level of the project or the site, often provide a means for getting over or around such problems. This is an important advantage in some respects, in that it provides an immediate solution to problems, but it may be an impediment too when it limits perceptions and narrows opportunities for recruitment – for example, amongst women, who have not traditionally been a part of the construction workforce.

One striking feature of the last 15 years in construction has been the decline in direct employment and the growth in self-employment, particularly amongst operatives. This is illustrated in the diagram below, based on statistics from the Department of Environment.

Figure 4   Construction: private-sector manpower

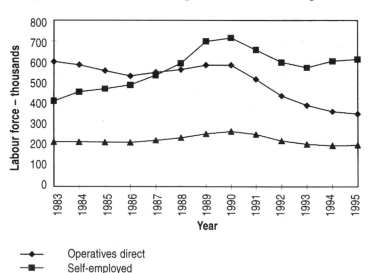

There is nothing new about self-employment within the construction industry. It is now almost 30 years since the Phelps Brown committee of enquiry considered the problem of 'lump' labour (Phelps Brown, 1968). However, the scale and the nature of self-employment in construction has changed significantly since that time. Self-employment grew significantly during the 1980s, and the balance between direct employment and self-employment in the private sector has been reversed. The majority of the workforce in construction is now described as 'self-employed' while a minority of operatives in the private sector are recognised as 'employees'.

The growth of new forms of contractual relationship between the client and contractor, with the development of management fee contracting, construction management, and techniques such as design and build, have been accompanied by new relationships between the main or management contractor and the workforce, mediated by the process of sub-contracting. The tendency to contract-out non-core activities – a tendency which has been widely adopted in industry and commercial life – seems to have been pioneered by the major contractors. In a competitive contractual climate, sub-contractors seek to download the costs and the responsibilities of employment, so that the construction process is highly fragmented and self-employed labour is preferred. This process increases the scope for specialist sub-contracting and 'supply-and-fix'.

It is sub-contractors who take the major part in managing the human resource planning process. In periods of more intensive activity, self-employment and labour-only sub-contracting have led to even more labour turnover on site as gangs of workers move from site to site to wherever the pay is highest (Beardsworth et al, 1988). In this sense, the development of self-employment may not have improved the levels of labour turnover within the industry. On the other hand, research conducted during the downturn of the 1990s suggests a less casual relationship with the main contractor (Druker and Macallan, 1996) – some self-employed workers are continuously engaged by the same contractor on a series of sites (and in reality might be considered permanent employees).

The use of self-employed labour is most common in the building trades, where labour-only sub-contracting is extensive, whereas by contrast in electrical contracting, direct employment remains more common although self-employment has grown significantly over the last decade. Many contractors and sub-contractors comment that they particularly value the skills of the general operative, who combines experience with flexibility. The almost universal trend has been to reduce the number of directly employed operatives, relying increasingly on sub-contractors.

Many sub-contractors prefer to engage self-employed labour, believing that they will not then incur the employment costs or the administrative burdens, which are feared particularly by small employers. Employers may only need a specialist category of labour for a short period – and so, they may argue, it is easier to use self-employed labour rather than employ people directly. Where they are competing for contracts, sub-contractors may be pressured to cut costs – and feel that using self-employed labour is a tax-efficient way of achieving that end. No National Insurance payments are made for self-employed operatives, who are expected to make their own contributions. It is widely (but sometimes erroneously) believed that no statutory employment rights obtain if an operative is engaged on a self-employed basis. Because construction work is dispersed over a wide geographical area, employers may argue, it is easier to find self-employed people who are close to the contract, rather than maintain a directly employed workforce which will have to be relocated for such scattered contracts.

The tax changes of the 1970s and the entrepreneurial climate of the 1980s gave a new legitimacy to the position of the self-employed, and the term 'lump labour' is nowadays rarely used. Self-employment is today more common than direct employment amongst operatives, and there is a strong financial imperative for sub-contractors and small builders to take on self-employed labour.

Yet the way in which labour is engaged for the construction trades remains a major issue for the industry and for those who make their living within it.

There are essentially four categories of labour engagement for construction operatives:

❏ the directly employed
  This group comprises those employees who have a contract of service with their employers and who are recognised as employees and describe themselves as such.

❏ the 'in-house' or long-term self-employed who remain with

34

a sub-contractor or contractor sometimes for many years
This is particularly attractive to those specialist sub-contractors who need to use high-quality labour but who fear the costs and the administration associated with direct employment. In the insecure climate of the 1990s, with fewer work opportunities available, many self-employed people prefer to retain the work they have rather than to risk their regular income for a brief period of more highly-paid work. Hence there is sometimes a surprising level of continuity of employment amongst people who describe themselves as self-employed. When the Inland Revenue and the courts look in detail at the situation, they redefine many of these people as employees.

❑ the casual self-employed
There are many self-employed people who move from job to job and from employer to employer, sometimes through the medium of an agency. The absence of continuity in engagement may suggest that this category is genuinely self-employed. However, the nature of the employment contract is not changed by virtue of its length. Casual employment remains 'employment' rather than 'self-employment'. Legal decisions as well as decisions from the Inland Revenue point in the same direction.

❑ the entrepreneurial self-employed
Within the construction workforce there are people who are in business on their own account and who rely on the success of the business. These are the genuinely self-employed who run their own business and who stand to gain or to lose from it.

This distinction within the workforce is illustrated in the diagram on the next page.

In order to understand the problems surrounding this use of self-employed labour, it is necessary to consider the current position with respect to taxation and the changes to the current tax scheme which are pending. We look at the legal position and recent legal decisions on self-employment, and at the implications for employers. Employer representatives have expressed concern at the ambiguities of the present situation, which has already generated problems for some firms and for their self-employed operatives. We conclude by offering a checklist to help distinguish between employment and self-employment.

Figure 5   Direct and indirect employment in construction

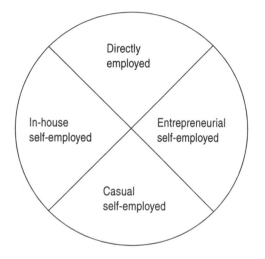

The tax situation – moving the goalposts?

Until 31 July 1998

The Construction Industry Tax deduction scheme has its origins in the 1970s, when the Labour government of the day endeavoured to wipe out the abuses associated with 'lump' labour. It applies to contractors, sub-contractors and workers who are designated as self-employed, and who are therefore not subject to Pay As You Earn (PAYE). Sub-contractors who qualify under the scheme are entitled to a tax certificate (often referred to as a '714'). There are four types of '714' certificate:

❏ the 714I – issued to individuals in business on their own
❏ the 714P – issued to partnerships and to directors of companies
❏ the 714C – issued to companies
❏ the 714S – issued to people such as school-leavers or new entrants to the industry who would not otherwise qualify.

In order to be eligible for a certificate, individuals must have been employed or self-employed in the UK for a continuous period of three years in the six years preceding the date of application, and must have been bona fide tax-payers during that time. Individuals who hold a 714 certificate are able to defer tax payments until the year's end, when they are processed for the whole of the period in question and allowances are made for the cost of the business operation.

When a sub-contractor does not hold a 714 certificate, the contractor must make a deduction on account of tax from all payments for labour. The contractor then provides the sub-contractor with an 'SC60' form detailing the deductions. At the end of the year individuals can submit the SC60s to their tax office, and if too much tax has been paid, a reimbursement is made.

There are real difficulties of identity posed by the current tax scheme: many employers assume that an individual is self-employed – or has the right to be paid as self-employed – because of the 714 certificate. Research shows that many so-called 'self-employed' are engaged continuously by their companies, on work which is the same as that undertaken by direct employees. The fact that someone holds a 714 certificate – or simply that they claim to be 'self-employed' – does not necessarily mean that they are really in business on their own account.

The Inland Revenue points out that employment status is not a question of choice. The fact that someone is engaged on a short-term or casual basis does not necessarily mean that they are self-employed either. Essentially, people are self-employed if they are in business and bear the responsibility for the success or the failure of that business. The employer cannot choose, simply because it is more convenient, to determine that the workers they have recruited are self-employed. Whether someone is self-employed fundamentally depends on the working arrangements which apply and the way in which the relationship is managed.

Nor is it the case that individuals when they join an employer are self-employed simply because they claim to be so and are already holders of a 714 certificate. It is the terms and conditions which apply to the job in question that must be considered.

From 1 August 1998

Concern about abuses of the 714 certificate scheme have led to proposals for change which will be implemented from 1 August 1998. From that date, a minimum turnover will be required in

Employment and self-employment: reference points suggested by the Inland Revenue

Tools

If the worker supplies only his or her own *small* tools, he or she is more likely to be an employee. Self-employment might be suggested where materials, plant or heavy equipment is provided.

Risk

Employment is suggested where the worker does not risk his or her own money and there is no possibility that he or she will suffer a financial loss. Genuine self-employment might involve the worker in bearing additional cost if the original bid for the job were too low.

Business organisation

Employment is suggested where the worker has no business organisation – for example, yard, stock, materials, or workers. If the worker has the right to hire other people who are paid by him or her and who are answerable to him or her to do the job, self-employment is suggested.

Payment

Payment on a time basis (hour, day, week or month) suggests employment, whereas payment of an agreed amount, regardless of how long the job takes, is an indicator of self-employment.

Control

The contractor has the right to control an employee in terms of what is done, and where, when, and how it is done – even if such control is rarely practised. The freedom to decide, within an overall deadline, how and when the work will be done may be taken as an indicator of self-employment.

Source: Inland Revenue: *Are Your Workers Employed or Self-employed? A guide to tax and National Insurance for contractors in the construction industry.* Business Series IR148/CA69

order for individuals to be eligible to apply for a 714. Applicants will also have to demonstrate that they have paid their tax bills in the three previous years. The validity of all 714s issued after January 1995 will end on 31 July 1998, from which point the new scheme will be brought into effect.

Tighter controls of tax payments reclaimed via SC60s are also proposed, with the intention of bringing such arrangements under more formal scrutiny. Employers will need to establish administrative arrangements for the deduction of tax for this group – and closer checks on employment status and National Insurance payments could follow.

The legal position: a contract of employment or a contract for services?

Legally, the test of whether someone is an employee or an independent operator, in business on their own account, is bound up with whether there is a contract of service (that is, a contract of employment) or a contract for services (that is, a commercial contract between two business organisations). This is an important distinction, for the existence of a contract of service means that the individual should benefit from statutory employment rights – and the employer owes a duty of care to the employee. What is more, the employer has an obligation to make National Insurance payments for an employee.

A confusion over employment status can leave employers with unexpected and expensive obligations – an obligation to pay arrears of National Insurance, for example, or statutory responsibilities towards the employee(s) in question.

Historically, the question of control over the work process has been seen as important, for an employer might reasonably be expected to have a knowledge of the tasks to be undertaken. Other points of reference have also been used to determine someone's work status. Although the question of control is still seen as important, recent legal decisions point to a more complex framework of reference in which overriding importance is attached to the question of 'whose business is it really?' The courts are no longer satisfied with the simple explanation that an individual holds a self-employed tax exemption certificate and that this determines his or her employment status. Like many others, Mr Lane (in the example opposite) had a tax status of 'self-employed' – but the Court of Appeal's decision means that he was, in effect, an employee.

The complexities of this situation are a source of concern to employers, who could find that their approach to employment matters has left them with financial liabilities that had not been anticipated. It is the smaller firms which are most likely to be

---

Court of Appeal decides that a 'self-employed' man is in fact an employee

The Court of Appeal considered the case of Mr Lane, a man who had his own building company, PJ Building, which undertook roofing work. Mr Lane was, for tax purposes, self-employed. He undertook some work for Shire Roofing, whose proprietor hired men for individual jobs. Mr Lane was hired for an all-in fee of £200 to do some roofing work, and suffered an accident which caused serious head injuries and brain damage. Following the accident Mr Lane made a claim for damages. The High Court found that Mr Lane was an independent contractor, and decided that Shire Roofing did not therefore owe the duty of care which is due to an employee. However, on appeal the Court of Appeal reversed this decision, saying that the question is, whose business is it? The test which they applied involved consideration of 'how far the workman has an opportunity of profiting from sound management in the performance of his task.' *Damages were awarded against the company, and leave to appeal to the House of Lords was refused.*

The Court of Appeal's decision was based on consideration of who controls the situation – who decides what is to be done, the way in which it should be done, the means by which it should be done, and when; who hires and fires the team which will do the work; and who provides the materials, plant, machinery and tools used.

Source: IRLR 1995: 493. *Lane* v. *Shire Roofing Company (Oxford) Ltd*

recruiting self-employed labour, and so it is this group who are most likely to find that they have fallen into the self-employment trap.

Advice on self-employment offered by an employers' association may help to clarify the situation.

An industrial relations perspective

Employers' associations have been increasingly concerned at the legal complexities surrounding self-employed status, and advise their members to distinguish carefully between their employees and those who are self-employed. Apart from the points already cited from the Inland Revenue, they highlight the following differences between the employed and the genuinely self-employed:

- ❏ Self-employed operatives are not on the payroll of the company. They should be paid in response to invoices – not as part of the normal arrangements for wages and salary payments.

- ❏ The self-employed are not normally covered by the employers' compulsory liability insurance cover – and contractors are advised to check whether the self-employed will be covered by their public liability insurance.

- ❏ Self-employed contractors would be expected to work for more than one contractor and have invoices and contractual documents which prove that this is what they do.

- ❏ Whereas employees are entitled to receive statutory sickness and maternity pay, this does not apply to the self-employed. Nor do the disciplinary rules and procedures – for example, dealing with timekeeping, absence and conduct – apply to the self-employed, whose work should be assessed against normal commercial and contractual criteria.

- ❏ Employees are entitled to statutory periods of notice to terminate the contract, but this does not apply to those who are self-employed, who are covered by the terms of the commercial contract.

- ❏ An employee has a right to statutory redundancy payments and to make a claim at an industrial tribunal for such things as unfair dismissal. The genuinely self-employed have no such rights, although those self-employed who are in reality 'quasi-employees' are able to make successful claims.

A new approach to employment – reviewing labour usage
Patterns of labour usage in construction during the 1980s and 1990s have been largely reactive as contractors and sub-contractors have sought to ride out the prolonged and destabilising recession. Employers have sought to minimise costs and to download responsibilities in response to workload fluctuations during this period. The preoccupation with downsizing has disguised the real need to develop and to consolidate construction teams which have the requisite skills and expertise for the type of work undertaken. Questions of quality and skill cannot

easily be separated out from the issues of predictability and reliability of labour supply. There is a real need for a review of labour usage with the following aims:

❑ to review the labour market and the image of the industry – to attract non-traditional sources of labour, particularly women recruits
❑ to review the balance of employment and self-employment – to avoid abuses of 'self-employed' status
❑ to generate new opportunities for training and professional development for all categories of employee.

The pace of change seems unlikely to decelerate, but the nature of change may shift as larger clients seek partnerships with contractors and sub-contractors, and as quality features still more strongly in the demands which clients put upon the industry. The public sector is once again to be encouraged to take on the role of being a 'model client', and firms may wish to demonstrate their credibility as employers by convincing potential clients of their inbuilt quality controls. In the light of a new interest from the Inland Revenue in what goes on in the name of self-employment, this would seem to be an appropriate time for contractors and sub-contractors to review their own pattern of labour usage, with a view to a more positive and pro-active approach to recruitment and retention. A commitment to equality of opportunity is a starting-point for firms which are seeking to differentiate their position and to take advantage of new areas of recruitment and skill potential.

The construction industry is notable for the high proportion of skill which goes into the construction product. The application of more advanced technology is still some way from superseding the value of experience and expertise on site. Sub-contractors need to retain a skilled workforce – why else would so many so-called 'self-employed' workers be given the rewards normally reserved for the directly employed, such as holiday money or sickness pay? As taxation arrangements provide fewer loopholes for administrative savings, and as legal decisions call the self-employed status into question, there are signs that some contractors and sub-contractors are already modifying their position on the use of self-employed labour.

There will always be financial pressures to reduce labour costs within a competitive contractual situation – but this is not a reason or a justification for the abuse of self-employed status. In other parts of northern Europe the proportion of self-employed labour is very much lower than in the UK, although contractors also compete for work. A balance needs to be found between the cost advantages which sub-contracting may offer the larger contractors and the abuses which have been associated with it. Moves to redress the balance in favour of direct employment can be made by smaller employers and by specialist sub-contractors as much as by the larger construction-based corporations. The benefits will be:

- ❏ recognition of the real costs of employment – including National Insurance and employment entitlements – without the risk of hidden extras
- ❏ greater possibilities for accurate and effective human resource planning
- ❏ new possibilities in skills development, multi-skilling and career progression for operatives – with real benefits in terms of quality and productivity
- ❏ reducing the damage which can be done by claims at industrial tribunals – and the unexpected additional costs which may result, relating to payments in favour of those self-employed workers who are really 'quasi-employees'
- ❏ changing marketing and management practice to take advantages of the 'in-house' skills and expertise which can be provided by direct labour.

Reference

1   Labour Force Survey figures are adjusted by the Department of the Environment, so that there is an apparent discrepancy in the figures quoted at the beginning of the chapter and those which are cited in table 1. The Department of the Environment's *Housing and Construction Statistics* allow comparison between different sections of the construction workforce.

CHAPTER 3

EFFECTIVE RECRUITMENT AND SELECTION

The project-based nature of the construction process means that many of the concerns about recruitment and selection occur at site level. Ensuring a ready supply of the various construction professionals and trades to make up project teams is a vital task.

This chapter looks at the practical issues involved in staff recruitment and selection. It identifies the norms of good practice in the recruitment and selection process within the construction sector, and points to the benefits for the industry of the recruitment of non-traditional sources of labour. It further indicates the importance of non-discrimination at every stage of the recruitment process.

Ensuring that an organisation has sufficient and adequately trained human resources is a vital part of management. It may sometimes seem to be a haphazard process as an organisation has to cope with unexpected successes in winning contracts or in developing work in new locations. In this chapter we concentrate on the recruitment and selection process, looking first at the priorities at site level in relation to the recruitment and selection of craft workers and operatives. We then look at resourcing the firm's needs for professional and management staff, including the recruitment and selection techniques which can be utilised to ensure that a 'best fit' is achieved in recruitment practice.

There is a clear divide between the resourcing of operatives on site and the supply of professional and management staff to project teams. In general, the supply of manual labour is carried out by the site manager with little intervention by the personnel manager. Basic guidelines may be provided by the personnel department on the legal requirements and basic employee records required, but in general the process is relatively informal.

Recruitment and selection have been areas for innovation in organisations where there has been a particular attention given to using HRM as a new approach. Research evidence suggests that this is not a major focus for new policies in the construction industry (Druker, White, Hegewisch and Mayne, 1996). Recruitment and selection decisions there are more likely to be taken by line managers than in other industries, and in many cases personnel departments have little or no input in recruitment decisions (Bresnan et al, 1985). There has been relatively little attention given to the use of psychometric tests, assessment centres or panel interviews, as compared with other sectors.

Ford et al (1982) pointed to the underdeveloped nature of selection processes on site. Workers were recruited through a 'selection by trial', which meant many workers left sites after very short periods. The main reasons for this rapid turnover were attributed to 'workers being engaged for jobs for which they have no competence (this is encouraged by an absence of skill certification among many workers) and a failure to inform workers adequately about the type of work and pay and conditions of employment' (Ford et al, 1982). The absence of any systems for establishing the quality and suitability of workers in advance of being hired was seen as a particular area of inefficiency within the industry, because of the inflationary effects on costs as recruitment had to be reactivated for each turnover. The use of self-employed labour does not automatically resolve this problem because self-employed workers may also be unsuitable for the tasks to be undertaken.

Some companies prefer to keep teams of skilled operatives together, whether of self-employed or employed status, and try to use the same teams on a series of contracts. This means that planning and provision for the transfer of existing staff between sites may be a more satisfactory solution than the recruitment of new employees. The degree to which construction operatives remain in the employment of a single contractor over a period of time depends largely on the type of labour market in which the operative is working. In Scotland and the north of England, direct employment is more common than in the south – and with it the potential for greater continuity in employment.

A labour needs analysis is required to establish what must be done when and by whom. The site manager or planners forecast the labour requirements of each stage of the project, taking into account the various trades required (eg bricklayers, structural engineers, electricians or painters), the need to avoid sharp fluctuations in employment levels, and the overall resource pattern of the project (Fryer, 1990). A shortage in one particular trade may lead to a hold-up in the whole process. Site labour (in the main sub-contractors today) has therefore to be brought on and off site in a planned order, without sudden changes in the numbers of workers of each trade. A staffing chart is used to plan this order of arrival and departure, based on the earliest and latest starts for each activity. The chart can show the balance of work and number of employees on site at any time, so that any correction needed can be made to keep to the schedule. Too much labour on site means that supervisors will be overloaded and workers may be idle for periods of time, leading to productivity problems. Not enough labour may mean delays, extra labour costs, and penalties for late completion. Planning of this type cannot take into account variations in the contract or additional work required by the client.

The recruitment and selection process

The process of recruitment and selection varies according to the level and type of vacancy being filled. As we note above, most on-site recruitment is carried out by project or site managers who decide the labour requirements for each stage of the construction process and have to plan the order in which events take place. Many construction sites may only have one or two contractor's staff present permanently, usually a project manager and possibly a general foreman, depending on the size of the job. Larger sites have a site manager and site agent.

A decision to use self-employed labour should take full account of the employment law implications and the potential liabilities of self-employment. The professional and technical labour requirements of each site will be decided by the heads of each department (eg surveying, planning, contracts manager), and these needs will be met from central pools at either head office or regional office level. The role of the personnel or human resource manager may be to act as conciliator between these different groups and to overcome divisions.

The main stages in the recruitment process are as follows:

❑ analysing the labour requirements (job analysis, job descriptions, person specifications, establishing criteria for selection, etc.)

❑ attracting applicants (internal and external markets, recruitment advertising, sources of applicants, etc.)

❑ assessing the candidate (application forms, curricula vitae, shortlisting, etc.)

❑ selecting the right candidate (interviews, group selection methods, psychological/personality testing, assessment centres, etc.)

❑ final assessment and placement (references, induction, recruitment administration).

Recruitment is a two-way process. Both the employer and potential employee should have clear expectations of how the process should operate. The organisation will have to sell itself to the potential candidates if it wishes to appoint the best possible candidates. It should be conducted on a basis which is effective, efficient and fair.

In the following pages we examine the stages in the recruitment process in terms of both the variety of techniques and best practice. However, we first look at the basic employment law requirements that apply to the recruitment, selection and engagement of employees.

The legal requirements

All managers with recruitment responsibilities should be familiar with the legal requirements that have to be observed. These are primarily designed to avoid the unfair treatment of applicants and, in particular, discrimination on the basis of gender or race. Other laws deal with the employment of disabled people, foreign nationals, children and young persons, and ex-offenders. Once a decision to appoint has been taken, there are legal requirements concerning the contract of employment and the issuing of terms and conditions.

Discrimination on the grounds of gender, race or trade union membership or non-membership is unlawful at any stage of the recruitment and selection process. It is unlawful to discriminate against a person because of sex, marital status or on the grounds of colour, race or ethnic or national origins.

Discrimination can be construed (in Lewis, 1992) as:

❏ *direct* – where a person is treated 'less favourably' than another person on one of the prohibited grounds (eg nationality). This includes segregation of jobs on racial grounds

❏ *indirect* – where a 'requirement or condition' which is or would be applied equally but where the proportion of one group (say, women) who can comply is considerably smaller than the proportion outside that group who can comply

❏ *victimisation* – where individuals are treated less favourably because they have, or are suspected of having, used the legislation or because they plan to use the law, or have alleged breaches of the law.

The statutes covering these areas of discrimination are the Sex Discrimination Act 1975; the Equal Pay Act 1970; and the Race Relations Act 1976. Sex discrimination law does not apply just to women – men are equally able to make a case. In recent times, sexual harassment has also been construed as unlawful sex discrimination. The Equal Pay Act is dealt with in the chapter on reward management.

Discrimination law applies to the recruitment and selection arrangements (eg a discriminatory interview); the terms on which a job is offered; refusals to offer employment; opportunities to apply for promotion, transfer or training, or access to other benefits, facilities or services; and to the circumstances of dismissal.

If an employee believes that he or she has been discriminated against on any of the above grounds, he or she may seek a remedy through the industrial tribunal system. Employees or applicants who claim discrimination do not have to have any minimum service before taking a case to the tribunal. It is up to the applicant to prove direct discrimination, but once a *prima facie* case has been made the employer must demonstrate that the different treatment was for reasons other than sex, race, etc. The issue of whether unlawful discrimination was intentional or not is irrelevant.

Discrimination may also be indirect – that, is the applicant must prove the discriminatory 'requirement or condition', the 'considerably smaller proportion' who can comply with it, and the fact that they have suffered detriment as a result of this condition. The employer must prove, in such cases, that the requirement or condition was justifiable, irrespective of the prohibited grounds. 'Justifiable' requires the employer to demonstrate a genuine need for the measures.

It is unlawful to use discriminatory advertisements, issue instructions to discriminate, pressure staff to discriminate, or aid and assist in the commission of illegal acts. Employers are is also responsible for the discriminatory actions of employees unless they can demonstrate that they took steps to prevent discrimination from taking place. Positive discrimination is also illegal (ie restricting a post to applicants from a group which is underrepresented or poorly represented within the workforce).

Certain types of discrimination are lawful, however. For example, single-race or single-sex training schemes are allowed, if that race or sex has been underrepresented in a particular type of work – and this provision underpins some training schemes for women who would like to take up a career in the construction industry. Moreover, both the Sex Discrimination and Race Relations Acts allow discrimination in the case of a 'genuine occupational qualification', where recruitment can be limited to a particular gender or race. The circumstances are limited but would apply, for example, to waiting staff in an Indian restaurant or to a prison officer in a women's prison.

Two regulatory bodies – the Equal Opportunities Commission (EOC) and the Commission for Racial Equality (CRE) – have the right to investigate any organisation which they suspect of operating discriminatory policies. The CRE investigation of the recruitment of craft trainees by the CITB (described in Chapter 5) indicates how some recruitment practices in the industry may be construed as discriminatory.

Recruitment methods

Before a vacancy is advertised, there must be some form of agreement or authorisation that the job can be filled. In most construction firms of any size, the personnel department has a procedure whereby the line manager responsible for the job has to fill in some type of requisition form stating the vacancy, the reason for the vacancy, and the need to fill the post. These may be approved by regional directors or regional personnel managers or head office personnel staff. Any vacancies must be within the staffing budget. Regions may have the authority to fill their own vacancies, but only if this is within the regional budget. Extra staff may have to be justified to head office. In smaller firms such decisions rest with the senior manager.

Once approval to fill the post has been given, an advertisement is drafted. Jobs may be advertised internally or externally. Internal trawling is the most likely method if the organisation is shedding staff. However, it is only where external trawling is applied that the composition of the workforce can be significantly changed.

Before an advertisement can be drafted, certain information about the vacancy and the qualities expected of the applicants must be decided. These have traditionally been:

❑ the job description

❑ the person specification.

The job description

Where jobs are fairly standardised, job descriptions may already be drafted. In particular where companies have job evaluation schemes in place, job analysis will have been carried out and job descriptions will already exist. Even where such job descriptions do exist, it may still be wise to review them if the job has not been filled recently. Job content, skills and responsibilities can change over time, and any such changes need to be updated in the job description. In many construction firms, the job content and responsibilities can vary widely between regions so that standardised job descriptions are problematical. In these cases, new job descriptions may be written for each vacancy.

The job description is drawn up by the line manager or supervisor responsible, possibly with the aid of the personnel department. A job description should contain enough detail to allow a reasonably accurate summary to be sent out to potential applicants. It may include the following:

❑ the job title, work location, purpose, and objects of the work

❑ the activities involved in the work, the responsibility for staff, equipment, public safety or budgets, and the standards of performance expected

❑ the training or qualifications required for the post

❑ the work circumstances, ie the work environment – office-based, mobile, or site-based; the pace and quantity of the work; physical working conditions

❑ the conditions of service and the career prospects.

Person specification

A job description should be purely descriptive and not attempt to include personal attributes which may be essential or desirable. It is important to use only 'action verbs' to describe the main tasks. Personal attributes are covered in the separate person specification. Clearly the job description should give enough information to deduce the personal qualities required for the tasks involved. The person specification is not a scientific tool but it does help to systematise the selection method, rather than rely on an unsubstantiated view of the interviewer. A variety of model forms of person specification have been designed. Two approaches found in the industry are Alex Rodgers' Seven-Point Plan and Munro Fraser's Five-Fold Grading Specification. These are shown in the box below.

Person specification models

a) Rodgers Seven-Point Plan	*b) Fraser's Five-Fold Grading*
Physical make-up	Impact on others
Attainment	Qualifications/acquired
General intelligence	knowledge
Special aptitudes	Innate abilities
Interests	Motivation
Disposition	Adjustment/emotional
Circumstances	balance

A more recent method of devising job criteria has been the use of competencies. These might include such competencies as self-confidence, thoroughness, interpersonal awareness, negotiation, communication, conceptualisation, analytical thinking, self-control, etc. (Torrington *et al*, 1991: 184). This level of complexity applies more to professional and managerial positions.

From the job description and person specification it should be possible to draw up criteria for shortlisting candidates. The next stage is to attract candidates. Various methods of attracting candidates may be used, but all of them require careful screening for any potential direct or indirect discrimination. The main methods of attracting candidates are:

- ❏ consulting a register of people who have approached the company for work in the past
- ❏ graduate recruitment through higher education institutions, or skills recruitment from schools and further education colleges
- ❏ government job centres
- ❏ private employment agencies
- ❏ recruitment consultants or executive search
- ❏ advertisements in the local, trade, professional or national press
- ❏ advertisements on company notice boards or outside sites or depots
- ❏ the 'grapevine'.

Clearly some of these methods are more appropriate for manual workers, and others more appropriate for administrative, technical, professional and managerial staff.

Manual workers are likely to be recruited through vacancy boards outside the site or depot, or through their own networks. In particular, labour-only sub-contractors use their own grapevines to recruit operatives. Other manual workers may come through job centres or private agencies, while some may be recruited through the local or trade press. Remember that informal recruitment methods such as grapevines and word-of-mouth are open to possible claims of discriminatory behaviour and may genuinely limit the potential for recruiting the best candidates.

Graduate and craft trainees are more likely to be recruited from the institutions at which they are undertaking their training or education. As already noted, many construction firms sponsor craft and technician trainees as well as graduates from university Built Environment Faculties.

Experienced craft workers and professionals are likely to use the trade and professional journals when looking for new jobs, whereas senior management jobs are dealt with either through the national press or through executive search (head hunting) by private recruitment consultants. Although the sophistication of the method used increases with the level of job, anecdotal evidence suggests that the construction industry operates at a fairly informal level at all ranges of the hierarchy. Personal introductions and contacts are seen as very important and, as one personnel manager in the industry described it, 'the recruitment process is different each time and is rather haphazard.' Whether jobs are advertised in the press or not depends to a large degree on the state of the labour market – when competition is stiff, companies spend money on elaborate advertising and open-day events to attract potential staff, but when the industry is in recession, vacancies are more likely to be filled by personal contacts or from the databank of previous applicants. Some of the newspapers used for job adverts include *The Times* and the *Daily Telegraph* for senior positions; *Building* magazine, *Contract Journal*, *Construction News* and *New Civil Engineer* for professional staff; and regional daily and evening papers for craft and administrative jobs.

It is essential to remember that it is unlawful to publish or cause to be published an advertisement which indicates or could imply an intention to commit unlawful discrimination. Use of job descriptions which have gender connotations – for example, craftsman or salesman – may be taken to be intended sex discrimination unless the advertisement indicates to the contrary. This rule applies equally to internal advertisements as to external adverts. It is therefore wise to include a statement to the effect that candidates of both sexes (or indeed all races, ethnic groups and nationalities) are welcome to apply. Many companies, including some major construction firms, include such statements plus another to the effect that the company is an equal opportunities employer.

Job applicants can be asked to send in a curriculum vitae (CV) or can ask for an application form. Again, in construction a large amount of recruitment is done by CV but some of the larger firms use an application form. Others ask for the application form to be filled in when the applicant comes for interview. The advantage of the application form is that all applicants must provide their details in a uniform manner. This may follow the format of the person specification so that candidates' details can be easily compared when shortlisting. The current 'state of the art' application forms, which seek to ensure that no direct or indirect discrimination takes place when selecting candidates for interview, often have tear-off sections so that the person's gender and personal circumstances are known only to the personnel department and not to the interviewers. However, in construction, where application forms exist, they tend to be fairly simple. Smaller firms who wish to compile an application form could confine it to the following:

- [ ] name and address, telephone number, etc.
- [ ] date of birth and title (Dr, Mr, Mrs, Ms, etc.)
- [ ] education and qualifications
- [ ] current employment details and salary
- [ ] previous employment and experience, in chronological order
- [ ] interests and hobbies
- [ ] reasons for applying for the post
- [ ] statement of general health
- [ ] names and addresses of referees.

Selection methods

Once the vacancies have been advertised and applications received, the next stage is to sift through the candidates to create a shortlist. This is usually done by the manager or supervisor in whose section or department the vacancy exists. In larger construction firms the personnel department may assist in this process by providing the documentation and checking that the candidates meet the criteria set out in the job description and person specification. The size of the shortlist will vary according to the number of vacancies (where a number of similar jobs are vacant) and according to the standard of the candidates. In general, too large a field is unwieldy while too small a field may make comparisons difficult. A minimum of three shortlisted candidates is common.

The shortlisting process is best done on paper. A simple form can be used which lists the main criteria for the post (taken from the person specification) across the top of the page and lists the candidates down the left-hand side of the page. A final column on the right-hand side can be used to record whether the candidate is to be called for interview or not. Each candidate's application form or CV is considered in turn against the criteria and a decision taken.

Once this process is completed, candidates can be invited for interview. A number of selection methods can be utilised in making the decision on whom to employ, but by far the most common method (and often the only method) is the interview. Other methods which have been developed include various forms of tests of applicants' skills or knowledge; psychological or personality testing; group assessment; and even trials with future colleagues. Below we look at three main areas – the interview, selection testing and group assessment. Although the interview remains the major selection method in construction, skills testing may be used for selecting craft workers, and other forms of testing may be used for technical, administrative, professional and clerical staff.

Interviews

Despite the fact that the interview is by far the most popular form of selection method (and this is true of all industries and services), research on the results of such interviews suggests that they provide only a slightly better prediction of future job performance than pure chance. Research at the University of Manchester's Institute of Science and Technology suggests that testing offers a more accurate assessment of future performance, and assessment centres even more. Other research has indicated that interviewers generally make up their minds about a candidate within four minutes of the start of the interview and then proceed to find reasons to justify this initial reaction; that this initial judgement was seldom changed; and that they communicated this judgement to the candidate.

Nevertheless, despite all such evidence, most employers continue to use the interview as the major selection method. This is perhaps because employers, understandably, place great value on the face-to-face encounter with potential employees. It is therefore unlikely that employees will be selected without some form of interview. The issue is how to ensure that such interviews are carried out in a fair manner so that the limitations of the interview method are minimised. Where care is taken, interviews can be very useful in enabling the interviewer to find out more information about the candidate and vice versa. It is vital that the interview is seen as an opportunity for dialogue.

A number of decisions need to be taken about the interview process. These are:

❑ Will the interviews all take place together on one day or on separate days? The advantage of the former is that all candidates can be compared ·while fresh in the mind. The advantage of the latter is that it does not require a block of time for busy staff and, perhaps more importantly, allows the candidate some choice of date and time of attendance.

However, where a number of people are required to sit on an interview panel, separate interviews are more difficult to arrange.

❑ Will the interview require a panel of people or will it be a small-scale affair with one or two interviewers? In local government and other public sector bodies, the panel interview is more common, but in smaller and more entrepreneurial firms, interviews tend to be conducted by smaller numbers of interviewers and sometimes through a series of one-to-one meetings with different people. The advantage of the panel interview is that the candidate is seen by all the interviewers at the same time, thus saving time, and moreover that any bias on the part of one or more interviewers can be compensated for within the group. The problem with panel interviews is that they can appear inquisitorial and do not give the candidate or each individual panel member much opportunity for dialogue. The advantages of the individual one-to-one interview are that the process is likely to be more informal and allow greater opportunity to develop a rapport between the two parties. If these individual interviews are carried out in sequence by a series of people, each interview can be used to investigate a particular aspect of the job or candidate's profile. Tandem interviews, where perhaps the line manager and the personnel manager interview together, can be less daunting for the candidate than a panel interview but may still inhibit the flow of the process.

❑ How is the interview to be structured? It is very important that interviewers are well briefed about the candidate before the interview, and have read all available documentation. If a number of people are involved in the process, a pre-meeting should be arranged to decide who is to cover what in the interview. It is useful for the candidate to be told the structure of the interview at the start of the event. If any tests are to be administered, candidates should be warned in the letter inviting them for interview. Interviewers should be issued with a brief note of the structure of the interview and encouraged to make notes along these lines.

Interviews are structured in three parts – a beginning, a middle, and an end. The start is usually used for introductions, 'ice breaking' and building up rapport. This stage often includes a question on the candidate's own view as to suitability for the post concerned. The middle section can either work through the questions in the order of the application form or be ordered according to the interviewer's preference. The final section of the interview usually includes an opportunity for the candidate to ask questions (although a dialogue should mean that this happens naturally), and for the interviewers to summarise the next steps and tell the candidate when he or she can expect to be notified about the decision. What is important is that interviewers should have good listening skills and not themselves spend too much time talking. The interview is primarily an opportunity for the candidate to demonstrate suitability for the job. The interviewer(s) should only talk for 30 per cent of the time available.

The type and content of the questions asked in an interview can vary widely but, in general, questions posed should be open and encourage the candidate to expand (they should start with What? Who? Why? When? Where? or How?) rather than closed, which simply require a Yes or No answer. Comparative questions can also be useful. It is in the types of questions that interviewers need to be most wary of discriminatory practices. Unfortunately, the boundary between what is lawful and what is not is rather hazy. Candidates should not be asked different questions because they are of a different race or gender or because they are members of a trade union. Such questioning will be construed as discriminatory. This does not mean that all candidates must be asked the same questions.

Selection tests

Tests can be an effective method of complementing the interview by providing more factual and observed evidence of the ability of the candidate to do the job. As mentioned above, tests fall into two main categories – those that test skills and/or knowledge, and those that assess the personality or the psychology of the candidate.

In general, the more sophisticated types of testing (both knowledge and psychological) are reserved for more senior jobs at professional and managerial level, whereas skills testing is more likely for manual and clerical employees. Research on selection methods suggests that the use of selection tests is not widespread within the construction industry, although some skills testing takes place where manual workers are directly employed. Psychological or personality tests are sometimes used for senior management positions. The absence of some of the tests being developed for manual workers in some other industries (such as 'trainability testing', competency testing, and tests to assess the ability of the worker for group working or multi-tasking) is partly explained by the decline of direct labour. Whereas parts of manufacturing industry are now using quite sophisticated methods to choose their directly employed manual workforce, with the objective of selecting those most likely to meet the company's needs for quality, flexibility and commitment, at present there is no spur to construction firms to follow suit. A return to direct labour might provide such a spur. The recent establishment of a voluntary construction industry skills register (see Chapter 5) may mean that skills testing becomes more common at company or site level.

In relation to professional and managerial staff, companies are more likely to be looking for knowledge, experience and managerial ability. The use of psychological testing has grown significantly in the UK over the last decade or so. Construction firms require people with technical skills and an understanding of the construction process, with the social skills needed for managing different types of people, and with the diplomatic skills needed for efficient project management. Some of these attributes are more easily tested than others. The main types of tests are:

❑ aptitude tests, which measure the potential of a person to develop certain skills or abilities

❑ attainment tests, which measure the current skills or abilities; these can be paper tests of knowledge (eg of construction technology) or practical tests of certain skills (eg computer skills)

❑ trainability tests, which measure the potential for the employee to learn new skills or his or her receptivity to new concepts

❑ intelligence tests, which measure overall mental ability (eg IQ tests)

❑ personality tests, which measure the candidate's aptitude for particular types of work (eg his or her leadership qualities).

The last two of these types of tests are controversial and some questions have been raised as to how such attributes as mental ability and personality traits can be measured effectively. A wide range of interpretations can be put on such data, and cultural implications are important. The IPD has provided a Code of Conduct for the use of such tests which stipulates that the tests should be administered only by a person trained and qualified in the interpretation of such data. A major problem with tests is that they may be open to cultural stereotyping and hence to allegations of racial discrimination. Setting educational standards which cannot be justified in terms of the job can also be construed as unlawful discrimination. For example, a requirement for a high standard of written English in a job largely concerned with technical skills or numerically-based skills might be seen as potentially discriminatory to certain applicants.

Group assessment

Another selection method which has gained in popularity in recent years is the use of group assessments or assessment centres. These began in the armed forces where they were used effectively to select candidates for officer (and particularly air crew) training. Many companies which recruit large numbers of graduates and other staff on a regular basis have established their own centres. Smaller firms may be able to make use of commercial recruitment and selection consultancies in a similar fashion. One reason for their growing popularity is the increasing need of companies to have staff who can work creatively in teams or groups. Nowhere is this more true than in the project-driven culture of construction.

Assessment centres have the advantage that candidates can be asked to attend for one or two days, which gives ample time for a variety of tests and exercises to be carried out. Moreover, they offer the opportunity to observe how a candidate behaves within a peer group. Group exercises and tests can be used to measure how well a candidate operates within a project group or team, as well as tests in which an individual candidate has to compete against other candidates. Such tests can give a good picture of how a candidate would operate in a real work situation – and how individuals behave and interact with others may be a better guide to future managerial potential than the psychological or intelligence tests. Again, however, cultural effects may mean that people from certain racial groups may be less happy with such tests (for example, from a culture which encourages more passive behaviour and deference to authority

59

or group consensus, rather than competition and conflict), and possible discriminatory practices must be guarded against. Given the international dimension of the construction industry (see Chapter 10), such concerns are important in selecting future managers.

The major obstacle to the use of assessment centres is the costs and the management time required. Such exercises involve expensive hotel accommodation and consultancy fees, and senior managers may be required to attend to assist in the observation process.

The selection decision

Once the final decision has been taken on which candidate(s) to appoint, a number of administrative procedures must follow. These include informing both the successful and unsuccessful candidates of the decision and calling for references. Medical checks and possibly verification of academic qualifications or professional membership may also be required before the appointment is confirmed. The letter of confirmation should include details of the location of the work (or the office or depot in the case of mobile workers); the hours of work; and the duties involved.

A contract of employment must also be created and written terms and conditions provided within two months of the start date. These may be included in the letter confirming the appointment or in the company handbook sent out with the letter. Normal practice is for two copies of the appointment letter to be sent to the person(s) selected with a request that one be signed and returned to the company.

The contract of employment is central to British employment law and forms the legal base on which the relationship between the employer and employee is founded. Once the employer makes an offer of employment, and the employee accepts the offer, a contract exists – although conditions may be applied to the offer (eg subject to references and a medical check). There is no statute that covers employment contracts so in essence the employment contract is an agreement (rather than a document as in a commercial contract). The employee agrees to work for a certain consideration (ie pay) and the employer agrees to pay for the work done. The contract does not have to be written down, therefore, in order to exist. Absence of a written contract does not make a contract unenforceable, although it may be more difficult to prove its existence. The contract begins once the employee accepts the employer's offer, and withdrawal from the agreement by either party can lead to a potential claim for breach of contract.

Given the nature of the construction industry, with its high levels of self-employment, casual employment and agency working, the precise definition of the employment relationship is very important (see Chapter 2). Many workers in the industry are not employees as such and therefore do not have contracts of employment. However, an inaccurate definition of the employment relationship may lead to problems with the Inland Revenue and National Insurance contributions, as well as with possible claims for injury.

The contract of employment thus has a number of sources:

❑ expressly agreed terms between the two parties either in writing or orally

❑ terms incorporated from collective agreements (eg the National Working Rules)

❑ the works rules (eg hours of attendance, holiday entitlement, etc.)

❑ custom and practice

❑ terms implied by common law (eg employer's duty of care for the employee's safety, to pay for work done, to act in good faith)

❑ terms imposed by statute (eg equal pay, minimum notice).

There are four main types of employment contract:

❑ a permanent contract (open-ended with no fixed date of expiry)

❑ a fixed-term contract (with a specific starting and finishing date)

❑ a performance contract (to carry out a specific task but without fixed dates) which ends with completion of the task

❑ a temporary contract (by which an employee is employed for a limited period but not under a fixed term or performance contract).

The last type of contract implies the same rights as for a permanent contract if sufficient service is completed to acquire employment rights (generally two years).

Written particulars required by law within the first two months of employment are as follows:

❑ the rate of pay or method of calculation
❑ the interval of payment
❑ any terms and conditions relating to hours of work, holiday pay, sick pay and pensions, including collective agreements, if any
❑ notice periods on both sides
❑ the title of the job
❑ the length of the contract, or date of termination if the contract is not a permanent one
❑ the place of work, or, if the employee is required to work in various places, an indication of this, and the employer's address
❑ details about work outside the UK if required.

The statement details do not have to be included in the statement if they are easily available in some other form (eg company handbook, collective agreement), but employees must be told where such details are available and have reasonable access to them. If no terms under the above headings exist (eg no specific hours of work), the statement should say so.

In conclusion

In conclusion, then, traditional methods of recruitment and selection still predominate within the construction industry. In part this reflects the size and composition of organisations in construction – the smaller the firm, the less likely it is that sophisticated selection techniques will be adopted. Although there is some evidence of increasing interest in assessment centres and in psychological profiling on the part of larger firms, this is still fairly unusual within the industry. Use of a network or a grapevine is more likely to provide the solution to recruitment problems, particularly where manual workers are concerned. Yet whatever the size of the organisation and whatever the nature of the job under consideration, it is essential that managers give careful attention to legislation concerning discrimination in employment, and ensure that recruitment and selection techniques are demonstrably non-discriminatory.

CHAPTER 4

REWARD MANAGEMENT

In this chapter we review the range of pay practices which can be used for employees in construction, including the currently changing attitudes to reward management and 'New Pay' ideas. The chapter sets out the results of a recent (1996) survey of reward practices in larger construction companies, considers the importance of pay as a means to motivate the workforce, and looks at some of the new developments in reward practice which may be appropriate for the industry. Profit-related pay, profit-sharing and SAYE share option schemes have been used by the most innovative construction organisations, although there are many who have not yet taken advantage of the tax concessions of such schemes. The chapter also looks at the potential pitfalls of unformalised grading systems in meeting equal-pay-for-equal-value claims.

Pay is a central feature of the relationship between employer and employee. As we note in Chapter 3 on recruitment and selection, the whole contract of employment hinges around the notion of exchange – the employee agrees to work for the employer, and in return the employer undertakes to pay the employee. It is the 'consideration', or exchange of money, which defines the relationship. Because exchange is at the heart of the pay relationship, it is an area which, if managed poorly, can lead to conflict between employer and employee. Where trade unions exist, and the major method of determining pay and conditions is through collective bargaining, such conflict can lead to major disruptions of work. But even where pay and conditions are determined by management discretion, poor pay management can lead to high labour turnover and poorly motivated employees.

What is reward management?

Reward management is a relatively new term for what used to be called pay and benefits administration (or remuneration planning, or compensation and benefits management). The new term has come into common usage with the spread of human resource management ideas and, like the term human resource planning (see Chapter 2), reflects a change in management philosophy. Traditional pay and benefits administration was largely a 'back office' function performed by specialist remuneration managers who administered systems which were largely handed down from on high from head office. Policies were mostly determined by central government decisions (in the form of incomes policies and various pay regulatory bodies) and by the process of joint regulation by employers and unions through collective bargaining. Many of the pay and benefits components were set at industry level through national agreements, although there was an increasing amount of local pay bargaining in the 1960s and 1970s. Line managers had little influence over, or 'ownership' of, pay systems.

The norm for manual workers was a system of industry wage rates topped up at local level by additional amounts of money, much of it the product of incentive payment by results (PBR) schemes and various premium payments for overtime, shift work, etc. In short, manual workers' pay was primarily aimed at rewarding productivity. In contrast, non-manual pay systems were largely aimed at rewarding loyalty and service. White-collar staff were salaried and often graded in accordance with elaborate job descriptions. Pay progression, apart from periodic cost-of-living increases, was largely based on service, seniority and promotion.

The change of government in Britain in 1979 heralded a major change in the environment in which pay was determined. Out went concepts of incomes control and pay regulation, and support for collective bargaining was removed. The result was a considerable decline in pay determination through joint regulation. Although much of this change was based on monetarist, neo-classical economic policies of market supply and demand, throughout the 1980s employers began to realise that pay could not be handled in such a simplistic manner. In particular, human resource management literature emanating from the United States suggested that pay could be a major lever in achieving organisational changes and establishing a sophisticated method of management control (Lawler, 1990). Two main themes emerged – that pay systems design has to be linked to business strategy, and that ideas of 'best practice' need to be discarded in favour of more contingent pay policies which take account of the organisational context and culture. Lastly, the term 'reward management' suggests a much more holistic approach to managing employee performance, which embraces not just the tangible rewards of pay and benefits but also the intangible rewards which employees could reap from the organisation (eg job satisfaction, good environmental working conditions, good training and development opportunities, friendly and supportive working relationships, job security, involvement in work decisions, etc.). Reward management is therefore about both extrinsic motivators – those things external to the employee, such as pay, promotion and praise – and intrinsic motivators – those things which are derived from within the individual employee, such as the level of job satisfaction, responsibility, freedom to use his or her own judgement and have control over his or her own work.

So far the development of more flexible and innovative reward strategies has been limited within the construction industry, and traditional systems of pay determination continue in many companies. For the manual workforce (or at least those who are in direct employment), wage rates, premium payments and allowances are all still largely determined at industry level, although supplemented at site level (see Chapter 8). In contrast, the pay of the non-manual staff is almost entirely determined at company level. Yet the pay systems for non-manual staff remain rather unformalised in comparison with other industries. Individual appraisal related performance pay and other 'variable' components are not common.

This chapter therefore provides an overview of both modern approaches to motivating employees and pay systems techniques which may help to improve the productivity of a workforce.

Designing a reward system

When designing a reward system a number of factors must be considered, notably:

❑ the business environment of the organisation. What are the major factors that influence the company's philosophy or 'culture' and its business strategy?

❑ the business strategy of the organisation. What are the key aspects of the business strategy? What stage of development has the company reached?

❑ the profile of the workforce. What types of people are employed? To what extent do occupational 'norms' apply to pay and benefits systems? From which external labour markets does the company draw its labour?

Each industry has characteristics common to most organisations within its sector, but there can be great differences in organisational practice, even within a single industry. In the construction industry there are clear differences between the smaller firms, which make up the majority, and the medium- and large-sized contractors. The larger firms may well be part of even larger conglomerates which include other manufacturing, quarrying and service companies, so that their pay systems may be influenced by wider considerations. Even the medium-sized organisations may have different divisions (such as construction, civil engineering, house-building and sales, joinery workshops, and plant hire) which employ different categories of staff, so that reward systems may differ between divisions. Some companies are largely professional practices (such as architects, surveyors or civil engineers) and hence employers of mostly white-collar professionals. In contrast, some small builders may employ significant numbers of manual workers. There are even differences between employment practices in the south of the UK and the rest of the country: direct employment of manual workers is more common in the north and Midlands, and self-employment more common in the south.

Ensuring the 'best fit' between the reward system and the organisation's needs is therefore an essential part of reward management. The choices which are available to employers relate to a number of components in the reward system:

❑ On what management criteria is the reward system to be based? For example, companies may choose to emphasise 'equity' of treatment between employees or to emphasise individual worth and performance. Pay equity can be interpreted simply to mean 'a fair day's pay for a fair day's work', but it can also mean that the level and type of reward reflects the contribution of each individual employee. In judging the level and type of reward, employees will not only compare their own circumstances with those of fellow employees but also with those of colleagues working in similar jobs in other organisations. If they perceive their own pay and conditions to be inferior to those of others, in comparison to the responsibility, skills and performance level required for their own jobs, employees will become dissatisfied. This can lead to high labour turnover. In particular employers need to be wary of any sex discrimination in their allocation of pay and benefits.

❏ How will decisions about internal 'ranking' of different types of staff be decided? Small organisations require only fairly simple grading systems, but once a company begins to grow, more formal systems of grading will be necessary to ensure that employees' expectations of fairness are met. In the past, job evaluation has been a major method of determining the relative value of each job. However, the American 'New Pay' writers (Schuster and Zingheim, 1992) have highlighted an important shift from 'job-related' pay, where employees tend to be paid according to rigid grade and job definitions, to more flexible 'person-related' pay systems, where the emphasis is on more flexible, broad-banded grading structures and the individual's worth. Nevertheless, there is little sign of any decline in the use of job evaluation in the UK, and the threat of equal-pay-for-equal-value cases has made such schemes more attractive.

❏ On what criteria is the form of pay to be based? Employees can be paid by task, by the time they spend at work, or on the basis of their performance. Manual workers have traditionally been paid on the basis of hourly, daily, or weekly wage rates but with considerable additional amounts of incentive pay based on the tasks accomplished. White-collar staff have had their pay primarily linked to the time spent at work (usually weekly rates or annual salaries). However, there is an increasing trend for such white-collar staff to have at least a proportion of their pay related to their individual performance so that their pay becomes more variable. 'New Pay' systems are about increasing the amount of variable pay or pay 'at risk' within the total pay package, so that a proportion of pay can increase or diminish in line with business circumstances. This view has much in common with the traditional approach to manual workers' pay. The

CBI recommends that pay should be made up of a number of components which are based on individual, team or group, and organisational measures of performance (CBI, 1995). Lastly, there has been some recent movement towards pay systems based on the acquisition of skills or professional competencies.

❑ On what basis will pay levels be changed? Once the reward structure is in place, there will be a periodic need to update pay levels. There are a number of criteria which can be used to assess the degree of increase in pay levels required. These include the rise in the cost of living (price inflation); the ability to pay (profitability); external labour market conditions; comparisons with competitor companies (the 'going rate'); increases in productivity; and increases in individual, group or company performance. Where trade unions are present, industry-wide collective agreements may also be an influence.

❑ What benefits will the company provide? There are a range of both 'welfare' measures which have become an expected part of the reward package (such as paid holidays, paid sick leave, pensions, and maternity/paternity leave) and fringe benefits. The latter are used either as incentives to the workforce or as status symbols (for example, a company car). The company must decide which of these benefits it wishes to provide and to what degree employees will have some choice over the benefits provided.

In the following sections we look at each of these areas in turn. But first we look briefly at current practice in the construction industry.

Pay and benefits in construction

As discussed in Chapter 8, the collective bargaining arrangements for manual workers remain largely still in place at national level, major industrial agreements continuing to be negotiated each year with the relevant trade unions. These include agreements that apply to building and civil engineering, electrical contracting, plumbing, heating and ventilating, glazing, demolition, environmental engineering, and engineering construction. In the main these agreements are traditional national agreements which lay down base wage rates, premium pay and allowances. For manual workers, benefits are limited:

there is only modest provision in the areas of pensions, life and accident insurance cover, sick pay and holiday pay. In general, earnings levels of directly employed workers have more or less followed overall average earnings levels for male manual workers (see Figure 6). However, given the large numbers of self-employed workers within the industry (for whom there is no measure of earnings increase), it is unclear what real levels of earnings may be. These industry-level agreements and conditions of service are covered in more detail in Chapter 8. At company and/or site level, managers will apply these agreements (the National Working Rules) where directly employed operatives are engaged. However, construction company personnel departments have little involvement in the setting of terms and conditions for manual workers at this level – largely because this happens at national level.

Figure 6   Average earnings in construction (UK) where pay is not affected by absence

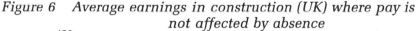
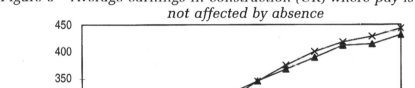
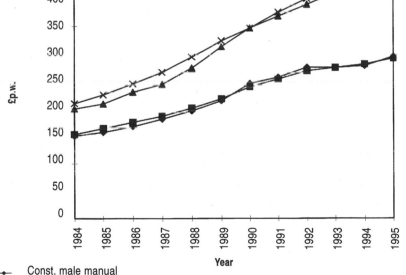

Source: New Earnings Survey

In contrast, personnel staff play a very important role in the design and administration of their non-manual staff's pay and benefits. The pay and benefits of non-manual staff are virtually all decided at company level. Average earnings for non-manual males in construction have more or less followed the trend for all such staff within the economy (see Figure 6).

Within the construction industry, pay and benefits tend to be the responsibility of generalist personnel managers or the company secretary. Companies are unlikely to have a specialist 'compensation and benefits manager' dedicated to designing and running the pay system – a survey of 41 construction companies in 1996 found that only three had compensation managers (Druker and White, 1996). In the following sections we concentrate on reward management at the level of the individual company. This chapter makes use of a survey of reward management practices in the construction industry carried out by the University of Greenwich in 1996.

Is pay a motivator?

Everybody has their own view on what motivates them and indeed what might motivate others. The big question for many managers is the degree to which employees can be motivated by financial means, and the degree to which other factors might be as or more important. Since the 1930s, business has basically been dominated by two separate schools of thought on the management of people – one which draws on the 'scientific management' school (starting with the American F. W. Taylor), and the other which draws on the 'human relations' school (starting with another American, Elton Mayo). At various times over the ensuing 70 years, these different schools of thought have been more or less influential on management practice. Even within modern human resource management, two approaches exist – 'Hard HRM', in which employees are treated on the one hand primarily as a commodity like any other raw material, and 'Soft HRM', which on the other hand emphasises the uniquely human aspect of labour compared with other commodities. Although these two schools of management thought have ramifications throughout the process of managing people, within the area of reward management they have particularly important roles – roles that relate primarily to the issue of employee motivation.

For the scientific management school, motivation is primarily about 'carrot and stick'. Employees will only work harder and more productively if they can be motivated through some form of incentive – either a reward for good behaviour or a penalty for poor behaviour. Although such rewards can be financial or non-financial, the concept remains the same. In contrast, the human relations school places the emphasis on the level of job satisfaction inherent in the work – employees will be motivated to work harder if they enjoy and take pride in their work, and if they feel that management cares about them. This is why the design of satisfying and interesting work by managers is essential if employees are to feel motivated.

The divide between these two management approaches was succinctly summarised by Macgregor (1960). Macgregor categorised these two approaches as Theory X and Theory Y. Theory X managers believe that the average person is lazy and prefers to be directed, and must be coerced into work through a system of penalties and control mechanisms. For Theory X managers the objective is to create discipline, conformity, obedience and dependence. In contrast, Theory Y managers believe that work is a natural and satisfying human activity, that people can be self-disciplined and seek out responsibility, and that the capacity for creativity and ingenuity is widely spread throughout the population. Most importantly, Theory Y suggests that employees will commit themselves to the organisation's objectives in proportion to the rewards received or on offer. Macgregor stresses the importance of participation and involvement in employee motivation.

A number of writers have developed theories to explain what motivates people at work. According to Maslow (1954), all employees have a hierarchy of needs. Those at the bottom of the hierarchy are physiological (hunger, sleep, thirst, sex), followed by the need for safety and security. These are followed by higher-level needs, such as social needs, esteem, and finally self-actualisation (the need to fulfil one's personal potential). Only when the basic-level needs have been met do the higher-level needs become important. For Maslow, pay was a means to achieving physiological and safety needs, and thus came fairly low in the hierarchy. Herzberg (1959) developed these ideas to suggest that there were two factors that affect human behaviour at work – dissatisifiers (or hygiene factors) and satisfiers (or motivators). Hygiene factors were those things which were expected by employees and which would lead to dissatisfaction

71

if not present. However, such factors were not motivators. In contrast, satisfiers were those factors which actually led to an employee's being motivated to work harder and achieve desired goals. For Herzberg, pay is a dissatisfier and not a motivator.

Within the construction industry, Maslow's hierarchy of needs may have some relevance. Given the insecure nature of employment for many manual workers within the industry, one might expect the satisfaction of lower-level needs to be paramount. However, this view would underestimate the very real job satisfaction which craft workers get from the practice of their skills. Nothing can upset a craft worker more than a poorly managed construction job, where there are delays in the delivery of materials or poorly designed processes or materials. Although such delays may limit the worker's ability to gain bonus payments and thereby hit earnings potential, there is also a pride in getting a job done to time and to appropriate levels of quality.

Other important influences upon reward management are the various so-called 'process theories' of motivation. These include expectancy theory, equity theory, goal theory, and attribution theory. Expectancy theory (Vroom, 1964) states that individuals will behave in a specific way where they expect to achieve a particular outcome (expectancy), but that the degree of employee satisfaction that results will depend on the outcome (valence). Outcomes can be either negative or positive. A negative outcome will not motivate, whereas a positive outcome will. Vroom also introduced the concept of instrumentality, which suggests that individuals will also be motivated by the degree to which additional personal goals are achieved in the process.

Equity theory (Adams, 1965) emphasises the fact that the work relationship is one of exchange. People expect certain outcomes in exchange for their contribution or inputs at work. They are motivated by the degree to which they feel that the exchange is a fair one. Where the individual perceives the exchange to be unequal, a feeling of inequity develops, causing tension in the employment relationship.

Attribution theory (Alderfer, 1972) is concerned with how people interpret and explain their success or failure. Employees are more likely to adjust their behaviour if they believe it to be something over which they have control. If they believe that their failure is due to circumstances beyond their control, they will be unlikely to change their behaviour.

Goal theory states that employee motivation can be influenced by the presence of a goal-setting process (Locke, 1968). Goals should be specific, realistic, challenging, but achievable, and seen as fair and reasonable by employees. Employees should participate in the goal-setting process, and feedback should be given on the degree to which the goals are achieved. Reinforcement theory suggests that success in achieving such goals acts as a positive incentive to performance and reinforces the likelihood of such behaviour in the future. Goal theory is important in explaining the degree of motivation associated with incentive pay; it has much in common with the 'management by objectives' (MBO) approach first explained by Peter Drucker in 1954 and popularised in the 1960s (Drucker, 1989). MBO is a process whereby clear goals are agreed between a superior and subordinate manager to assess the subordinate's contribution to the area of work for which he or she is responsible.

It is expectancy theory which has most relevance to reward management. Porter and Lawler (1968) adapted Vroom's original concepts to provide a model of how employers can influence employee motivation. In contrast to the human relations school approach, which tends to assume that job satisfaction leads to improved performance, Porter and Lawler suggest that satisfaction is an effect rather than a cause of performance. It is performance that leads to job satisfaction, rather than vice versa. Their theory brings together a number of the motivational factors discussed above.

This model states that a person's motivation is based on three elements:

❑ *the effort-to-performance expectancies* – What is the perceived likelihood that the amount of effort required will result in the desired level of reward?

❑ *the performance-to-outcomes expectancies* – What does the employee expect to put in in order to achieve the required level of performance? The input that employees make to a task is dependent on both their own abilities and personal traits and on their perception of what is expected of them. Clearly, if an employee does not have the required abilities or traits or does not have a clear set of objectives, it is unlikely that the desired level of performance will be achieved.

❑ *the perceived attractiveness of the outcomes* – Does the

73

outcome constitute what is desired and expected by the
employee? The reward can be either extrinsic or intrinsic,
but in either case its value will depend on the employee's
perception of what constitutes a fair reward for the effort
delivered.

Figure 7   Expectancy theory

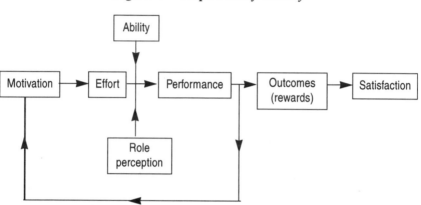

Expectancy theory can be a vital tool in designing a reward
system. Because it embraces a number of dimensions of motivation, it can be applied to virtually any level of employee
within a construction firm. However, as with many business
processes, it is important to realise that the expectations of
employers and those of employees may differ. It is the media-
tion of these different expectations which is at the heart of
reward management techniques. The managerial criteria for pay
are (in Child, 1984) as follows:

❑ to attract and retain staff
❑ to encourage dependable behaviour
❑ to secure high commitment and effort
❑ to foster flexibility
❑ to foster innovation.

For employees, in contrast, the criteria are:

❑ intrinsic rewards
❑ extrinsic rewards

74

❑ fairness (internal equity)

❑ external comparability.

Of course these two separate sets of objectives are not mutually exclusive. For example, achieving both fairness and external comparability for employees will undoubtedly aid recruitment and retention and secure high commitment and effort for management. Fostering innovation for management may well help meet the intrinsic needs of employees for job satisfaction and feelings of achievement.

Grading systems and job evaluation

The starting-point in the design of a reward system is the establishment of some form of grading system which denotes the value each job has within the organisation. This is normally done by comparing the content of jobs within the organisation so that a hierarchy of grades is created. Such grading structures can be anything from very simple to highly complex. Grading is used to determine the rates of pay for particular jobs, the relationships (or relativities) between jobs, and the basis on which job holders are paid.

In small firms this process of grading may happen without much conscious effort – the owner of the business will know the capabilities and contribution of each member of staff intimately from day-to-day contact at work. Pay rates will therefore be decided on the basis of either managerial discretion or some form of agreement between the employer and the individual employee. However, once organisations increase in size, so that the owner devolves day-to-day management to a number of individual managers, such intimacy ends. In order to ensure fair treatment of all employees, irrespective of their managers, systems have to be installed to ensure that the pay systems truly reflect the value of each employee, both within the internal structure of the company and externally in terms of the market rate.

Given that construction is an industry of many small firms (see Chapter 1), it is perhaps not surprising that formal grading systems and the use of job evaluation are rare. In the average small building sub-contractor, the owner may know all the employees by name and operate in the 'owner-manager' mode. This is not to say that such small firms do not use grading systems at all – indeed, many small firms are party to the industry national agreements and see the advantage of having their pay rates fixed through some national forum and grading structure for craft and non-craft tasks. The large and medium-sized contractors employ people in such numbers that formal systems are more likely. Even so, the evidence suggests that pay systems in the major contractors tend to be relatively unformalised. In the 1996 Greenwich Survey, only 12 companies out of 41 had a formal grading system for manual workers, and only 15 for non-manuals. More importantly, only two companies out of 41 used job evaluation for manual workers, and only eight for non-manuals. Three companies used the same grading system for manual and non-manual workers, but the great majority had separate arrangements for the two groups. This absence of formal grading systems reflects the general picture of construction as an industry relatively lacking in human resource management systems.

However, there are several reasons that more formal grading systems may be beneficial to the industry. The first is that, with the growth of National/Scottish Vocational Qualifications (N/SVQ) awards, the opportunity exists for the first time to secure a structured approach to career development and pay throughout the industry. It is now possible, at least in theory, for an employee to join an organisation with a first-level vocational qualification (N/SVQ 1) and progress through to management (N/SVQ 5) (see Chapter 6). Increasingly, construction employers may need to link pay to the competencies required for N/SVQs. Moreover, this means that grading systems which include both manual and non-manual workers – harmonised or single-status systems – will be necessary. Secondly, more formal grading systems imply a concern to achieve fairness and internal equity within an organisation. Organisations need to ask themselves to what extent they can afford to rely on purely subjective assessments of differences in the value of jobs. This is of increasing importance because of the legal requirements to demonstrate that equal pay for work of equal value has been taken into account in the distribution of rewards (see below). Lastly, the use of job evaluation schemes can be used to make sector-wide comparisons – and indeed wider comparisons with the external labour market. Companies which use 'patent' job evaluation systems, provided by management consultancies such as Hay, Wyatt, PE International, PA Consulting Group, etc., usually have the opportunity to update their pay information each year from surveys conducted by the consultancy. By being able to compare jobs across companies and industries, pay levels can be more easily linked to the market.

Job evaluation is the process of assessing the relative 'size' of jobs within an organisation (Armstrong and Murlis, 1994). Its primary purpose is to provide a rational basis for determining and managing internal relationships between jobs and for the design of pay structures. The information collected for a job evaluation exercise can be used for a variety of other purposes as well as pay – organisation design, human resource planning (see Chapter 3), training and continuous development. It is important to understand five facts about job evaluation – it is:

❑ comparative

❑ judgemental

❑ analytical

❑ structured

❑ job-centred.

The major types of job evaluation system can be grouped into two main types – but all of them start, however, with the process of job analysis. Each job must be examined in turn and some form of job description written. This may involve skills or competency analysis, and can be carried out in a number of ways – through questionnaires, interviews and checklists, critical incident techniques and repertory grids (Armstrong and Murlis, 1994). Generic job descriptions can be used where a number of employees carry out similar tasks, but otherwise individual job descriptions are necessary. A first step is to separate out the total employee population into job families of basically similar jobs.

The two major types of job evaluation in use are non-analytical and analytical job evaluation schemes.

Non-analytical job evaluation schemes

These schemes are known as non-analytical because jobs are examined and compared without any analysis of their component parts.

❑ *Job ranking* determines the position of jobs in a hierarchy by placing them in rank order according to views on their relative size. This is the simplest system of job evaluation but suffers from the absence of any rationale to defend the rank order because no defined standards are used to estimate the relative size of job. Such schemes may suit a small company in which there are few employees to grade.

❑ *Paired comparisons* is a more refined method of job ranking. The underlying principle is to compare each benchmark job in turn with another job. If the job is considered to be more important than its comparator, the job scores two points; if it is the same value it scores one point; and if it has a lower value it scores zero. The total score is added for each job and produces its rank order in the hierarchy. The problem with this method is that it is difficult to carry out for large numbers of posts, even with the aid of computers. The process is also open to allegations of subjective bias because decisions about jobs are not based on any independent breakdown of job qualities and values. However, again the small building company may find such schemes attractive because they are simple to administer and easy to communicate to staff.

❑ *Job classification* starts from the point of a ready-made grading system. A system of grades is established with sample job descriptions for each grade, and individual benchmark jobs are then compared against the criteria for each grade to establish to which grade the job should be allocated. Some companies use the Institute of Administrative Management (IAM) scheme, which is a good example of job classification, to grade their clerical and secretarial staff.

Analytical job evaluation schemes
Unlike non-analytical schemes, analytical job evaluation schemes analyse jobs by one or more criteria, factors or elements. In an analytical scheme, each job is examined against a number of criteria and sub-criteria. This more scientific approach helps to mitigate any subjective bias among the evaluators and in particular helps to overcome gender stereotyping of jobs.

❑ *A points factor scheme* uses job scales. Jobs are broken down into factors or key elements, on the assumption that each factor contributes in some degree to job size. Using numerical scales, points are allocated to a job under each factor heading according to the degree to which the job exhibits the factor. The key parts of a factor-rating scheme are the factor plan, the factor-rating scales, and factor weighting. Factors may include such things as the knowledge and skills required to do the job; the processes required (such as mental effort, problem-solving, etc.) and the outputs (the contribution impact which the job holder can make on end results, such as responsibility for staff, for resources and budgets, and the effect of errors). Each factor or sub-factor is scored to a maximum determined by the factor weighting. In other words, some factors are considered to be more important than others and are scored appropriately. Points progression is usually arithmetical (eg 20, 40, 60, 80, 100) but it can be geometric (ie each number increases by a percentage over the previous one).

❑ *Graduated factor comparison* is similar to points factor schemes, but the scale is a graduated one in which the descriptive level definitions are scored as high, medium or low.

❑ *Factor comparison* compares jobs with jobs using a number of factors but not using a scale. In other words, there is no fixed weighting between the scales and they are not necessarily the same length or spread.

❑ *Single-factor analytical methods* use just one factor, such as skills, competencies, decision-bands or time-spans of discretion.

The advantages of points factor schemes are that evaluators are forced to consider more than one aspect of each job, allowing more objectivity and consistency. Most importantly, they are acceptable in the case of legal challenges under equal pay law.

Very few construction firms currently operate such factor-based job evaluation schemes, but this may be changing. A good example of a factor-based job evaluation scheme has recently been agreed for the environmental engineering industry, one of the few areas of non-manual employment in the construction industry covered by collective bargaining. A new unified grading system for the industry's 30,000 technical, supervisory and administrative staff covered by the Environmental Engineering National Joint Council has been developed to commence in January 1998. This new grading scheme uses four factor headings to assess jobs – job knowledge, decisions, contacts, and supervision. A job evaluation exercise will take place over the next two years to re-grade staff following the new structure.

Equal pay and equal value

Although the construction industry remains very much a majority male sector at present, as we discuss elsewhere in this book this may not continue in the future. Labour force projections indicate that the number of women in the workforce has increased dramatically and will increase further in the near future. The demographic changes which were concerns in the late 1980s, especially the shortage of school-leavers (see Chapters 5 and 6), may have been obscured temporarily by the economic downturn of the first half of the 1990s but are forecast to return to prominence when the economy recovers. Already women have made inroads into the construction professions, and this may spread to the skilled areas too. For this reason, construction firms need to look very carefully at their grading and pay systems to ensure that they genuinely reflect the value of employees, irrespective of gender.

The Equal Pay Act 1970 (as amended by the Equal Value amendment in 1984) states that there should be equality between men and women where they are employed

❑ on 'like work' – work of the same or broadly similar nature
❑ on 'work rated as equivalent' – work of equal value under a non-discriminatory job evaluation system
❑ on work which is of equal value.

'Like work' does not have to mean that the work has to be the same. It can be broadly 'similar' but the differences must not be of any 'practical importance'. What must be examined in an equal-value case is what work is actually done, rather than what could be done under the contract. Job evaluation schemes allow a comparison of different jobs for the purposes of equal-pay claims. Such a job evaluation scheme must be non-discriminatory, impartial, and must constitute a proper analysis. The Equal Value amendment means that equal pay can be claimed, irrespective of whether the jobs are completely different, provided that the demands made under such headings as effort, skill and decision-making are of equal value. The Act does not deal just with pay but extends to other terms, although a defence cannot be based on arguments about the total remuneration package. The basic rate must be the same, irrespective of benefits. The comparator has to be in the 'same employment' as the claimant, meaning employed by the same (or an associated) employer at the same establishment, or at a different establishment if there are common terms. A woman may compare herself with a male predecessor but cannot argue a case based on a 'notional man' – ie cannot argue that a man doing the same job would have been paid more.

In defence, an employer may argue that the variation in conditions between the man and the woman is not due to gender and that the difference is 'genuinely due to a material factor'. The onus is on the employer to show what the material factor is.

Payment structures and methods

Once a grading system has been established, a pay structure can be created. Pay structures vary greatly between industries and companies, and largely reflect the norms of behaviour in each sector. A pay structure in a small advertising company is very different from that in a local authority or indeed an airline. Pay structures reflect the organisational structure of the company, so that bureaucratic structures create rather rigidly structured payment systems which emphasise service, seniority and internal equity, whereas fast-moving entrepreneurial organisations tend to have much less structured systems which emphasise the individual's performance, the profitability of the company, and the external market rate for the particular job. Within the construction industry, smaller organisations have relatively informal systems but the larger companies, especially where staff may move between divisions, tend to have more formal pay structures.

In general, there is still a strong divide between the payment systems for manual workers and those for non-manual workers, and nowhere is this more true than in construction. For directly employed manual workers, pay structures tend to be very simple: there are few grades, and hourly and weekly wage rates are set at industry level. These rates of pay may be enhanced through various allowances (such as abnormal conditions, tool allowances, etc.) and through overtime or shift premiums. Financial incentive schemes were introduced into the construction industry after World War II as a mechanism to increase output, and were common up to the 1970s. The frameworks for these payment by results (PBR) incentive schemes are covered by the industry-level national agreements, but there is some evidence of a decline in this area, mainly because of the growth of self-employed labour. Incentive pay appears to be a more significant pay component in construction than elsewhere. According to the government's annual New Earnings Survey for 1995, PBR makes up around 8 per cent of total earnings in the construction industry, compared to around 5 per cent for all production industries. The Greenwich Survey found that few construction firms link the pay of their manual workers to individual performance measurement (only 13 companies) and only 11 companies used group- or team-based incentives. Site productivity and completion bonuses were provided by 12 companies. Three companies include their manual workers in company-wide bonus schemes, and two have bonuses for achieving quality standard targets (Druker and White, 1996).

Most construction PBR schemes are work-measured (ie the tasks are timed and operatives' work is measured on completion against standards). Schemes can be either individual-based or group-based. Another common feature of the industry in the past was the 'end-of-contract' or 'completion' bonus which rewarded employees for completing the contract ahead of schedule or, where work was slipping behind, completion to the deadline.

For non-manual workers, payment systems are generally composed of annual salaries with an annual cost-of-living increase and/or performance-related bonus. Grades tend to be broad-banded (wide gaps between minimum and maximum salaries for each grade) and sometimes grouped into job families (eg all surveyors will be on one structure and all planners on another). The Greenwich Survey found not a single company which used age-related or service-based salary progression. Some 14 out of the sample used performance-based incremental progression, and 19 used individual managers' discretion. Four used 'all-merit' appraisal-based spot salaries, and three used competency-based systems. Although 10 companies said that individual salaries were linked to formal performance appraisals, 30 out of the 40 companies did not have appraisal-related performance pay. This suggests that many construction firms have fairly informal salary progression systems, increases being decided largely at management's discretion.

Although such systems may fit the informal culture of the industry, there may be good reasons for introducing more structured systems. Such reasons would include the fact that management discretion may be open to challenge in the future.

Employers are more exposed to equal-value claims and companies will need to justify their pay decisions on more scientific grounds than simply management discretion. More importantly, research has demonstrated that for employees to have their salaries based on their individual performance will only work if the individual is set clear targets against which his or her performance can be measured. As expectancy theory states, failure to make clear links between the targets set and the outcomes achieved will not motivate employees. Systems based on management discretion may give managers a great deal of power over individual employees, but such arrangements suggest a poor method of handling employee performance. It also suggests a system prone to favouritism and bias, and is certainly not one which encourages the fair treatment, involvement and partnership suggested by modern human resource management techniques.

Performance-related pay
There is an on-going debate about whether performance appraisal should be used for making pay decisions. Some writers argue that it is best suited to assessing employees' training and career development needs, while others argue that linking it to pay is an effective method of improving performance. There has yet to be any academic research which proves conclusively that individual performance-related pay leads to improved performance, and some organisations have begun to question its value. On the other hand, there is no sign of any shift away from more variable pay systems. The process of individual performance appraisal is dealt with in Chapter 6. If a company wishes to link its pay system to individual performance appraisals, it is a relatively easy step to develop a system.

Individual employee performance can be assessed using two main methods which, broadly speaking, relate to either inputs to or outputs from a job. Input measures are generally more qualitative – such as personal qualities (eg diligence, punctuality, enthusiasm, etc.) – while output measures are usually based on more quantitative and specific targets (eg reaching a required level of sales, generating a certain amount of income, keeping to budgets, developing new products or services, etc.). In recent times, output measures have become the more popular method of assessing employee performance because they usually have clear financial implications for the organisation. It may also be argued that such outputs can be more easily set as targets at the start, and measured at the end, of the appraisal period. What is clear is that such targets must be fair and achievable, must be within the individual's ability and span of control, and must be limited in number.

Some form of box marking must be utilised so that employees can be given a score or grade. The important point here is that such box marking schemes should not have very many boxes – it is recommended that such marking schemes should have no more than six grades. Even numbers of boxes are better than odd numbers because many managers tend to mark in the middle if they can. Four or six boxes will stop managers from picking the middle box.

One observed problem with individual performance-related pay, like any other form of incentive scheme, is the tendency for salaries to drift upwards over time. If all individuals' performance continues to improve, as expected, all employees will tend to drift towards the top of the grade range, especially as many managers have been found to mark on the generous side. For this reason, some organisations operate a system of 'forced distribution' where the numbers of employees who can be given each box mark is limited, obliging managers to show more discretion in their marking. Alternatively, each line manager may be given a budget for merit increases which they must decide how to allocate according to the appraisal results. In order to ensure fair and equitable standards of assessment are being utilised by managers right across an organisation, many companies appoint an independent senior manager to act as 'grandfather' and make adjustments at company-wide level before any final decisions are taken. This individual may also play the role of adjudicator in any dispute between the manager and employee over the award given. In some cases, appeal procedures are in place to serve this function.

Once a company has an appraisal system in place and a system of measuring individual performance, the last step is to decide on the payment system and how the pay level is to be linked to the appraisal mark. There is one big decision to make – will the performance rating be used to assess the whole salary level (eg will the base salary be increased each year in line with the performance rating?) or just a proportion? Alternatively, companies may decide to make the reward a merit bonus which is unconsolidated into base salary and must be re-earned each year. If salary progression is to be performance-related, there are further decisions to be made. Will progression be based on a scale of fixed incremental steps, the increments varying in size according the rating? Or will there be additional performance-based increments at the top of basic service-related scales? Or will salaries be increased by different percentage amounts within broad salary bands. In the last example, the mid-point of the band may increase by the cost of living but any other progression is performance-based. Many organisations provide a cost-of-living increase for all but the unsatisfactory performers, adding varying increases on top according to individual performance.

Apart from individual performance-related pay schemes, a construction company may also choose to provide group or team incentives, again based on clear target-setting arrangements, and indeed company-wide bonuses based on financial turnover or profit levels. The Greenwich Survey found that the most common additions to salary for non-manual staff in construction were one-off merit bonuses and overtime pay. A small number of firms had profit-related pay and profit-share bonuses, SAYE share option schemes, shift/unsocial hours payments, and team/project completion bonuses. The survey also found that for non-manual staff the proportion of variable pay to fixed was relatively small. Most companies said that between 80 per cent and 100 per cent of pay was fixed. The various forms of financial participation schemes are dealt with briefly later in this section. For those staff employed in a sales function within a construction company – and this may be more likely in house-building than elsewhere – companies may have a sales bonus which relates to the amount of business conducted or sales achieved. Commission is yet another incentive which may be used to encourage sales staff.

Keeping pay levels competitive

All companies need to keep their payment structures up to date, in particular in ensuring that pay levels do not exceed or fall too much out of line with competitor firms. Although the cost of living (ie price inflation measured by the Retail Price Index) is an important benchmark for both employers and employees, other factors are as, if not more, important. The Greenwich Survey found that, for manual workers, matching the industry collective agreement increases was most important. For non-manual employees the survey found that 'ability to pay' was foremost, followed by matching labour market conditions and linking pay to performance/productivity. The cost of living came relatively low in their consideration. The Greenwich Survey shows that the frequency of salary reviews is almost entirely annual, only one company reviewing pay more frequently than that.

The main criteria used to determine pay levels are:

- ❑ cost of living
- ❑ matching external labour market conditions
- ❑ linking pay to productivity/performance
- ❑ ability to pay
- ❑ matching competitor companies' reward levels
- ❑ rewarding the development of skills or competencies
- ❑ collective bargaining.

The degree of importance which each company places on each of these criteria varies according to the business circumstances. Companies can afford to ignore the cost of living when the industry is in recession and jobs are under threat. In construction the early 1990s were marked by pay freezes at both industry bargaining level and at company level. However, when the industry's fortunes improve and labour turnover increases, companies normally use pay increases as the most common method of combating skill shortages (Agapiou *et al*, 1995b). This can lead to major wage and salary drift, and push up the industry's costs. More stable and structured pay systems may help to reduce labour turnover in times of boom, but non-financial rewards (such as good training and development and job security) may be as important in keeping valuable staff in the longer term. As mentioned above, collective bargaining remains the major influence upon the pay levels of manual employees in the construction industry, despite the decline in the numbers of directly employed workers. Collective bargaining has never applied to the non-manual workforce in any significant degree, but the size of the annual industry wage agreement does have an indirect influence upon the levels of pay for non-manual workers within the industry. Average earnings figures (as at April 1995) for a number of construction occupations are shown in Table 2.

Table 2   Average earnings by occupation

Occupation (Males only)	Total average gross weekly pay £p.w.	Overtime £p.w.	Payment by results £p.w.	Shift etc. pay £p.w.	Total weekly working hours (inc. overtime)
Non-manual Employees					
Civil, structural, municipal, mining and quarrying engineers	508.0	13.6	10.4	7.1	39.2
Architects	483.0	6.3	10.8	–	37.7
Building, land, mining and general practice surveyors	447.9	2.6	12.2	–	37.9
Architecture and town planning technicians	322.6	6.7	2.0	0.3	37.6
Building and civil engineering technicians	310.7	10.6	1.2	–	38.5
Quantity surveyors	418.2	8.3	7.5	–	39.0
Manual Employees					
Bricklayers, masons	262.7	21.0	29.4	0.8	42.7
Roofers, slaters, tilers, sheeters, cladders	254.8	12.7	37.7	0.4	41.5
Builders, building contractors	269.0	29.0	8.8	1.8	43.3
Painters and decorators	262.1	26.5	21.1	1.2	43.3
Other const. trades	269.4	28.3	12.9	2.3	43.7

Source: New Earnings Survey 1996

Financial participation schemes

Although the construction industry is not usually in the vanguard of new types of remuneration practice, in one case the industry is in line with national trends. Construction firms appear to be making significant use of the government's financial participation initiatives: the Inland-Revenue-approved Profit-Related Pay (PRP) scheme, profit-share bonuses, and SAYE share option schemes.

According to the Inland Revenue, at March 1995 there were 399 approved PRP schemes operating in construction, covering some 55,000 employees. No figures are available on a sectoral basis for other government-approved financial participation schemes, but the Greenwich Survey found significant numbers of construction companies with profit-share cash bonuses, SAYE share option schemes and discretionary share option schemes. Such schemes offer companies the opportunity to provide a longer-term financial incentive to employees which links their pay to the success of the company over a specified period of time. The degree to which such bonus schemes improve productivity and encourage worker commitment is hotly disputed – some argue that the effects are minimal. Few employers appear to see the schemes as providing more pay flexibility during recession, and hence protecting jobs, but they do say that they focus employees' attention more closely on the link between pay and company performance. More importantly, there are clear tax advantages for the employee in such schemes, which can increase the amount of take-home pay without any consequent increase in cost to the employer, and some argue that it is this aspect which makes the schemes popular with both employers and employees.

There has been a rapid growth in PRP schemes generally over recent years. By September 1995 there were some 10,500 schemes covering 2.6 million people. This is three times the number in 1992. The idea of PRP is that an employee's pay varies in line with changes in the company's profitability. Where a PRP scheme is approved by the Inland Revenue, PRP payments are exempt from income tax up to a limit of 20 per cent of total pay or £4,000 a year, whichever is the lower. There is no overall limit on the amount of PRP which can be paid to employees, only that portion which can gain tax relief. The tax relief is worth up to £960 each year to a basic-rate tax-payer and up to £1,600 a year to a higher-rate tax-payer. PRP can operate either as a bonus addition to basic pay or as a salary conversion scheme. Although employees have to put a significant element of their salaries at risk, companies seem to have encountered few problems in gaining their support for such schemes (IDS Study 603, 1996). Further details about PRP are available from the Inland Revenue Profit-Related Pay Unit, St Mungo's Road, Cumbernauld, Glasgow G67 1YZ (Tel: 01236 736121).

Other forms of financial participation available to companies include profit-sharing schemes and share option schemes. These schemes may or may not attract tax relief and may be available for all employees or at management discretion. The Inland Revenue estimates that over 1.4 million employees and directors received shares or share options worth over £3.8 billion during 1992–93. The total number of tax-approved profit-sharing schemes was 1,111 at March 1994, and around 740,000 employees were allocated shares in 1992–93. There are also SAYE (Save As You Earn) share option schemes, of which there were 1,257 registered at March 1994. Around 590,000 employees were granted share options under SAYE schemes in 1992–93 (IDS, 1995). No figures are available separately for the construction industry.

To gain tax concessions, any profit-sharing or share option scheme must be approved by the Inland Revenue. Under an approved profit-sharing scheme, an employee is set aside, or appropriated, shares which are held in trust for a minimum of two years. After this period, the employee may dispose of the shares, but is liable for income tax on their value at the time of setting aside unless the shares remain in trust for a further three years. After five years in trust they may be disposed of without any income tax charge. The share bonus does not attract National Insurance contributions either.

Savings-related share option schemes were introduced in 1980. Under these schemes, employees are given options to buy shares in their company on a specified future date at, or within an allowed discount to, the share price at the beginning of the contract. The shares can be bought only from the proceeds of the SAYE contract. These contracts last for a period of five or seven years, at which time employees may either use the proceeds to buy shares or withdraw their savings plus a bonus. Employees must choose at the outset whether to take a five-year or seven-year share contract. If share prices have risen over the contract period, the option price will be below the market price and so a profit is made. Whether employees choose to opt for shares or cash, there is no income tax to pay.

Further details on both profit-sharing schemes and SAYE share option schemes are available from the Public Enquiry Room, Inland Revenue, Room G1 West Wing, Somerset House, Strand, London WC2R 1LB (Tel: 0171 438 7772).

Benefits

The last but very important part of the reward package considered in this chapter is the benefits on offer. Often overlooked and taken for granted by employees, but potentially adding substantially to an employer's overall payroll costs, the benefits provided can be an important element in both attracting and retaining employees. There are various types of benefits, some of which employees might see as essential in any modern workplace (eg paid holidays, sick pay, and life insurance) whereas others might be more discretionary and dependent on service, merit or status. Some are basically reimbursement of money spent in the employer's interest (eg travel and subsistence allowances, tool allowances) while others may be for working in unpleasant, unsocial or dangerous conditions. Both of these latter two types are common in construction.

In general, the divide between manual and non-manual employees which we have noted elsewhere in the construction industry also exists in the area of benefits. Although working conditions allowances are set at industry level through the working rule agreements, there are few other benefits provided for manual workers. The mobile nature of construction work means that few manual employees at site level have enough service to accrue significant amounts of service-related benefits such as holidays, sick pay and pensions. Instead, as explained in Chapter 8, arrangements exist at national level for the employers of directly employed manual workers to buy 'holiday stamps' which can be traded in by the employee (irrespective of whether he or she is still employed by the same employer) to provide holiday pay when an employee wishes to take a vacation. A similar scheme exists to provide a lump sum retirement benefit. In the electrical contracting industry the AEEU trade union has negotiated an industry-wide private health insurance scheme. Most construction workers have to be fairly self-reliant in terms of their main welfare benefits, and put money aside to cover any long-term period of sickness or injury. The employers provide basic statutory sick-pay entitlement but in the main no enhanced company benefit.

Nevertheless, the table of benefits provided by 41 construction companies shown below (Table 3) shows that this picture may be changing. At least 18 companies provide company sick pay for manual workers; 11 provide a company pension; eight a company retirement benefit; three company private health; 27 company paid holidays; and 19 company redundancy pay. Clearly, where companies employ a substantial direct workforce rather than self-employed or labour-only sub-contractors, there is an incentive to provide good benefits because they will help to recruit and retain highly skilled workers (who may indeed have the option of becoming self-employed but thereby lose such benefits). Elsewhere the number of manual workers employed may be so small that they are treated as part of the non-manual workforce and hence receive similar benefits.

For non-manual workers the position is more similar to other industries: there is a range of company-provided welfare benefits, such as sick pay, pension, life insurance, paid holidays and private medical insurance. In addition, office-based workers may have the usual range of allowances such as assisted house purchase, company loans, season ticket loans, and a sports and social club. Site-based professional, technical and managerial staff may either be provided with an essential-user company car or be able to claim mileage allowance on their own cars. Office-based management staff may also have essential-user cars if their jobs involve some travel around sites or regional offices, while others may have non-essential-user 'status' or 'perk' cars. Anecdotal accounts suggest that construction industry personnel managers spend a great deal of time on the administration of car fleets, and the choice of car can be a major source of conflict with an employee!

It is interesting that few construction companies provide female-centred benefits such as childcare allowances or career breaks. This attitude probably reflects the small proportion of women employed in the industry – but this may need to change if construction firms are to attract women into the industry. An optimistic sign of changing attitudes can be found in the fact that maternity pay for manual workers now exists in 16 companies, and at least three now provide paternity leave for non-manual fathers.

The changing nature and composition of the workforce has

led some companies to review their benefits practices. Instead of all staff receiving the same benefits irrespective of their individual needs, companies are introducing flexible or 'cafeteria' benefits systems. Under these schemes, employees can choose from a menu of benefits up to a specified budget figure. Some limits to this flexibility are imposed by tax considerations, and any employer who wishes to introduce such a scheme would be well advised to consult a tax and benefits advisor. The administration can be quite complicated too, and significant discounts on certain benefits (such as pensions and private

Table 3   Benefits provision in the construction industry

Benefit	Manual	Non-manual
Company sick pay scheme	18	39
Company pension scheme	11	41
Company retirement scheme	8	19
Industry retirement scheme	25	2
Company private health insurance	3	36
Industry private health	5	2
Tool allowances	24	2
Working conditions allowances	26	3
Travel and subsistence	27	29
Essential-user cars	5	37
Non-essential-user cars	1	34
Company paid holidays	27	41
Sabbaticals/career breaks	1	8
Company maternity	16	28
Company paternity	0	3
Relocation	4	31
Company redundancy pay	19	31
Long service awards	23	34
House purchase assistance	1	10
Company loans	2	7
Financial advice	0	5
Benefit	**Manual**	**Non-manual**
Sports and social club	8	14
Season ticket loan	4	16
Childcare allowance	0	1

Sample size: 41 companies
Source: Druker and White, *University of Greenwich Survey of Reward Practices in the Construction Industry, 1996*

medical insurance) may be lost if staff are allowed to opt for alternative benefits to the extent that the numbers in the group decline. However, such flexibility does suggest a more employee-centred approach to benefits, and certainly allows staff a choice of benefits to suit their personal circumstances at particular points in their careers. Eight of the companies in the Greenwich Survey allowed employees some degree of flexibility in their choice of benefits.

Building reward systems for the future

As we have discussed in this chapter, the practice of reward management has changed significantly in the UK over recent years. Although some of these developments may appear inappropriate for the construction industry, a number of lessons can be learned from other sectors. Firstly, a more formalised reward system does not necessarily imply either increased administration or extra costs. A well designed reward system which meets both employer and employee expectations can save money by ensuring that salary drift is controlled and by reducing labour turnover. An effective system of performance management, in which employees are set clear targets against which they are measured, can increase productivity and aid employee development. If pay is to be related to performance, it is important that such a performance management system is in place first. Performance-related pay only works if employees are clear about what is required of them, if the objectives are seen as fair and achievable by each employee, and if the size of the reward reflects the size of the employee's contribution. Most importantly, employees should be given a 'voice' in any discussion of changes to their pay systems. Employee involvement in the design of pay systems is vital if such changes are to be accepted and 'owned' by those to whom they are applied. Where trade unions are present, the process of collective bargaining should help achieve this involvement.

More formal grading systems will be essential if the number of women working in the industry increases. An employer must be able to demonstrate clearly that the allocation of rewards is based on a fair system of assessing the value of individual jobs. There is a growing body of equal-pay law which can be brought to bear on an employer who ignores such requirements. Lastly, the sharp divide between the reward systems for manual and for non-manual employees may need to be eroded if companies are to meet the competitive market conditions of the next century. Not only will there have to be greater opportunities for advancement for manual workers if the skills shortages are to be addressed, but the need for increasing quality at site level will mean creating more multi-skilled and flexible teams of both manual and non-manual workers.

Skills-based or competency-related pay systems may offer opportunities for new harmonised pay structures at company level.

CHAPTER 5

CONSTRUCTION SKILLS TRAINING

One of the most important aspects of managing human resources is the provision of an adequate supply of skilled labour to meet the needs of an organisation. The construction industry has a tradition of skills training for craft operatives and technical education for the various construction professions. Although traditional training routes have been abandoned elsewhere in the economy, in the construction industry there is still a statutory training board, supported by a levy on employers. A similar arrangement also survives in engineering construction. As with so many aspects of construction personnel management, there is currently a strong divide between the training of the manual and non-manual workforces, although the establishment of National Vocational Qualifications for the industry is creating a unified set of standards which could lead to a more integrated system of employee development.

This chapter provides information about the institutional structures of skills training within the industry, indicates the major routes through which operatives can enter the industry, and advises of the support available from the Construction Industry Training Board (CITB). It looks at the recent introduction of 'modern apprenticeships' and skills certification. It also discusses the issues currently affecting training provision in the industry, especially the problems of the image of the industry in attracting trainees, the question of equal opportunities, health and safety, and the growing use of self-employed labour and its effect on training provision. The training and development of professional and managerial staff is dealt with separately in Chapter 6.

Craft training in the construction industry is a vital element in the provision of skilled labour at site level. Yet, despite extensive training arrangements, skills shortages have been a perennial problem in the industry whenever economic activity increases. As mentioned in Chapter 3, the major method for dealing with such skills shortages has been through wage inflation, which has increased costs and tender prices. The amount of skills training therefore has important financial implications for employers in the industry.

Because of the volatile nature of the industry, skills training in construction is rather different from that in other industries. Most importantly, the training of craft workers has been largely co-ordinated for many years through a national training board – the Construction Industry Training Board (CITB). In addition, there are continuing strong occupational, and hence training, divisions within the industry at both craft and professional level, whereas there is a relative absence of training and education for manual workers beyond induction/basic training. Concepts of employee or 'career' development are not common for operatives in the industry. This absence of employee development routes has been aggravated by the rise in the numbers of self-employed operatives. Contractors employ so few operatives that they have little need for programmes of operative development or re-skilling/re-training.

In terms of overall training comparisons, the UK construction industry has seen a decline in both the number and the proportion of trainees to total workers over recent years. The number of trainees overall has fallen from 32,000 in 1984 to around 24,000 in 1993 (Clarke and Wall, 1996), while the proportion of trainees to operatives has fallen from 2 per 100 operatives in 1984 to 1.5 per 100 in 1993. This compares with 2.5 per 100 in western Germany and Holland in 1993. The decline in training provision in Britain has been exacerbated by the fall in public-sector construction training. The substantial fall in employment in local authority direct labour organisations – down from 63,955 in 1983 to 37,778 in 1993 – has been accompanied by a consequent fall in trainee numbers – down from 4,618 in 1983 to 1,675 in 1993 (Clarke and Wall, 1996).

In this chapter we explain the role of the Construction Industry Training Board in co-ordinating skills training across the sector. We look at the major routes through which a construction trainee can progress, and at how an employer can claim grants for training employees. We explain the new National Vocational Qualification system for the industry and the Modern Apprenticeship scheme. For those seeking to recognise the skills of their existing workforce we discuss the new skills register. Finally, we discuss the importance of equal-opportunities policies in meeting future skill requirements, and the other issues affecting the continued supply of trainees in the future.

The Construction Industry Training Board

The major co-ordinating body for craft and supervisory training in the industry is the Construction Industry Training Board (CITB), established under the 1964 Industrial Training Act. Given the precarious nature of the construction industry, with a large mobile workforce employed by numerous small firms, a national system of training has always made sense. The CITB is controlled by a board of 18 members appointed by the Secretary of State for Education and Employment. All employers in the industry above a certain size of payroll (and therefore deemed to be 'in scope' of the board) are required to pay an annual levy based on a percentage of payroll and a percentage of all payments made for labour-only services. Levy rates and proposals must be approved by the Secretary of State, with an annual assessment each January. This levy is used to pay grants to those firms which carry out training to the CITB's approved standards. The CITB is not the only training institution in the industry – the electrical contracting, plumbing, heating and ventilating, and environmental engineering sectors have their own training schemes. Moreover, building operatives employed by local authority and NHS direct service organisations are not normally covered by the CITB. The public sector bodies, although responsible for a significant amount of craft training, at least until recent years, have their own arrangements.

The CITB has been engaged in training programmes for young people since the 1970s. New entrant training is offered through both youth training schemes and full-time courses in colleges, with periods of sponsored site experience. Trainees may progress from these courses into full-time employment or on to further and higher education. Around 50 per cent of these trainees are of employed status at any one time, and the rest are on youth training allowances. Of those who complete the training programmes, around 90 per cent go into employment in the construction industry. The CITB provides subsidised new entrant training from its levy income and makes grants towards trainees' wages and payment of tuition fees at colleges and training centres.

A large proportion of the grant aid is awarded for off-the-job training of craft apprentices at either CITB training centres (of which there are four) or in further education colleges. Grants are also paid for trainees who attend approved training courses run by companies (see the Mowlem case study at the end of this chapter) and independent organisations (training agents), and for the accreditation of National Vocational Qualifications (NVQs) and equivalents. Other grants are available for group training, safety courses, the development of learning programmes, and the encouragement of employers to develop their own training programmes. Grants are not intended to fully cover all the costs, nor are they automatically available for all types of training.

One of the particular features of the industry already noted (see Chapter 1) is the large and increasing proportion of small firms within the industry. If a company is too small to provide its own training specialist, the CITB has an arrangement whereby it can link with other small firms to provide a pooled training facility. These groups may be serviced by a CITB training advisor or they may employ their own training specialist for which CITB financial support is available. The Board has also begun to address the problems associated with the growth of labour-only sub-contracting and self-employment.

One of the advantages of having a centralised training organisation for the industry is the CITB's ability to compensate for the decline in employer training provision during periods of recession. To deal with this problem, the CITB has a programme of 'counter-cyclical' measures, introduced in 1991, to help offset the effects of recession on recruitment. Under these measures, the Board recruits directly onto its courses. In 1994–95 the board approved the recruitment of 750 first-year award holders and the continuation of training for existing award holders entering their second year.

Training is available in some 31 separate trades, but the largest groups are in carpentry and joinery (3,460 trainees), bricklaying (1,950), and painting and decorating (1,340) (1994–95). Other trades include those of roofers, ceiling fixers, demolition workers, dry lining workers, fencers, floor layers, formworkers, glaziers, mastic asphalters, plant mechanics, plant operators, plasterers, plumbers, scaffolders, stonemasons, tilers, woodworking machinists and shop fitters.

The total number of trainees as at 31 March 1995 was 10,987. Around 52 per cent of the current trainees are of employed status (see Table 4 below).

Table 4   Entrant training (as at 31 March 1995)

Sector	Employed	Non-employed
Building crafts	1,963	1,767
Specialist building crafts	122	106
Civil engineering	85	95
Building engineering services (BES)	46	40
Building technician	64	42
Civil engineering technician	4	0
Totals	2,284	2,050

Source: CITB Annual Report 1994–95

What types of training are available?

There are six main routes through which a construction trainee can progress, of which the most common are routes 2, 3 and 4. These are:

❑ *Route 1* – Direct employment from commencement on an industry-based training scheme as an apprentice/trainee under any of the recognised industry apprentice registration schemes. Training can be by the CITB Youth Training (YT) agency or day/block release in colleges of further education, leading to achievement of relevant N/SVQ.

❑ *Route 2* – Full-time course of two years' duration in a college of further education as a student, with the option to transfer to another route at the end of year 1. This is followed by employment as an apprentice/trainee, taking routes 1, 3 or 4 depending on progress made and standard reached, leading to achievement of the relevant N/SVQ and GN/SVQ.

❑ *Route 3* – The CITB's Youth Training (YT) agency with a two-year apprenticeship/traineeship foundation course, followed by employment as an apprentice/trainee, leading to the achievement of the relevant N/SVQ.

❑ *Route 4* – Construction industry training contractor – YT agency. Two-year apprenticeship/traineeship foundation course followed by employment as an apprentice/trainee, leading to the achievement of the relevant N/SVQ.

❑ *Route 5* – On-the-job training, leading to the achievement of the relevant N/SVQ.

❑ *Route 6* – Adult training – up-skilling existing employees with training under existing priority categories.

How does an employer claim a grant?

All companies with a turnover of £61,000 per annum and above were 'in scope' to the Board as at 1994–95. The levy provides around 60 per cent of the CITB's income. For main contractors the levy is 0.25 per cent of PAYE payroll and for labour-only (LOSC) payments it is 2 per cent. Labour-only payments make up 77 per cent of the total levy income. In March 1994 there were 58,406 companies 'in scope' to the Board, of which about a third were paying the levy.

Various types of grants are available from the CITB. Any employer in scope to, and registered with, the CITB is eligible to apply for one of these grants. Employers claiming a grant must be able to satisfy the Board that a suitably planned programme of training is being followed for each trainee for whom the grant is made. Details of the training programme must be open to inspection. Safety is an integral part of any training given and, where appropriate, instruction in health and welfare should be provided. Records must be kept and be open to inspection by the CITB.

The grants available fall into three main types:

❑ *Long-duration off-the-job training courses.* Grants may be claimed for initial craft, operative, and technical training courses which lead towards a nationally recognised qualification (eg NVQ/SVQ/CGLI/BTEC/SCOTVEC). These courses usually last one academic year.

❑ *Short-duration off-the-job training courses.* Grants may be claimed for training courses which reinforce, complement, or update initial training. These usually last from one day up to about four weeks.

❑ *On-the-job training.* Grants may be claimed for on-the-job training schemes where off-the-job training facilities are uneconomic, impractical, or not available.

In addition to these three types of grant, the CITB provides financial support for youth new entrant training, run under its managing agency, by way of tuition fees, travel, subsistence, and other costs. Allowances towards travel and accommodation costs may also be payable where there are no local courses and trainees are required to lodge away from home. A grant is also available to Independent

Group Training Associations for the production of a satisfactory group training plan. An 'adoption grant' may be payable where an employer adopts, under a formal contract of employment, an apprentice/trainee who has been made redundant by another employer.

Employers wishing to apply for a CITB grant should apply to the Board (see Useful Addresses at the rear of the book). A booklet detailing the grants scheme is available on request from the Board.

National Vocational Qualifications

The CITB is the lead body for National Vocational Qualifications (NVQs) 1 to 3 in construction and has been developing the new construction standards since 1986. This has involved the development of craft- and operative-level qualifications for the industry. In addition, the CITB is a member of the Construction Industry Standing Conference (CISC), which is a collective venture involving over 50 other construction organisations, charged with developing technical, professional and management qualifications for the industry. These NVQs (or SVQs in Scotland) are competency-based qualifications which measure the ability of a person to perform a task rather than measure academic knowledge. Most assessment therefore takes place in the workplace or a simulated work situation, not in a classroom. In order to achieve an NVQ award, a person must demonstrate the skill, knowledge, and understanding to do the job to the standards required by employers.

All such qualifications have to be accepted and approved or 'accredited' by the National Council for Vocational Qualifications (NCVQ) so that there is compatibility of NVQ levels, and hence transferability, across industry sectors. For example, a painter who decides to change career to work on an offshore oil rig is able to have his or her construction NVQ level recognised immediately. Similarly, all elements and units gained in plant repair and maintenance are recognised in all industries where they are relevant. There is no time limit or age limit, and there is no pass mark. The qualification is made up of units of competence which individuals can acquire at their own pace at work, in college, or in their own time. Like all other NVQs, construction NVQs are at five levels.

These five levels are:

❑ *Level 1* – Competence in the performance of a range of varied work activities, most of which may be routine and predictable.

❏ *Level 2* – Competence in a significant range of varied work activities, performed in a variety of contexts. Some of the activities are complex or non-routine, and there is some individual responsibility or autonomy. Collaboration with others, perhaps through membership of a work group or team, may be a requirement.

❏ *Level 3* – Competence in a broad range of varied work activities, performed in a wide variety of contexts, most of which are complex and non-routine. There is considerable responsibility and autonomy, and control or guidance of others is often required.

❏ *Level 4* – Competence in a broad range of complex, technical or professional work activities, performed in a wide variety of contexts and with a substantial degree of personal responsibility and autonomy. Responsibility for the work of others and the allocation of resources is often present.

❏ *Level 5* – Competence which involves the application of a significant range of fundamental principles and complex techniques across a wide and often unpredictable variety of contexts. Very substantial personal autonomy and often significant responsibility for the work of others and for the allocation of substantial resources feature strongly, as do personal accountabilities for analysis and diagnosis, design, planning, execution and evaluation.

Progression through the units can be on either a vertical or a horizontal track. A person may acquire additional units at the same level from the NVQs of other occupations. For example, in theory, a bricklayer might take one or two units from the plastering or wall- and floor-tiling NVQs. Alternatively, a bricklayer could take units from a completely different NVQ – for example, after a Level 3 Craft NVQ he or she might switch to Level 3 Building Site Supervision.

As well as being a lead body for construction industry standards, the CITB is also an awarding body responsible for establishing quality control systems, keeping records of people who gain NVQs, and checking the standards and qualifications of assessors as necessary. The CITB does this in conjunction with the City and Guilds of London Institute. The CITB has also combined with the Chartered Institute of Building (CIOB) to form a joint awarding body partnership for NVQ Levels 3 and 4 Building Site

Supervision and Management awards. There are similar arrangements in Scotland.

Under the NVQ system, the CITB maintains a computerised register of people who hold the construction NVQs detailed above. Records are kept of which qualifications are held and at which level. Applications for 'once in a lifetime' registration can be made by an individual or through an employer, training provider, assessment centre or local CITB office. Applicants pay a one-off fee plus the price of at least one unit, although applicants are expected to purchase units in blocks.

NVQs achieved by 31 March 1995	
Level 1	14,516
Level 2	34,968
Level 3	8,020
Total	57,504

Source: CITB Annual Report 1994–95

Achievement of an NVQ for a particular construction skill or occupation requires the candidate to provide evidence that he or she is capable of carrying out the tasks to the satisfaction of the assessor. The CITB says that this may be best delivered by colleges or training centres, although firms with the necessary qualified staff and resources can deliver NVQs themselves. Because few firms have the staff and other resources needed to train adequately on site, the CITB expects off-the-job training to continue to be a critical factor. 'Where possible, block release is better than day release because it allows time for realistic, "life size" practical exercises,' says the CITB (CITB NVQ Factsheets).

Although the industry is committed to the new NVQ system, its introduction has not been without problems. This system of qualifications is not well understood or widely recognised in the industry (CITB, 1994: 48). However, the total number of NVQ registrations at 31 March 1995 was 104,640, a considerable increase on the figure of 9,769 in 1991. By March 1995, over 57,500 people had been awarded an NVQ since the start of the scheme. The Board has some concerns, nevertheless, regarding the validity of the N/SVQ assessment process, partly because training providers are 'under considerable pressure to demonstrate achievement to at least Level

2, in order to obtain the output-related funding from the TECs or LECs for the training provided' (CITB, 1994: 12).

Modern Apprenticeships

The government's Modern Apprenticeship initiative was announced in November 1993. Fourteen industry sectors were chosen for the pilot year, which commenced in the autumn of 1994 and included construction. The national scheme was launched in September 1995. Key aspects of the new initiative are that

❑ it requires a firm commitment to training from employer, local Training and Enterprise Council (TEC) and apprentice
❑ it is based on ability, not time serving
❑ it results in a recognised Level 3 NVQ
❑ it provides personal development skills
❑ it leads to a career in the chosen industry
❑ it is flexible and adaptable to company requirements.

The initiative is designed to achieve a higher level of skills than existing trainee schemes. A Modern Apprenticeship leads to a NVQ Level 3, rather than NVQ 2 under Youth Training, and applicants need higher entry qualifications such as a minimum number of GCSEs. Modern apprentices may be employed either by an individual employer or by a group of employers and receive wages as an employee. An alternative is that the apprentice is not employed but linked to an employer or group of employers and is paid an allowance. In either case, the employer or group of employers makes an agreement with the apprentice to provide training to a minimum of NVQ Level 3 in the chosen occupation. This agreement is signed by the apprentice, the employer and the local TEC. A Modern Apprenticeship normally lasts around three years. Accelerated Modern Apprenticeships are available for older entrants aged between 18 and 19 who are leaving school or college, but these entrants have employed status from the start of their apprenticeships.

The CITB, in conjunction with Manchester TEC, has developed a Modern Apprenticeship Framework for the construction industry. This framework was designed around the New Entrant Training Policy mentioned above and currently covers five of the six entry routes. An initial 42 trainees were signed up in January 1995.

The skills register

'There is a growing need for firms to be able to provide evidence of a skilled workforce which is aware of health and safety requirements. The ability of firms to compete and of individuals to obtain work is becoming more dependent upon the evidence of skills that can be demonstrated.'

Chairman of the CSCS Board, 1995

Concerns about the skills deficit within the industry have recently led to a voluntary scheme to register skills. This new scheme, which builds on the existing certification schemes for Construction Plant Operatives and Scaffolders, is designed to ensure that such workers are properly trained to an acceptable standard of basic skills and, very importantly, to ensure the safe operation of construction plant on site. The Construction Skills Certification Scheme (CSCS) was launched in 1995 and is administered by the CITB. The scheme is controlled by a management board of the main employers' bodies and the trade unions within the industry. It provides a voluntary register of the skills, competencies and qualifications of individual workers within the industry in order to identify its trained and experienced operatives and craft workers, and thus give confidence to the industry's customers.

The scheme allows those who do not possess N/SVQs to become members of the scheme through industry accreditation, but only for a limited period. An important requirement for membership of the scheme is the need for evidence of valid health and safety awareness training. Another aim of the scheme is that it should encourage the improvement of skills by setting benchmarks for future achievement.

The benefit of the scheme for the individual is that he or she can achieve recognition for skills, competencies and qualifications, develop greater health and safety awareness, understand personal training needs, and possibly improve employment prospects. For employers the benefits of the scheme are that it helps to identify and recruit the right people, raises standards of health and safety awareness, and helps to raise quality standards which in turn will give clients greater confidence when awarding contracts.

The scheme is open to anyone, including those currently undergoing recognised formal training programmes, who is not already covered by one of the industry's specific occupational skill certification schemes (such as those for scaffolders and plant operators). Applications can be made by individuals, trade unions or employers. Labour-only sub-contractors, the self-employed and unemployed can also apply to join the scheme. No figures are available for the number of individuals covered by the scheme, but anecdotal evidence suggests that take-up was initially low. The *Construction News* reported in February 1996 that only 1,150 workers had signed up. However, the scheme subsequently acquired the support of some of the major contractors, and there are signs that major clients of the industry will in future require evidence of skills registration when awarding contracts. This may act as the catalyst to get the scheme off the ground. If it fails, there has been talk of a compulsory statutory scheme.

Each certified worker is issued with his or her own personal CSCS card showing occupation, qualifications, and skill level. The registration card carries photographic identification, a registration number and an expiry date. For those who have not achieved N/SVQ, evidence of satisfactory completion of an approved one-day (minimum) health and safety course within the previous two years is mandatory. A special one-day health and safety course has been developed by the CITB to support the CSCS requirement.

The scheme is being introduced in phases. The first tranche, launched on 3 April 1995, covers five occupational groups – bricklayers, roof slaters and tilers, painters and decorators, partitioning fixers, and piling operatives. In total, 26 occupations will finally be covered by the scheme.

Industry accreditation is a temporary measure to accommodate the many people working within the industry who do not possess formal qualifications. For a transition period of 18 months following the introduction of an occupation into the scheme, individuals (including labour-only, self-employed and unemployed) can seek membership via industry accreditation. They must obtain a recommendation from their present or any other bona fide employer for whom they have worked, who is able to judge their level of ability. Employers who provide such a recommendation must take into account the relevant industry standards, the satisfactory completion of a recognised apprenticeship, a pass in a skills test (where appropriate), and any City and Guilds or SCOTVEC qualifications held by the individual. After the 18-month transition period, entry to the scheme – other than for trainees – will be through achievement of N/SVQs.

Details of the CSCS scheme are available from: CSCS, PO Box 114, Bircham, King's Lynn, Norfolk, PE31 6XD (Tel: 01485 578777).

Equal opportunities in skills training

Women and people from ethnic minorities are poorly represented in the echelons of skilled workers within the construction industry. Only 11 per cent of full-time employees in the industry are female, according to LFS data (March 1996). As stated in one report, 'It is clear that while women are making inroads into construction professions, they are still represented mostly in secretarial and clerical occupations. There is far greater under-representation in manual and craft trades' (CIB, 1995). In the case of women, this is because the industry has traditionally been viewed as a dangerous and physically demanding industry in which employees are expected to put up with few creature comforts and work in both dirty and inhospitable conditions and outdoors in all weathers. The industry's view has been that construction is 'men's work' unsuitable for females. This is in spite of the fact that women construction workers were used extensively during the last war, and the fact that many of the skilled jobs in construction do not require physical strength so much as manual dexterity. Many of the heavy labouring jobs are now done by machine.

The poor representation of women in construction has been highlighted as problematical, not least within the training dimension. The declining number of school-leavers and the difficulty in attracting recruits to skills training courses because of the industry's poor image suggest that employers will have to consider changing their recruitment practices in the future. The industry is likely to remain labour-intensive, and this means a continuing requirement for a large volume of skilled employees. Women constitute a growing proportion of the labour force, yet at present they are an untapped resource in construction. There is thus a clear business case for improving the activity rates of women within the industry at both craft and professional levels. Apart from any business consideration, there may also be other benefits to be gained from employing women. In general, the presence of females within a workforce has often gone hand in hand with an improvement in working conditions because, in general, women's expectations of such conditions are higher. This improvement in working conditions, including a potential change in attitude to health and safety issues among the workforce, would help improve the industry's image for attracting recruits, both male and female.

The case of ethnic minorities has been investigated by the Commission for Racial Equality (CRE, 1995) because ethnic minority groups appear to have less access to training opportunities than white youngsters. The CRE Report on the CITB found that, according to the 1991 census, 8 per cent of 16–17-year-olds in Britain were from ethnic minority groups but only 1.1 per cent of the CITB trainees in 1991 were from these groups. This was despite the CITB's adopting a number of initiatives in the 1980s – including the appointment of an Equal Opportunities Officer – to attract young people from ethnic minorities into the industry. The CRE's concerns revolved around two questions. Firstly, why did black and Asian candidates for traineeships fare worse than white candidates? Secondly, why were ethnic minority candidates disproportionately unlikely to get workplace experience placements with building firms? The CRE found no evidence of discrimination in the selection tests used to choose trainees, but it did conclude that the method of finding placements adversely affected the ethnic minority candidates. This was because the three approaches used – 'do it yourself' (where candidates approach potential employers directly themselves), 'kith and kin' (where candidates use family contacts) and local residence requirements (where some employers lay down rules that candidates must live within a certain radius of the workplace) – were all potentially indirectly discriminatory. When the CITB provided assistance in finding placements, ethnic minority candidates benefited slightly more than white candidates. The CRE recommended that the CITB should reduce its dependence on the 'kith and kin' approach to placements, and that any local residence requirement must be valid and justifiable. It also recommended that the CITB should move towards a more systematic process of placement over which the Board should play an effective central role. Employers should be actively encouraged to provide placements for ethnic minorities and the CITB should recommend that all candidates go through its own selection process, even if employers had their own recruitment process.

The CITB reinforced its commitment to promoting equal opportunities in its new entrant training provision following publication of the CRE findings. It has set national and regional targets for the recruitment of women and ethnic minorities, established a national and seven regional Equal Opportunities Working Groups, and developed national and regional action plans that detail equal opportunities programmes to be carried out. The CITB national equal opportunities policy says that

CITB is committed to the provision of equal opportunities within its training for craft, operative and technician new entrants. CITB's equal opportunities policy aims to ensure that no applicant for training or trainee receives less favourable treatment than any other on the grounds of race, colour, nationality, ethnic origin, gender, religion, marital status, sexuality, political belief or disability. Furthermore, no applicant or trainee should be disadvantaged by any conditions or requirements which cannot be shown to be justified.

The CITB has its own Equal Opportunities Officer to advise CITB management and staff, and who is a member of the Equal Opportunities Commission's Equality Exchange and the European Commission's IRIS network of training for young women. The Board has also developed a range of literature and videos aimed at encouraging careers in the construction industry for non-traditional entrants.

At local level the CITB actively supports and helps fund collaborative work with other organisations on equal opportunities in construction training. Recent examples have included

❏ a pre-vocational course for ethnic minority young people (Black Contractors Association, London)
❏ the New Ethnic Minority and Careers Guidance Project (BBC)
❏ a presentation skills course for women employed in the industry who discuss construction at careers events and schools (Women and Manual Trades, London)
❏ special careers events with an equal opportunities focus.

The future of skills training

If the future supply of craft skills to the industry is to be assured, a number of issues must be addressed. These include changes in the structure and employment patterns of the industry, issues relating to the industry's public image, the need for training to standards, and the impact of self-employment on training provision.

Changes in the industry

The wide and fluctuating pattern of demand in the industry will not change, so that any training strategy must address the problems caused by this turbulence. The reduction in the size of the labour force brought about by recent improvements in productivity and

109

by reductions in output has caused problems for the industry's training arrangements. This decline has led to a fall in levy income coupled to sudden and large variations in the number of first-year trainees. The CITB forecasts that productivity will continue to increase, which has implications for training needs, and the industry will continue to be a national industry such that training requirements can only be satisfactorily met on a national basis. The introduction of locally-based Training and Enterprise Councils (TECs) has underlined the fact that construction training cannot be easily administered at local level. The need for a national training framework will persist.

The need to improve the industry's image

The increase in the number of school students who decide to stay on at school beyond the age of 16 has reduced the number of available trainees for the industry. The staying-on rate has increased from 47 per cent in 1986 to 70 per cent in 1993. This has intensified the competition between the construction and other industries for the declining number of school-leavers. The staying-on rate at school is likely to increase to 75 per cent by 1999, a change that is likely to affect the industry in three ways: young people are unlikely to revert to entering employment at 16, even if the current situation of poor job opportunities improves; those employers who used to recruit school-leavers with few or no qualifications will have to change their recruitment practices; and the industry will have to work harder to attract under-16s towards the industry.

Although the use of Youth Training schemes in the industry has made a successful contribution to training for the industry's needs, the CITB believes that the term 'Youth Training' has operated as a disincentive to many parents/guardians of potential trainees, and that the term 'apprenticeship' would be a more attractive term. Given the decline in the industry's traditional intake group, both in numbers and in quality, the Board sees the promotion of Modern Apprenticeships as a key to attracting more and better recruits. The public perception of the industry as one of limited opportunities is a major disincentive to potential trainees and their families. Coupled to this return to the concept of apprenticeship, the CITB sees the change in employment status of such trainees from their current YT unemployed status to employed status as a desirable means to improving the image of training in the industry.

The issue of equal opportunities is also related to this problem. The untapped potential of the female and ethnic minority workforce could also be more fully explored, with possible accompanying improvements in working conditions and therewith the image of the industry. The reluctance of women and ethnic minority people to enter the industry means that a significant source of labour is being neglected. The Board has undertaken to set targets for the participation of women and ethnic minorities on new entrant training, and to implement an action programme to encourage applicants from these groups.

Training to standards

The Board sees the future of new entrant training as being based on National Vocational Qualifications (NVQs) although there is clear evidence that the new system of qualifications is not well understood or widely recognised in the industry. The Board wishes to see the integration of skills tests into the N/SVQ assessments, and also suggests the introduction of suitable externally-assessed written knowledge tests to emphasise the importance of underpinning knowledge. The introduction of the Construction Skills Certification Scheme (CSCS) will enable those who are already at the required NVQ standard but have no qualification as such to be registered, but this scheme may require stronger support from the industry's clients if it is to work effectively.

The impact of self-employment

The CITB feels that the rise of self-employment in the industry means that it cannot meet its requirements for work experience for trainees and apprentices without the use of labour-only sub-contractors and the self-employed. The Board has therefore focused on those sub-contractors who undertake labour-only contracts whether using directly employed or self-employed operatives. Labour-only sub-contractors are in reality employers of labour (either direct employees or self-employed people where they are quasi-employees) and should be registered with the Board. The levy for these LOSCs should be paid by the main contractor rather than the sub-contractor.

The major obstacle to the provision of training placements by LOSCs has been identified as the administrative burden. For this reason the CITB has introduced the new LOSC administration grant for the main contractors, who undertake to administer the placement of the individual trainee with the LOSC or with a self-employed person.

CASE STUDY – **Mowlem Training, East London**

Mowlem Training is a division of John Mowlem Construction Plc, and operates construction training centres in East London, Rotherham, Speke, Cardiff, Toxteth, Bristol and Birkenhead. Mowlem has operated its own training division for the last 20 years. Trainees work to NVQ Levels 1 to 3 in a wide variety of occupational trades. At the East London training centre in Silvertown, NVQ courses in brickwork, solid plastering, carpentry and joinery, wall and floor tiling, and for general building operatives are provided. Mowlem Training has full accreditation from City and Guilds, CITB and NCVQ, and draws on a broad range of expertise in construction management, craft and basic skills training. All trainees with a basic skills requirement are able to take advantage of the on-site Literacy and Numeracy Unit at the East London Centre, which opened in 1989 to develop and deliver occupational basic skills within construction crafts. The Centre has also developed an extensive Jobsearch programme for trainees.

Health and safety training

Mowlem Training also operates a comprehensive health and safety policy designed to encourage trainees to be aware of the responsibility for their own safety and to ensure that safe working practices are followed both during directed training at the Centre and while undertaking on-site training. The health and safety policy is monitored by the group safety officer at the Centre. In addition to basic health and safety training carried out during induction and the practical training elements of the course, trainees also participate in training sessions conducted by the group safety officer.

Training delivery

The training provided at the Centre is designed to meet not only the requirements of the individual trainee and the accrediting bodies but also the needs of local employers. These local needs are identified through close liaison with the Centre's employment officer. The NCVQ syllabus is then augmented to guarantee the relevance of the training to potential employment possibilities. This ensures that all trainees carry out the standard occupational activities and also benefit from flexible training delivery.

CHAPTER 6

PROFESSIONAL AND MANAGEMENT DEVELOPMENT

The training and development of managers and professional staff is a key to improving company performance. The construction industry has a tradition of professional education and training which has been fostered by the major professional bodies. Each body has a long history stretching back over 150 years, and each has been involved in the training and professional education of its members for many decades. Compartmentalisation between the various construction professions has produced a rather demarcated system of employee development in the past. However, the establishment of the Construction Industry Standing Conference (CISC) specifically to introduce a set of common vocational standards has helped to produce a more unified approach.

Training and development are seen by many construction firms primarily in terms of basic training or professional education for new employees. The notion of 'career development' is perhaps less common than in other industries. This is because the typical construction firm has a relatively flat structure, involving few levels of hierarchy, and the majority of companies are small to medium-sized. Opportunities for advancement up a long career path are therefore unusual, and professional staffs may switch employers in times of high economic activity both to gain new experience and to improve salary levels. In contrast, some construction firms are now seeing the advantage of developing their managers and professional staff as a key to competitive advantage, and utilising ideas closer to 'employee development' (see the Shepherd Construction case study on page 140, and the Drivers Jonas case study on page 15).

This chapter considers the concepts of employee development

and the 'learning organisation', and their relevance to the construction industry. It offers a step-by-step approach to mapping an organisation's employee development needs and setting up a training programme. Recent developments in the training and education of professional and managerial staff are considered. Lastly, the chapter explores the benefits that some companies have found in the Investors in People initiative in encouraging employee development.

First we must put forward a definition of employee development.

> Employee development as part of the organisation's overall human resource strategy means the skilful provision and organisation of learning experiences in the workplace in order that performance can be improved, that work goals can be achieved, and that, through enhancing skills, knowledge, the learning ability and the enthusiasm of people at every level, there can be continuous organisational as well as individual growth. Employee development must, therefore, be part of a wider strategy for the business, aligned with the organisation's corporate mission and goals.
>
> Harrison, 1992a

In other words, training and development is as much about the individual employee's needs as the organisation's. Among industries other than construction, this need for continuous professional development has been encapsulated in the concept of the 'learning organisation'. Coupled to the total quality management idea of continuous improvement, the learning organisation concept is based on Kolb's learning cycle (which views the learning experience as a circular and perpetual process). The learning organisation has a wider vision than simply to provide the right training to meet the organisation's requirements – it includes the entire work environment. It starts from the view that experience has a fundamental influence on people's learning. This is the experience 'not simply of the work that people do, but also of the way they interact with others in the organisation, and the behaviour, attitudes and values of those others' (Harrison, 1992a: 156). The practical points which arise from this assumption are:

❑ Everyday experience should be carefully examined, because it affects learning.

❑ The organisation should be viewed and managed as a continuous learning system.

❑ There must be a conscious decision to develop an organisational environment that will promote and sustain the desired kinds of organisational learning.

Kolb sees learning as an explicit organisational objective which should be pursued as consciously and actively as profit or productivity.

As we explained in Chapter 5, where we considered operative training, the training function in the construction industry is sharply divided between the responsibility for operative or 'blue-collar' training and that for the 'white-collar' staff.

In the case of professional, technical and managerial staff, the responsibility for training lies, in the larger firms, with the training or personnel department. Anecdotal evidence suggests that there has been a considerable decline in the presence of specialist training managers in construction firms: some firms have actually closed their management training units. This reflects the recent recession in the industry and the considerable reductions in staffing which have occurred in many firms. Despite this, many companies continue to provide both graduate entry training and management development for staff already in employment. In recent times there has been increased attention to site supervision courses and the development of new management programmes, including some for senior managers in the industry.

The obstacles to management and professional training within the industry are considerable. In particular, the cyclical nature of the industry's workload has militated against a long-term and continuous approach to employee development. Employee development programmes are often among the first items to go when recession hits. But when the economy recovers, and skill shortages emerge, construction firms complain that they do not have sufficient qualified staff to meet demands. A study of management development by the Industrial Society in 1985 found that construction firms spent less than 0.5 per cent of their annual turnover on development activities. A later survey (Mphake, 1989) estimated that the average expenditure on management development in construction was only £300 per head per annum. Most companies operate within very tight staffing budgets. Moreover, the project nature of much of the work means that staff are very mobile and often heavily committed, with no spare time between projects to attend training courses. There has also been the 'cultural' obstacle that many construction managers, especially at senior level, believe that the best form of development is through experience on site rather than through academic or classroom-based study.

However, there is evidence that things are beginning to change. There have been some important shifts towards action learning-based systems, in which theory and practice are more closely linked. Another trend has been the development of special, jointly designed management development programmes by university built environment faculties and individual construction companies (for an example see the Shepherd case study on

---

'Forward through quality' at Barratt Plc

Barratt Plc, the North-East based international house-building and construction firm, provides a good example of the vital connection between the development of more customer-focused business strategies and employee development programmes. In 1989 Barratt decided to appoint a group training manager to define its employee development needs and to formulate a corporate strategy to improve the contribution of all its employees. The company had no specialist personnel function, despite employing 2,000 people. In 1990 the formulation of this employee development plan coincided with the parallel development of a projected total quality management (TQM) programme. The company decided to integrate the two programmes under the banner 'Forward through quality'. This led to a clear statement of the role of employee development as a strategic objective – 'By linking the strategy for employee development with the business aim, to achieve competitive advantage through total quality'. The strategy was to be achieved by building an effective infrastructure for employee development, monitoring and reviewing work performance and identifying employee development needs (through annual employee appraisals), organising company-wide training and development initiatives to meet key corporate training needs, and facilitating TQM through appropriate forms of employee development.

Source: Harrison (1992b), in Winstanley and Woodall, *Case Studies in Personnel*, IPD

page 140). These allow managers to attend block-release or day-release courses at diploma or master's level, which relate closely to the needs of the particular company. Although these are limited in number at present, they do offer a guide to the possibilities.

Despite the 'stop-go' approach to employee development in many companies, the advantages of continuous professional development and management training within the industry are clear. Increasingly, clients are asking for information on the expertise of the staff allocated to their work, and there is an obvious market edge for those companies that can demonstrate the competence and qualifications of their staff to do the job. This is particularly important when clients are seeking long-term partners for their construction requirements. The increased attention to quality control systems has drawn attention to the importance of high-quality human resources (see the Barratt Plc example opposite).

The Investors in People initiative has been used by some other companies within the industry to underpin such quality improvement programmes (as discussed later in this chapter).

Assessing the organisation's training needs

In developing a programme of employee development, an organisation has to consider three levels of analysis.

☐ the requirements of the organisation as a whole
☐ the job or occupational requirements
☐ the individual employee's requirements.

The first stage in creating an employee development programme is an assessment of the construction firm's existing level of skills and qualified staff. This is done through a process of identifying the major development needs of the company. There are two main approaches to this process – the global approach, and the 'critical incident' or 'priority problem' approach (Kenney and Reid, 1988).

The global approach

The global approach represents the system by which the training needs of the industry are decided by some central body, such as an industry training board, and then filtered down to individual companies. Companies therefore use pre-prepared forms for analysing their training needs. This system has been criticised for its tendency towards bureaucratic form-filling, even if it has the advantage of providing companies with ready-made programmes for analysing training needs.

The 'critical incident' approach

The 'critical incident' or 'priority problem' approach is much more common today. The aim here is to identify and record those business problems that have a training solution and which are important from the individual organisation's stand-point. This approach should avoid the 'training for training's sake' tendency inherent in the global systems.

As we have already noted, within the construction industry it is the CITB that provides a global solution to the training requirements of the industry for craft skills. For professional and management groups, the alternative company-centred approach is used.

Although there is little evidence of a sophisticated organisa-tional appraisal of training needs in construction companies, most link their training plans to perceived gaps between what project managers require and what is available within the exist-ing workforce. To some extent, these training gaps may be remedied through the recruitment process (see Chapter 3), but there is also scope for developing existing staff. Whereas in the past the industry may have had a clear divide between its craft and operative employees and its professional and management staff, the introduction of N/SVQs allows for the concept of continuous development from operative up to site manager, providing a real career path (see later in this chapter).

Following this identification of training needs, a corporate training plan can be developed.

Assessing occupational training needs

Once the organisation is aware of where its training is deficient, further investigation should determine the requirements for individual employees. From the overall business plan, clear training and development needs may be identified which can then be translated into particular craft, professional, technical or management competencies. To do this, some method of job training analysis is required, which will involve looking at job descriptions and person specifications (see also Chapter 3 on recruitment and selection) to draw up some training specification for the job, and which compares the job specification with the trainee's current level of competence.

There are four main methods of job training analysis (Kenney and Reid, 1988):

☐ *The comprehensive analysis*, in which all facets of the job are examined with the aim of producing a complete record of what is required for the successful execution of the tasks. This is perhaps most appropriate at the lower-level jobs within an organisation, where tasks require little discretion and are fairly static in content.

☐ *Key task analysis*, in which only the most important areas of the job are identified. This may be more appropriate where jobs cannot be described or prescribed accurately, as is the case with many professional or management jobs.

☐ *Problem-centred analysis*. This approach seeks to provide a comprehensive description neither of the training needs nor of the key tasks. Rather the analysis is limited to a particular difficulty to which training can provide a solution. This is used either where resources for a wider analysis are not available or where an employee's work is satisfactory apart from one particular area. Such an approach has been labelled 'training by exception'.

☐ *Core analysis*. This approach concentrates on the core skills that may be transferable from one employer to another. This type of training analysis is common where there are national systems of training (as in the case of the CITB skills training courses).

Identifying individual training needs
Once the occupational training needs for the organisation have been identified, the final stage is to design individual training plans. The training gaps revealed may be due to a number of reasons – factors operating in the learners themselves, their managers, or in their work and organisational environment (Harrison, 1992a). Training needs can be identified at the individual level in relation to:

☐ induction and basic training
☐ the improvement of current performance

❏ a response to the demands of business strategy and of change in the workplace

❏ ensuring effective continuous development and career planning.

The training needs of an individual can be identified through observation of the employee by the manager, from records of work performance or productivity, or by the employee himself or herself. One major method by which an individual's training needs may be identified is the annual appraisal process.

At Barratt Plc, under the strategy adopted in 1991, all the 17 subsidiaries' directors have to complete and send back to headquarters a manpower and training plan before the start of each budget year (Harrison, 1992b). The data required is fairly simple – a projection of the main staffing issues and demands, with a focus on anticipated training needs in each occupational group. Personal reviews have also been introduced, which operate on a self-appraisal basis. These provide an opportunity for a discussion of work performance and joint target-setting between managers and employees. This is confidential to the two parties, but a report of the agreed training needs of each individual has to be sent to the group training manager so that a business-wide view can be taken of common employee development needs across the company.

The appraisal

Appraisal is now a common feature of the management of people in many organisations, and can serve a number of functions – as a means to objective-setting and feedback within the performance management process; as a means to establishing the level or amount of performance-related pay; and, very importantly, as a means to identify employee development requirements. Whereas there is a continuing debate about the effectiveness of linking individual appraisal with pay (see Chapter 4), there is no dissent about the effectiveness of appraisal systems in managing performance and planning for employee development.

Appraisal involves a meeting of one person with another for a discussion which is focused on the performance of one of them. It enables objectives to be set and counselling to be provided. It offers a context within which approval can be conferred on the employee, and confirmation given that he or she is doing the right thing. Such recognition is an essential human need.

Appraisal interviews are useful only if they are systematically managed and carefully planned. For this reason, the employer or manager should be very clear about the purpose to which appraisal is being put. Appraisal can be motivated by two very different views – as a system of management control (as in the case of appraisal-related reward systems), or as a system of employee development. Problems can arise if the appraisal is expected to cover a number of very different objectives. Although that may be an economical approach to the task, it may result in communicating different messages to the appraisee (eg 'First the good news, now the bad!'). The method of appraisal must be chosen with care. The aim should be to ensure clarity of purpose and to encourage motivation and participation (Young, 1990).

There are four keys to successful appraisal (Harrison, 1992a):

❑ *A shared perception of purpose.* Both parties to the process – the appraiser and appraisee – must have a shared understanding of the aims and objectives of the process and a shared commitment.

❑ *Mutual learning and understanding.* In the course of the appraisal, performance should be examined in the light of the employee's views on the constraints and opportunities affecting it, so that the appraiser gains increased understanding of the issues influencing performance.

❑ *Objectivity.* The discussion should not seek to apportion blame or criticism but seek to be supportive, centre on work objectives, and be future-oriented rather than raking over the past. Poor performance should not be left until the annual appraisal but dealt with by the manager concerned on a regular basis or, in more serious cases, through the disciplinary procedure.

❑ *Diagnosis, planning and action.* There should be a clear outcome from the appraisal in the form of an agreed plan of action, with achievable objectives and a mechanism for monitoring and review.

Key to the success of the appraisal is the relationship between the appraiser and appraisee: difficulties here can obstruct the whole purpose. The most common problems are that the appraiser is not convinced of the value of the exercise, or is not given sufficient time to carry out the task effectively; that the appraiser does not have the skills to do the job; and, lastly, that the basic relationship between appraiser and appraisee is so poor that no trust exists between the parties. An employee is unlikely to be open about his or her own perception of training and development needs, which suggest weaknesses or gaps in performance, if there is a low trust environment. Further difficulties may emerge if the appraisal is seen as a cosmetic, public relations exercise which fails to deliver on any of the promised support, and if identified outcomes are ignored.

One particular problem identified in the construction industry is the fact that much of the work is carried out at remote locations, and only infrequent meetings occur between the manager and the employee on site. A chief surveyor, responsible for five surveyors who spend most of their time on different sites, will see very little of their day-to-day performance (Fryer, 1990). Although appraisal systems exist in many construction companies, they are often ad hoc and very informal, reflecting the culture of the industry. For example, the appraisal system described in a case study of 'Joiner Construction' (Lord, 1992) – the UK branch of a large multinational engineering construction contractor employing 2,500 people – provides a classic example of how *not* to run an appraisal system. At this company,

> All staff may be appraised annually in informal ad hoc interviews exclusively with their direct line manager. There is no standard form for doing this and, when it happens at all, it is usually as a means of disciplining particularly poor, or rewarding particularly good, workers. In general, line managers see little direct benefit in the appraisal process and have scant respect for Personnel.

Appraisals must operate realistically, given the constraints of the external environment. The objectives set must be achievable and limited in scope and number. If the scheme is designed as an employee development exercise, there is no need for complex forms or ranking systems, and only basic information should be recorded. It is also important that the line managers who operate the scheme have 'ownership' of it, which implies that they must be involved from the start in the design, planning, and implementation of the scheme. Such line managers must also be given adequate training in appraisal techniques and sufficient time by senior management to carry out the task.

This means: time to prepare for the appraisal interview, an uninterrupted period during which to conduct the interview, and time to write up their report at the end. Schemes must also be monitored and regularly evaluated by both the participants and senior management. Most importantly, appraisal schemes must have the active support of top management, because it has to be recognised as an expensive process in terms of the time that must be allocated to its operation. It will only work if top management is convinced of the contribution of this process to investment in the organisation's human resources.

The process of training

The completion of the individual training needs assessments will feed into the training plan. Examples of the sort of issues that a construction firm might address include the retention of managers, shortages of key personnel such as contracts managers, slow contract completion, and poor product quality.

As with any business activity, the process of training follows a number of stages.

Training checklist

- ❏ Confirm training needs. Once the training plan has been developed, the plan will need to be agreed by senior management and adequate funding allocated.
- ❏ Agree on overall purpose and objectives. A clear statement of the purpose and objectives of the training planned should be created and communicated to all involved, including the trainees.
- ❏ Identify the profile of the intended participants. The type, grade or occupations of the employees to be trained will need to be selected and these details conveyed to those who will be undertaking the training, so that the trainers have a clear picture of the clientele.
- ❏ Select the strategy and agree on the direction and management of the training. Once the methods of training have been agreed, a decision will need to be taken on who is to undertake the training and who will manage the process. This means deciding either to employ an external consultant or to provide the training in-house with current staff.
- ❏ Select participants and produce a detailed specification of the training to be done. Where a large number of staff

requires the same or similar training, it may be inappropriate to train all of them at the same time. A decision must be taken on who is to be trained and at which event. A clear statement of the learning objectives, methods of training, and sequence of events should be provided for the participants.

☐ Design the training event(s). As above, this will entail a clear timetable of events during each period of training, and for the learning objectives to be broken down into sub-units. The secret of a well-designed training programme is a clear plan of what is to happen and when. Variety in the training methods and activities is essential. Ensure that there are sufficient opportunities for breaks but also that the pace is right for the trainees. The training exercises should not be too fast or too slow.

☐ Deliver the training.

☐ Monitor and evaluate the event. Once the training has been carried out, some form of monitoring of its effects will be necessary. The individuals who have been trained will need to provide an evaluation of what they have learned and their view of the training provided. There will also be a need for more long-term evaluation of the benefits to the individual and the organisation of the training provided.

☐ Assess the organisational payback. Some form of assessment by the managers of those trained is necessary if there are to be clear calculations of the effects of the training on performance and productivity. Although it is often difficult to measure the benefits of training directly in financial terms, senior managers will need to be assured that the money is well spent and that there is some form of financial payback.

Training programmes for non-manual staff

Having explained the major stages in the development of a training and development programme, we now turn to some of the types of training which are most common. For many construction firms, their small size will limit their capacity to undertake elaborate training policies and programmes of the types outlined above. Only the medium- and larger-sized contractors have the resources and staff numbers to operate at this level. However, companies can work together to provide training, and the CITB can help set up such joint training arrangements. It may even be possible for smaller firms to place their staff on the programmes of larger contractors. In some cases, the larger firms can provide training consultancy (eg Shepherd Construction now has a training consultancy).

Apart from the skills training programmes dealt with in Chapter 5, there are a number of other levels at which training and development can take place in the industry:

❏ technician training in quantity surveying, planning and construction management (four-year courses leading to BTEC higher national diploma)

❏ industrial attachments for undergraduates on university construction courses

❏ sponsorship of undergraduates on university construction courses

❏ graduate training courses leading to the appropriate professional qualification

❏ site supervision courses leading to NVQ Level 4 in site supervision

❏ site management courses leading to NVQ level 5 in site management

❏ post-graduate development leading to diplomas and masters' degrees

❏ management development courses for middle managers.

Now let us examine some of the various types of training provided for management and the non-manual workforce.

Training craft supervisors

One of the most important roles requiring training is that of the site supervisor. The term 'craft supervision' covers a number of occupational titles in the construction industry, including charge-hand, trade foreman, craft foreman, ganger, and supervisor. In general the term refers to the first line of supervision located at the site or workshop, comprising those who are responsible for the construction process. They may be employed by general contractors, specialist contractors, manufacturers of components to be used on site or public sector direct service organisations. Such staff are usually recruited from the ranks of the operatives whom they supervise, and traditionally the majority of first line supervisors have received little or no specialised training. Yet wherever they are employed, such supervisors have traditionally been a key link in the management of the construction process. Many such supervisors have been promoted to contracts managers and senior construction firm managers. With the decline of direct labour and the increased use of sub-contract labour, the need for such supervisors has declined among general contractors, but there are still many general contractors who continue to provide long-term employment and career progression opportunities for craft supervisors (Hatchett, 1992).

Craft supervisors also exist in single-trade or specialist contracting, and have experienced something of a resurgence with the shift to more sub-contracting and management contracting arrangements. Such specialist sub-contracting companies are often relatively small, involving few levels of management, so that the craft supervisor enjoys a higher status than those employed by general contractors. Although the opportunities for career progression may be less because of the restricted numbers involved, in the larger firms there are opportunities to move on to more technical occupations, particularly as estimators and surveyors (Hatchett, 1992). Others may become small employers in their own right, and some supervisors will shift back and forth between employee and employer status during their working lives.

A third area of supervision is in the various types of construction workshops manufacturing components for assembly on site (eg joinery, plastering, stonemasonry and metalwork fabrication). In such companies there are two types of supervisor – those responsible for workshop operatives, and those responsible for supervising the assembly of components by operatives on site.

In recent years, the CITB, the Chartered Institute of Building and the Institution of Civil Engineers have paid increasing attention to the training of supervisory and site management staff. Site supervision qualifications are now available at NVQ Levels 3 and 4. These qualifications are delivered through a Joint Awarding Body in a number of approved training centres. The CITB offers courses in site management, setting out and surveying, and safety. The site management course covers management principles, communication, planning and organisation, employment procedures and contract law, and site safety. In addition, the CITB has produced a range of flexible learning materials on general site supervision. Each module is self-contained and can be used in a number of ways – for self-development, as in-house company training, and by colleges and universities.

Educating the professionals

The construction firm also requires a range of professional and technical staff who make up the project teams. The training and professional development of these staffs is a major concern for any construction manager, and graduate recruitment is a vital task. In addition, many companies provide the opportunity for such staff to gain their qualifications while in employment, and there is increasing emphasis on continuous professional development to keep up to date with new processes and practices. The Chartered Institute of Building (CIOB) has recently begun a development programme for company directors (see later this chapter).

The various chartered and professional bodies play a very important role in the design of education schemes and the monitoring of standards among providers of construction training. There are many such bodies, but the major professional institutions are the Royal Institution of Chartered Surveyors (RICS), the Chartered Institute of Building (CIOB); the Institution of Civil Engineers (ICE), and the Royal Institute of British Architects (RIBA). In recent years all of these institutions have tended to concentrate their professional education programmes on full-time undergraduates in universities, with a consequent decline in the number of evening study courses for those already in work.

In membership terms, the largest of these professional institutions is the RICS, founded in 1868, which has 93,000 members, including students. However, this institution covers a far wider range of sectors than just the construction process. Chartered surveyors are responsible for all aspects of the life-cycle of property – managing its physical and financial performance for owners and occupiers. This can mean managing agriculture, construction, workspace or homes. The RICS has members in six main markets – commercial property, construction, infrastructure, minerals, residential property, and rural property. Of the 93,000 RICS members, 12 per cent are female. The total membership includes 10,400 building surveyors and 33,700 quantity surveyors. The majority of entrants to the profession (around 75 per cent) join the profession after gaining the necessary A-level GCEs/Highers and enrolling on a RICS-accredited degree or diploma course. Students who leave school at 16 can opt to take either a vocationally-oriented BTEC National certificate or diploma, which can also lead to enrolment on an accredited degree or diploma programme. Alternatively, they may choose to progress to a BTEC Higher National Certificate or Diploma (HNC/D). The majority of students take a full-time three-year or four-year sandwich course leading to a degree or diploma that allows entry to the Assessment of Professional Competence (APC). Part-time mode and distance learning are also available. All students, whatever route is taken, must complete the APC. At least one year of professional qualifying experience is required after obtaining a RICS-approved degree or diploma. Increasingly, graduates from other disciplines are being encouraged to join the profession, and a number of graduate conversion courses have been established.

The CIOB has 33,000 members, of whom one third are at Chartered level. There are also around 300 Chartered Building Companies that have institutional membership. Although its Royal Charter was granted only in 1980, the Institute's origins go back to 1834. Its membership has grown eight-fold over the last 30 years. The CIOB views itself as the major organisation for construction managers. Its membership includes a wide range of construction occupations, but around half are surveyors, both in building and quantity surveying. However, the CIOB's members tend to be among contractors rather than in professional practices, and it has a high profile among project managers and senior managers at director and general manager level. In the past, most members entered by studying, usually part-time, for the CIOB's own examinations, but today the majority enter via accredited university courses (the number taking university courses is five times those taking the CIOB exams). The Professional Development Programme, designed for new entrants to the industry, covers the education, experience, training, competence and professional assessment of those aiming to become corporate members of the institute. Under the new scheme, those seeking corporate membership must provide evidence of learning, evidence of performance from the workplace, and evidence of commitment to professionalism.

For those wishing to study for the CIOB examination route, courses are offered on a day-release basis by further and higher education establishments. Graduates who wish to achieve Chartered status must have three years' approved professional experience and produce a dissertation. The CIOB has developed its own competency route and uses 50 assessment centres to accredit these competencies. CIOB is a joint awarding member for NVQ Level 5 in project management. In addition, it has recently launched a new programme in construction directorial skills development for very senior managers in conjunction with Henley Management Centre.

CIOB Professional Development Programme

Occupational and Personal Competences

Unit	Title
1	Personnel management at work
2	Decision-making
3	Communicating
4	Managing information
5	Planning work
6	Managing work quality
7	Managing health and safety
8	Managing resources
9	Assessing environmental risk factors.

Source: CIOB Professional Development Programme Scheme Document

The Institution of Civil Engineers (ICE), founded in 1818, is a UK-based international organisation that has 80,000 members (64,000 in the UK). It has three main functions – as a learned society, as a qualifying body, and as a voice for the civil engineering profession. The ICE provides three principal levels of qualification: Corporate member, Associate member, and Technician. Civil engineers who have passed the Institution's incorporated professional review are admitted as Associates, whereas those who pass the chartered professional review are admitted as Corporate members. The ICE approves a number of UK degree courses in civil engineering.

The RIBA, founded in 1837, is the main professional body for architects: nobody can practise using that title unless they are on the statutory register. Membership is around 27,000. Around

70 per cent of registered architects are members of RIBA. To qualify for RIBA membership and for statutory registration, a minimum of seven years' higher education and training are required. The usual pattern is five years in an academic institution (there are 38 recognised schools of architecture in the UK), followed by two years approved practical training (usually undertaken in architects' practices, although part may be spent in the offices of associated professions or with other members of the building team). At the end of the seventh year, candidates for entry to the profession sit an examination in Professional Practice and Practical Experience, which they must pass before entry to membership of RIBA or the statutory register. In most academic institutions a first degree is awarded at the end of three years, but this does not signify any professional qualification.

All four professional bodies described above have embraced continuous professional development (CPD), and all oblige members to provide evidence of CPD activities.

Professional, technical and management standards

In recent years the development of N/SVQs has led to greater integration of this higher level of training. The Construction Industry Standing Conference (CISC) was established in 1990 as the forum for Standards/NVQ/SVQ development at professional, managerial and technical levels in planning, construction, property and related engineering services. CISC – funded by the DfEE and supported voluntarily by the industry – is charged with producing a framework of N/SVQs. CISC is the first sector-wide body in construction to develop occupational standards at higher levels. For the first time there is a single, national, industry-wide qualification structure. It encourages career progression and skill transfer from bottom to top and from side to side. The framework for Construction Standards brings together both the craft and professional groups into a single progression route (see below). Although NVQ 1 and 2 remain introductory and trade standards, at NVQ 3 there is an overlap between the craft and supervisory standards and the technician standards. This new structure not only creates for the first time a single progression route for the industry but also brings all the various professional qualification routes together.

The first N/SVQs were accredited in 1993. Further areas are

being developed, with particular attention to gaps in the existing qualification structure, where there is a population of unqualified practitioners.

CISC says that it is likely that there will be a range of N/SVQs to reflect the breadth of professional practice. For example, in civil engineering there will be separate N/SVQs for design, site management, project management and business management. Professional institutions are considering how N/SVQ units can be absorbed into their existing qualification structures. There are clear differences in approach between the two. For example, the bestowing of Chartered status by a professional body can be viewed as a long-range forecast of an individual's future performance, whereas an N/SVQ at Level 5, on the other hand, is a public statement of an individual's current competence. CISC believes that the achievement of selected N/SVQ units will 'be stepping stones to charterdom'. In terms of integrating the current academic programmes with N/SVQs, learning centres will be able to match their provision against the evidence demanded by the standards. This should enable an academic qualification to provide evidence of much of the knowledge requirement of an N/SVQ. CISC is also involved in developing GNVQ/GSVQs in construction and the built environment.

Encouraging diversity

Although the proportion of females among the construction professions has been increasing in recent times, there are still

---

A framework for construction standards

N/SVQ Level	CISC	CITB
	Professional, managerial and technical	Craft and operative
5	Chartered equivalent	–
4	Incorporated equivalent	–
3	Technician equivalent	Craft and supervision
2	–	Trade
1	–	Introductory

Source: CISC, 1995

131

major problems in attracting women into the professions. According to a recent report by the Construction Industry Board (CIB, 1995), women make up 43 per cent of the working population but less than 10 per cent of the construction workforce. Most of those employed in construction are employed in office jobs as clerical and secretarial staff. This makes the industry the most male-dominated of all the major industries. In the surveying profession, in 1991, fewer than 5 per cent of practising surveyors were women, and most of those were employed in the public sector – although 20 per cent of surveying students were female (Greed, 1991).

However, as we note elsewhere in this book, the industry faces increasing problems of labour supply in the future. The number of school-leavers who are entering the industry is declining, and attracting graduates is also proving difficult. According to the CIB report (CIB, 1995), in order to cope with even moderate growth in output as the economy recovers, the construction industry will need to recruit from a wider skills base. The economic activity rate of women is expected to increase to 75 per cent by 2006, while the activity rate of men is expected to continue to fall. Women will therefore be an important source of labour for all types of organisation. While the industry currently has a poor image as a career for women, the dangers inherent in the work are a threat to both sexes. The employment of more women would probably serve to improve safety on sites, and should certainly improve employee facilities. For the professions a further barrier to women is the long hours expected of the staff, a culture that puts a strain on all staff, but particularly women 'who believe that if they do not match the hours put in by their male colleagues they will be perceived as not being sufficiently committed to their job' and suffer in promotion prospects (CIB, 1995: 19). The CIB report argues that, although it is difficult to provide flexible hours on site for crafts and trades, 'the project nature of construction should, with effective management, provide an opportunity for innovative working practices within some disciplines.'

The CIB suggests that what might help the industry improve its image and attract women would be to

❑ accentuate the positive
❑ encourage the development of a variety of management styles

- improve site conditions for all
- develop flexible working patterns
- recognise the real cost of replacing rather than retaining skilled staff
- acknowledge the effects of working conditions on social and family life
- take advantage of experience in other industries and other countries.

Management development

Management development has been defined as 'the planned process of ensuring, through an appropriate learning environment and experiences, the continuous supply and retention of effective managers at all levels to meet the requirements of an organisation and enhance its strategic capability' (Harrison, 1992a). It can focus on either of two areas – manager development, which is designed simply to provide a continuous supply of competent managers; or management development, which has the wider objective of building a shared culture across the whole management group and enhancing management capability throughout the organisation.

Management development is therefore very much concerned with organisational values, culture, and the management of change. Programmes correspondingly focus on opportunities for self-reflection as well as other forms of learning. The intention of such management development courses is to provide an environment in which managers can feel free to express their opinions, experiment with new ideas, and allow creativity to surface. It is not to impose an authoritarian company view on all matters. Such courses accordingly use teaching methods that involve project work, case studies, role playing, sensitivity training, action learning, and self-development.

The traditional belief in construction has been that 'only experience develops construction managers', but this view has been challenged in more recent times (Langford *et al*, 1995), and both the professional bodies and individual companies have begun to see the importance of increasing the level of management development to improve the industry's performance. All the major professional bodies encourage continuous professional development. Moreover, the demand for more management development has been increased by the growth of such staff within the industry. While the number of directly employed operatives has continued to fall, the proportion of administrative, professional, technical and clerical staff has continued to rise. This increase has been attributed to three factors: the increased use of sub-contractors on site, the greater technical sophistication within buildings (eg the requirements for information technology services), and the different procurement methods that have become more legally and financially complex (Langford and Newcombe, 1992).

Yet the evidence suggests that few construction firms have such management development programmes. A survey of 38 of the top 100 UK construction firms in 1989 found that only 17 had formal management development policies (Mphake, 1989). The evidence also suggests that those organisations which do have such a programme prefer to offer internal courses that gain credits towards a professional qualification, and there is therefore a strong technical element. Such courses are supported by coaching but there is little use of project attachments, job rotation and self-directed learning, as used more widely in other sectors. Nevertheless, there is some evidence of increasing emphasis on management techniques (Langford *et al*, 1995), although the importance of people skills in managing the various employment relationships within the industry is perhaps not so strongly reflected as one might expect. Langford *et al* (1995) comment that the skills of 'empathy and understanding are not well evidenced'.

The types of courses offered to construction managers have been found to fall into three main categories – functional management (ie the various business functions), management techniques (eg communications, negotiation, leadership), and general management (eg business policy, strategy and decision-making) (Mphake, 1989). These exist at all levels of management – senior, middle and junior.

One very recent development in the industry has been the establishment of a course for company directors by the CIOB. Such senior executives have tended to be recruited from the specialist construction professions, which may guarantee technical expertise but not necessarily the general management skills needed to run a company. The CIOB has recognised this 'paucity of high-level training and development programmes' in the industry, and for that reason has designed a programme to prepare professionals for directorship by developing the skills needed to run a contracting organisation. The course simulates the board room environment, involving interactive learning methods that draw upon the wide experience of the participants. Because of the time constraints on such top managers, the modules are presented as self-contained two-day blocks, combined with self-development activities in between the blocks. The modules include such areas as construction in the national economy, marketing, selling, business communications, strategic planning, risk assessment and management, company finance, leadership styles and organisational culture, human resourcing and development policy, the statutory responsibilities of companies and senior executives, organisation design and development, and performance indicators.

Investors in People

Obtaining the support of senior management for an employee development programme is essential. Within the construction industry this has always meant a fairly hard-headed approach, such that clear business paybacks are required from the investment. One way in which such support can be gained is through the Investors in People initiative. The Investors in People (IIP) initiative was started by the Department of Employment in November 1990. Its aim was to raise the level of commitment to training and development among British employers. A 'National Standard' has been developed against which employers can be formally assessed for official recognition of their IIP status. The scheme is run by the local Training and Enterprise Councils (TECs) and in Scotland by Local Enterprise Councils (LECs). Both the TECs and LECs are eligible for extra funding if they can achieve a specified level of IIP commitments. The national training target was that at least half of the country's medium- and large-scale organisations should be recognised as having IIP status by 1996. By the end of 1995 18,000 organisations had committed themselves to IIP, and some 3,000 had achieved recognition. Of these, some 44 per cent of organisations employ fewer than 50 people, around 33 per cent employ 50 to 200, and a further 23 per cent employ over 200.

The benefits of IIP can be wide-ranging and may include:

❑ improved earnings, productivity and profitability through benefiting from more skilled and motivated employees

135

- reduced costs and wastage because employees are committed to such objectives
- enhanced quality because investment in people can add considerable value to 'kite mark' schemes such as BS5750 and ISO9000
- improved motivation because greater involvement, personal development and recognition can lead to higher morale, reduced absenteeism, readier acceptance of change, and greater identification with the organisation beyond the confines of the job
- customer satisfaction because employees become more customer-focused in their work
- public recognition, which itself may attract the best-quality job applicants
- an improvement in the competitive edge to secure future prosperity for the organisation.

The primary attraction of IIP for employers is the opportunity to audit existing training and development practices against a national benchmark (IDS, 1993). This enables gaps to be identified in existing provision, and focuses attention on the strategic benefits of linking training to business objectives. Employers have also found that it complements their moves towards total quality management and the achievement of the BS5750 quality standard. Research also suggests that the achievement of IIP can demonstrate commitment to employees which can itself lead to greater motivation, especially if the organisation is undergoing change. It can also serve to improve recruitment and retention of staff.

The IIP initiative is defined as 'a planned approach to setting and communicating business goals and developing people to meet these goals, so that what people can do, and are motivated to do, matches what the business needs them to do.' There are four IIP principles: commitment, planning, action and evaluation. A company that aims to achieve IIP status must demonstrate:

- *commitment* – it makes a public commitment from the top to develop all employees in order to achieve its business objectives
- *planning* – it regularly reviews the training and development needs of all employees

❑ *action* – it initiates action to train and develop individuals on recruitment and throughout their employment

❑ *evaluation* – it evaluates the investment in training and development in order to assess achievement and the benefits to the company, and to improve future effectiveness.

The National Standard expands these principles into more general policy statements and requirements. Each of the four principles has a number of indicators (eg 'commitment' has six indicators). Although the same indicators are used for all types of employers in all industries, there is no suggestion that all organisations should adopt the same approach to training. Companies have to demonstrate the existence of some form of training needs assessment system. The CITB can help smaller companies to do this through the introduction of basic systems, while for larger firms the board can, where necessary, provide help in developing a full-scale staff appraisal system.

Assessment for IIP is undertaken by an assessor appointed by the local TEC/LEC who first reviews a portfolio of evidence compiled by the organisation. CITB staff have been trained to help organisations prepare for such IIP applications. The assessor then visits the company to talk to employees selected on a random basis. These employees are expected to demonstrate an awareness of IIP and to confirm that the company's declared policies on employee development are being carried out. The only direct cost of IIP to the employer is the cost of assessment, which varies from organisation to organisation depending on the size and structure of the company and the number of employees. However, in the longer term, argues IIP UK, companies may actually make savings as a result of IIP. According to research by IDS, the cost of assessment varied between £1,300 and £2,500, although larger organisations paid more. Assessor fees are usually around £500 per day.

The CITB actively encourages employers to make a public commitment through a TEC/LEC to the IIP programme. The CITB itself, as an employer, is fully committed to IIP, and during 1993 it was decided that each of the board's seven regions and the Bircham Newton Training Centre should apply for an award with the most appropriate TEC/LEC. To date around 40 construction sector organisations have achieved IIP status, covering in total over 12,700 employees. A further 412 construction companies have committed themselves to IIP. However, in terms of the overall penetration of IIP, construction remains one of the lowest sectors (just over 8 per cent of potential coverage). The companies recognised to date range from small companies which employ fewer than 10 people to large national contractors such as Shepherd Construction (1,600) and Laing Engineering (2,006).

Shepherd Construction (see the case study at the end of this chapter) has attained IIP for both its construction arm (1,500 employees) and its housebuilding division (240 employees). The company – one of the largest privately-owned businesses in building – was the first construction firm to achieve the IIP Standard, which it was awarded in June 1992, six months after making the IIP commitment. The company has a long history of training and won a National Training award for its safety training; it introduced a Total Excellence Programme shortly prior to its commitment to IIP. Shepherd claims that IIP has helped them achieve an increased market share, a high level of repeat business, a reduction in accidents and the winning of a National Training Award.

Another example, Laing Engineering, is part of the John Laing Plc group and undertakes mechanical engineering and construction contracts across the UK. The company introduced IIP as part of a three-year programme to address declining competitiveness. The company says that a commitment to IIP and TQM helped transform the firm from a directive to a participative culture. Between 1992 and 1993, the company maintained turnover despite the recession, quadrupled its operating margin, increased productivity by 45 per cent, improved repeat business by 24 per cent, raised the annual value of contracts finalised by 4 per cent, and reduced the frequency of accidents by 10 per cent.

Employee development as a key to success
Although the construction industry has not been known for continuous professional development in the past, this is now a major target for all the professional bodies within the industry. With the development of NVQ Standards for the industry, for the first time some form of employee progression is now possible from the most basic introductory level for new entrants at operative level up to senior management and chartered status. This development has significant human resource management

implications for both pay and grading systems and for employee development. The new Standards have also helped to break down the occupational demarcation lines between the various construction professions which had been created by professional rivalries in the past.

Most importantly, the industry has recognised and begun to remedy the absence of management development for existing managers and professional staff. Whereas in the past the emphasis was placed firmly on technical knowledge and experience of the construction process, employers have begun to recognise the advantages of more practical management training for supervisors, middle managers and top executives, many of whom have been promoted into management posts from technical backgrounds but with little or no training in management skills. The contribution that higher education institutions can make to this process has also been acknowledged. In particular, the issues of business strategy and marketing have been incorporated into management development programmes. However, human resource management skills and knowledge are still seen, perhaps, as less important by many managers in the industry.

This attitude may need to change in the future as the labour market changes and the traditional sources of trained labour for the industry begin to dissolve. We have stressed the importance of tackling the issues of diversity in the workforce and of extending the available pool of labour to women and ethnic minorities. Raising the quality of the existing workforce is also important in the increasingly competitive construction markets of the future. Some construction firms have begun to see the value of developing their human resources as a business asset. The use of Investors in People may be a useful mechanism for focusing attention on this important element and winning top management support for a more strategic approach to managing people in the industry.

CASE STUDY – Investors in People at Shepherd Construction

Shepherd Construction is part of the York-based Shepherd Building Group, one of the largest privately-owned building businesses in the UK. The Group includes three divisions:

construction (five companies), manufacturing (Portakabin Ltd and Portasilo Ltd), and housing, commercial and industrial development (Shepherd Development Co. Ltd and Shepherd Homes Ltd). Shepherd Construction Ltd was founded as a family business in 1890, and still is, for members of the Shepherd family are involved in the management of the company today. It operates throughout the UK and has regional offices in York, Manchester, Northampton, Birmingham, Nottingham, London, Leeds, Cardiff and Darlington. The company is known as a pioneer in Design and Build techniques and has successfully met the exacting demands of clients in the public sector (eg hospitals, universities, law courts, prisons) and the private sector (factories, shopping centres, hotels and office developments). The company has worked for such companies as Glaxo, ICI, Coca-Cola, Vickers, Panasonic, Nestlé, Boots, Asda and W H Smith. It recently completed the new hotel at Alton Towers theme park.

The Group as a whole employs around 2,500 people, of whom 1,400 are employed in Shepherd Construction. The company is unusual for the construction industry in that it employs a substantial direct workforce of operatives (around two-thirds of the workforce). This commitment to direct labour is based on a number of factors – not least the ability of the company to find a succession of projects for its operatives, enabling them to be employed continuously. Another factor stated by the company in support of direct labour is that such operatives do not have to be retrained for each job and know the company's quality standards. The investment in specialist skills training therefore provides a payback over the longer term. The directly employed need less supervision because the job security provided is an incentive to work productively and to high standards. According to the company, directly employed labour is not more costly than self-employment if it is managed correctly, because the workers can be more productive, although there may be higher administrative costs. The company says that its reputation for employing operatives on a longer-term basis than elsewhere in the industry means that it attracts many adult job applicants and young people looking for career opportunities.

Company philosophy
The company has a well established reputation for reliability and integrity and, as a privately-owned family business, is able to

take a long-term view. In the words of the managing director, Paul Shepherd, the company thinks 'long-term rather than in terms of quick profit'. This applies as much to its employment policies as to other business matters. The company has had a strong commitment to training and developing its employees for around 35 years, from the time Sir Peter Shepherd helped to develop construction industry training through the Chartered Institute of Building and the Construction Industry Training Board. Today the company has highly developed personnel, training and safety policies. These include an appraisal system for all staff, including site-based operatives. The company has a strong belief in the competitive advantage of good human resource management policies, especially in the training and development of its workforce. The aim is to seek constant and continuous incremental improvement which can be measured. The company mission statement includes commitments to personal involvement, constant improvement, quality management, the measurement of progress, and the selection of sub-contractors and suppliers on the grounds of excellence. The chairman and managing director, Paul Shepherd, believes that the company 'is not just here for the boom times, nor are we going to disappear when things get tough'. He says that 'long-term progress is more likely to come from continual action in a small way rather than by occasional great leaps forward'. The company's mission is to be 'not the biggest but the best' building company.

The personnel department

The Construction Division personnel function is centralised in York and serves the four companies nationally. The department consists of the chief personnel services manager, the training and development manager, the health and safety manager, the security manager and four personnel managers. Each of the personnel managers has responsibility for a region or company. There are also three health and safety officers. The training and development manager has an assistant plus two training administrators, one of whom was employed recently to help with Shepherd's external training courses provision.

The company has employee handbooks for both staff and operative employees. The company states that it 'places a high value on good staff relations and believes that effective communication plays an important part in this'. For operatives the company follows the NJCBI working rule agreement and contributes to the national holiday and lump sum retirement schemes for its employees. It has good relations with the local UCATT trade union officials but does not have any formal collective relationships at company level. Subscriptions are deducted at source where employees choose to belong to a union. Staff employees are not unionised and are not covered by collective bargaining.

The company's commitment to good employee relations manifests itself in the low turnover and length of service of employees. Almost 55 per cent of the operatives and 60 per cent of the salaried staff have been with the company for six years and over. Around 70 per cent of the salaried staff have had a substantial promotion since they joined the company, and about 40 per cent started with the company as apprentices, students or graduate trainees.

Training and development

Shepherd's training activities are organised by the training and development manager and his staff. Policy statements cover the broad approach to training and development. The company 'encourages members of staff to develop their abilities in order to improve efficiency in their present positions and, where appropriate, to equip themselves for more senior positions'. In the view of the managing director, Paul Shepherd, it takes time to produce results – in the case of middle management training up to five years before a payback is seen. However, in his view, 'Training is rather like breathing – you have to keep breathing to stay alive, and you have to keep training to remain success-ful commercially.' The company has won two national training awards over the last four years. In addition, it became the first national contractor to achieve the Investors in People (IIP) stan-dard in 1992, and was successfully reassessed in 1995.

Staff are encouraged to study for relevant qualifications: continuous personal development is seen as very important. Each employee, including operatives, has an annual appraisal to set training needs and development plans. This appraisal system is designed to focus on the concept of continuous devel-opment and improvement as a route towards higher-quality delivery to the customer. At present, some 126 employees are currently attending external courses which lead to vocational qualifications, in addition to the company's 80-plus annual in-house training courses.

The company provides a wide range of training programmes, both internal and external. Craft training is seen as very important and the chief executive, Paul Shepherd, has encouraged greater attention in this area. There are around 60 craft apprentices (mainly located in the north, where direct labour is more common and there is therefore a ready supply of mentors) who are recruited at the age of 16 for a three-and-a-half-year course. Most of these are now classified as Modern Apprenticeships and the apprentices are of employed status (they are also paid at National Agreement rates of pay). These apprentices are studying towards NVQ Levels 2 and 3. The training is a mix of on-the-job training and block release. The appraisal of operatives at site level is used to plan development for such staff, and the company has issued a guide to operative training for site managers. Training is also available for technicians, who take four-year courses in such qualifications as HNC/D quantity surveying, planning, and site management. Most of these students progress on to professional qualifications, and some are sponsored for degree courses.

Shepherd provides industrial placements for undergraduates studying relevant degrees, usually for one year. The training plans for such students are agreed with the universities before the start of the training, and jointly monitored. Such placements may lead to company sponsorship of the student during the final year of study. The company jointly sponsors degree courses and individual students. Courses include Commercial Management and Quantity Surveying at Loughborough University and UMIST, and Construction Management at Salford University. These are four-year sandwich courses with a guaranteed one-year attachment to the company. There is also a two-year graduate training programme for university graduates in relevant disciplines. The aim is to widen rapidly their knowledge and competence, and they are also encouraged to gain their appropriate professional qualification.

There are both site supervision and site management courses. Some 15 years ago the firm started in-company site supervision and site management courses which are CIOB-accredited. These courses are run in-house in block-release mode, and are now being revamped to update and focus them towards the new NVQ Levels 3 and 4. Shepherd Construction was the first company to register as an assessment centre for the new CIOB/CITB NVQ 3 site supervisory and NVQ 4 site management programmes in 1994. An in-house NVQ 4 pilot undertaken in 1994 indicated that the NVQ led to a new emphasis on managers' responsibilities for expenditure and recovery, encouraged the pursuit of information, and helped managers reconsider the development of teams, individuals and themselves.

In conjunction with Leeds Metropolitan University, a postgraduate development programme has been developed by the company, which leads to the award of an advanced professional diploma. The core course is jointly delivered by both the company's own staff and external specialists. Reflective learning assignments are managed and assessed by the University.

Finally, a Management Development Programme for middle managers was developed with Leeds Metropolitan University; it was first run in 1992. The programme leads to a post-graduate diploma and allows participants to progress to an MSc in Construction Management. This course includes accreditation of prior learning, work-based learning as well as seven short block modules taught by university staff, company staff and external specialists. Participants have included staff from a variety of backgrounds. Indeed, some members of staff started with Shepherd as craft apprentices at the age of 16. Nine trainees gained the diploma in 1994, and three have since been promoted to construction manager and three to project manager. This programme has won a national training award.

The training and development manager has his own budget to cover courses and the cost of graduate sponsorship. In addition, each region has its own budget to cover apprentice training, external courses and building students' fees. The figures are collated centrally. Including the cost of administration, courses, time and travel expenses for those attending courses, as well as the full cost of young trainees (apprentices, students and graduate trainees), Shepherd's expenditure on training is around 7 per cent of payroll and salary bill. The company estimates that two-thirds of the cost of training is directly recovered from the work of young trainees and the CITB grants. Moreover, the company believes that the payback on its training investment is considerably more than this sum in terms of improved company performance.

Shepherd Training and Development Services was formed in 1996 to market and deliver Shepherd expertise externally. This includes short courses linked to post-graduate qualifications.

Total Excellence Programme

The development of the Investors in People programme within the company was initiated in tandem with a total quality management programme – 'Shepherd's Total Excellence Programme'. The Total Excellence Programme was prompted by increasing competition within the industry and the possibility of a recession after the building boom of the late 1980s. The programme was designed as a means of achieving constant improvement in the quality of the company's services and in the building process and products. It was adopted at board level in 1990, and has been worked down through the organisation with target dates for implementation of the various stages. At present the programme is confined to salaried staff.

One of the main elements of the programme is the encouragement of the personal involvement of employees in raising standards and understanding the company's objectives. Communication, involvement and training opportunities are seen as key elements in the process. The programme also concerns the selection of sub-contractors and suppliers on the grounds of their ability to meet the company's excellent standards of performance as well as price.

The Total Excellence Programme was launched in 1991 with a workshop for senior managers; it was followed by a half-day workshop for team leaders and all staff in 1992. Shepherd produced its own video to sell the programme to employees.

Parts of the Shepherd Group are working towards the quality standard ISO9000, but the company says that this only audits the company's systems and procedures. In its view, people are as important as systems and a successful company needs strength in both areas. Investors in People was therefore seen as a useful adjunct to the total quality programme in that it provided an audit of the quality of the employees.

The commitment to IIP

The company became aware of IIP in 1991 and IIP commitment was made in January 1992. The full standard was achieved within six months in June 1992. This rapid success demonstrated the degree to which Shepherd had already achieved high levels of investment in training and development before committing itself to IIP.

The company decided to commit itself to IIP for a number of reasons:

145

❑ the training plan was directly linked to the business plan
❑ identification of individual training needs was improved
❑ simple messages were communicated across the company
❑ consistency was achieved in carrying out appraisals
❑ company-wide communication from the chairman on the need to develop all employees to achieve business objectives was achieved
❑ more vigorous evaluation of training was possible, including the monitoring of training's contribution to general business objectives
❑ a manager guide to operative training gave a new focus to the importance of this level of training
❑ it encouraged a 'right first time' approach
❑ it encouraged the further development of site supervision and management training
❑ it linked management and supervisory training to continuous improvement through projects
❑ training was linked to NVQ standards
❑ it encouraged a quality culture within the company.

The evidence for the IIP assessment was completed almost at the same time that the company committed itself to the standard. The assessment was undertaken by a consultant on behalf of the then National Training Task Force, who visited all the regional offices and a number of construction sites. Altogether, some 120 interviews were conducted at all levels of employee, starting with the chief executive. Each region provided a list of all employees, from which the assessor could select interviewees. The process of assessment took two weeks and cost the company £2,175. The company was successfully reassessed in 1995.

The outcomes of IIP

The main advantage for the company in going through the IIP assessment was that it led to critical review of the training being undertaken and its usefulness. This meant examining in detail how the training being undertaken related to the company's needs, and led to more focus on particular areas. The company is not spending more money on training as a result of gaining IIP but is getting better value for money. The three-year review of IIP status is also seen as a useful device for keeping the company on its toes and looking for continuous improvement. This fits in with the long-term approach adopted by Shepherd.

Linked to the Total Excellence Programme, IIP is seen as providing important benefits for both the company and employees. Together they have contributed toward a number of outcomes:

- market share has been increased
- the objective of completing contracts on time and to the required quality has been reinforced, thereby improving the company's image with clients
- the business has weathered the recent recession in the industry well and with relatively strong order-books
- the high level of repeat business has been improved
- accidents at work have been reduced
- the policy of concentrating on seeking widespread incremental improvements has yielded consistent cost savings
- staff turnover is very low in relation to the norm in the construction industry
- the average length of service is well above the average for the industry
- the company has few problems recruiting and retaining staff because of its reputation for fair dealing and good career development opportunities
- employees are motivated and committed to the company.

The benefits for employees are:

- there is relatively good job security in an industry known for its insecurity, especially among operatives
- there are good opportunities for progression within the company – the majority of Shepherd's middle and senior managers started their careers with the company
- there are good opportunities for achieving vocational, professional and academic qualifications
- the training budget is secure, irrespective of the state of the industry, so employees know that there is a long-term commitment to their development
- there have been improved employment opportunities with the company for apprentices, graduates and technicians, thereby benefiting the local economy

❏ the culture is friendly and supportive of employees in a tough industry.

A major benefit of IIP is that it demonstrated that Shepherd's training and development was audited against a national standard which applied to all sectors of industry and commerce. The process helps to highlight areas for improvements to be undertaken before assessment. According to the company, 'Perhaps the single most important contribution which IIP can make towards business success is that it provides a clear focus on the value of training within the context of strategic business planning.' It means that managers concentrate on whether the training programmes meet the company's medium- and long-term needs. The achievement of IIP has also sent a message to all employees that the company values their contribution and their involvement in improving the business.

Note: Sources for this case study include both Investors In People UK and IDS Study 530/May 1993, 'Investors In People'. Special thanks go to John Foreman, chief personnel services manager, and Peter Blackburn, training and development manager at Shepherd Construction.

CHAPTER 7

MANAGING PERFORMANCE AND MINIMISING CONFLICT

Building the 'softer' human resource management skills within a construction organisation may be one of the most challenging tasks a manager can face. Yet it can also be one of the most worthwhile. Motivated and committed employees are likely to be the most productive and effective, and with workforce size cut so dramatically it makes sense for managers to review the way in which they handle their relationships with individual employees. One purpose of this chapter is to consider how to improve on management practice at the individual level. It focuses on the levers for improving individual performance through effective communications and teambuilding, and looks at the role of coaching and mentoring in this process. The chapter also considers the procedures which apply in the event of unsatisfactory performance – particularly disciplinary procedures. It highlights the provisions of collective agreements and of the code of practice of the Advisory, Conciliation and Arbitration Service (ACAS). It also points to the importance of observing these arrangements as a means of avoiding unfair dismissal claims, and to recent developments in redundancy handling.

A construction professional or a manager is expected to have the capacity to face in a number of different directions at once! Meeting diverse and sometimes conflicting demands is not always easy. Within the scope of a specific project, attention to client needs is a key requirement. Yet individuals have responsibilities to their own organisation and are answerable to more senior managers for their actions. At the same time they must be able to co-ordinate work with colleagues and those working for them at the level of the site or the project. To complicate matters further, the increase in sub-contracting may require extensive liaison across organisational boundaries.

Each of these relationships is concerned with communications. Much has been written about the subject of partnership within the construction industry. Yet there can be no partnership without the establishment of effective communications – both within and between organisations. Technical and professional knowledge is undoubtedly important, but there is evidence that the softer, interpersonal skills are particularly valued – for example, by clients reviewing the work of project managers.

Effective communication

The term 'communication' is used here to mean the giving out of messages by one person and the receiving of those messages by another. Communication can be undertaken verbally, in writing, or through audio-visual or electronic means such as e-mail and the Internet. At corporate level, most of the larger construction firms issue new employees with a staff handbook. They also have their own journal or newsletter. News boards or bulletin-board information are widely circulated too, to keep people at regional offices and sites in touch with developments.

At the individual level it is important to recognise that communication is not just words which are said or written. It is also the way in which they are heard and how they are understood. An effective manager is one who is able to communicate at a number of different levels and in a variety of ways.

Communication can be formal – for example, in the context of a meeting; or it can be informal – for example, in face-to-face discussion on site. Familiarity with the people around you – a willingness to share informal and sometimes non-work-related exchanges – may be as important to building a culture of shared experience and understanding as the formal communications established in the context of a meeting.

Communication can be a one-way process or it can be two-way. It may often seem easier to tell people what they are going to do rather than invite their contribution. But the more complex interaction, which involves feedback, questions, comment and discussion, may ensure a more thorough understanding and a more thought-through approach to the task in hand. Managers can contribute to effective teamwork by creating an environment which is participative – in which comments and suggestions are welcomed and taken into account. It is often the case that the person who is going to do the job can most easily see the problems or the pitfalls which it involves. If problems can be anticipated and avoided, there can be savings in time and possibly in cost – for example, it may be possible to improve on health and safety standards and to resolve some problems in this area. Although the thought and the care which is required for communications may seem to be onerous – particularly when set in the context of the deadlines for a major building project, there can be long-term benefits – not the least of which is quality of the work process and improvement to the quality of working life for the individuals concerned.

However clear the message may be, there may be impediments to comprehension or full communication. One impediment which may emerge is that the listener may not receive the message which the speaker believes he or she is communicating – or may receive a hidden message which is conveyed by the manner of the speaker. Background 'noise' which results from the environment may intervene in such a way that the message does not get through. This can happen because of preconceptions or stereotypes. While words are being spoken, other messages may be communicated through body language. If you think that a colleague or a subordinate is lazy or inadequate, it is all too easy to communicate this impression without actually expressing it in words! There can be no advantages to you or to your organisation in conveying such an impression if the purpose of your communication is not concerned with this issue. If these are your real concerns, though, maybe the issue should be more openly considered.

A subtle communication of negative attitudes may undermine communication. Guirdham (1990) points to six barriers which can be put up and create problems (see next page).

Any of these attitudes can be detrimental to teambuilding and to constructive communication. If you can avoid putting up barriers to communication, it will help to create a climate within which others – from your own organisation and from organisations with which you are working, such as sub-contractors – can listen more effectively to what is being said.

A message can be lost for a number of reasons. If it is not clearly formulated or expressed, it is less likely to be understood. But there can be distractions, interruptions or misunderstandings which intervene. The recipient may

---

Six barriers to communication

'I'm judging you'
'I'm in charge'
'I can manipulate you'
'I don't give a damn about you'
'I'm superior to you'
'My mind is made up. Nothing you can say will alter it'

Source: Guirdham, M. *Interpersonal Skills at Work*, 1990: 173.

misconstrue the meaning because she or he has a different background or way of thinking. For example, younger graduate managers may have difficulty in communicating with older employees who have acquired their skills and knowledge on site because in terms of education and framework of reference these two groups may be very different.

Managers at all levels need to consider the different types of skills and expertise which the various actors bring to the project in order to be able to find ways of bringing people together to work effectively.

One way in which communication can be impaired is when we allow a stereotype to influence our expectations of the communication we receive from a person. Because women are underrepresented in the construction industry, some people may have stereotyped views of the way in which they may behave – expecting them to be unable to cope with the demands of the work, or unwilling to work late to get the job done because of family commitments. Women entrants to the industry may be conscious of their minority position and have different perceptions or priorities from those of their male counterparts, but this will not always be the case. Such views should not be assumed, and communications should be aimed to reinforce the confidence and capacity of all of the workforce to participate effectively.

Another impediment to communication arises simply because people fail to pay attention to what is being said. We all forget many of the things said to us, so important information requires clear communication, probably in a variety of forms, so that the message is reinforced.

So what can be done to improve communication? Guirdham (1990) suggests that a positive approach can help to create the climate needed – emphasising the pleasant aspects of a situation – telling someone what you will do as well as what you will not.

Try to think about the needs and the point of view of the person you are talking to as well as emphasising your own point of view. Expressions involving the word 'You' may be better than those involving 'I' in some circumstances – 'Could you have this job done by tomorrow?' may be better than 'I want this job done by tomorrow.'

Ask questions, and use the knowledge of others to reach conclusions, rather than imposing your own views. Try to use questions which probe the situation or improve your understanding. Much may be lost if you preclude comment or contributions from those who are working with you.

Remember that the person who is listening may be influenced by the way the message is communicated.

The message

❏ Is it useful or important to the recipient? (Messages are more likely to be absorbed if they have some personal relevance)

❏ Does it correspond to the recipient's existing beliefs? (Messages which conform to current beliefs are more likely to be assimilated)

❏ Is it novel? (Unusual messages carry more influence)

❏ Is it for the second time? (Repeated messages also carry influence)

Adapted from Williams, Dobson and Walters, *Changing Culture*, IPM, 1989.

The importance of culture

The prevailing attitudes and beliefs within the organisation – sometimes referred to as the organisation culture – may have an impact on the way in which individuals perceive their role and responsibilities. Organisational culture includes the formal practices such as the structure and the written policies within organisations. It also embraces the informal practices, the day-to-day behaviour and assumptions, including the rituals, stories and the workplace humour (Hendry, 1995: 124). These factors may consciously or unconsciously also affect the perception and understanding of messages.

Culture in organisations is something which is historically-based and which is learnt. It may have its origins in the demands of the work environment as much as in the values of individuals. Different market sectors operate with different technologies and with variations in the physical environment, and with diverse needs for skills and resources (Williams, Dobson and Walters, 1989: 14). It is interesting to reflect on the demands which have been transmitted through the tough competitive and physical environment within the construction sector. It could be argued that there is little evidence of continuity in culture within organisations, in that there may be significant differences in the sub-culture of the different occupations and groups through larger organisations. Yet in contracting, at least, there may be a dominant influence stemming from the immediacy of the requirements of task or project completion – on getting the job done regardless of the impediments.

Four main culture types have been defined (Handy, 1985) and it is useful to reflect on their relevance to different sections of the industry. They are:

❑ power culture
❑ role culture
❑ task culture
❑ people culture.

Power culture is evident in the early days of an organisation. It is dependent on a strong leader who dominates the company (or a project or department). The leader is expected to be closely involved in all areas of business – either directly or through lieutenants. It is a model which is relevant to the operations of the smaller enterprise, which often carries the mark of a central or founding figure, and it may have echoes in larger organisations which can trace their origins back to these small beginnings.

Role culture becomes more likely as organisations grow, because they require functional specialists who fulfil a prescribed role. The organisation is expected to operate to rational principles, and power within the organisation may rest on expert or specialist knowledge. Although offering the advantages of predictability, the role culture may be less adaptive to change. As a model, the role culture is recognisable within traditional local authorities.

Task culture provides a focus on the project or the job in hand. It brings appropriate expertise and resources to a project team to lay a flexible working base towards the achievement of a shared goal – the completion of the task. The team or task culture is most suitable for markets which are competitive, where product life-spans are short. The task culture would seem to be appropriate to the requirements of contracting activity.

Person culture may result from a voluntary decision by a group of people to co-operate as a means to shared goals. This may be the case for a group of professionals, such as architects, who may group together in order to maximise the benefits of shared administrative facilities while maintaining a degree of individual autonomy and control of the work which they undertake.

The question of organisational culture is particularly relevant because the needs of the industry are changing rapidly. The renewed focus on partnership in contracts, on quality and competencies, and on effective performance, are indicators of change in the business environment which can be expected to feed through to the attitudes and values within the industry.

Some writers suggest that there is a link between culture and organisational effectiveness – that a 'performance culture' or a 'learning culture' can make a contribution to success. Peters and Waterman, writing about 'excellent' organisations, were arguing that a strong culture can be generated with a view to stimulating success (Peters and Waterman, 1982). Yet culture may be deep-rooted and may itself encourage resistance to change. Although there are doubts about the extent to which culture can be managed, the question is an interesting one at site level, where the impact of received culture may be minimised. Each contract creates new opportunities for a unique project-based culture, as the culture of individual organisations may be diluted or adapted within a temporary alliance across organisational boundaries. Precisely because of the short-lived nature of many construction projects, project and contracts managers, together with clients, may have more than the usual opportunity to impact on the culture of their immediate work environment.

Coaching and Mentoring

Coaching and mentoring can provide important ways for a manager to develop the skills and the confidence of people in the project or work team. Coaching and mentoring are not intended as alternatives to more formal training programmes – rather they can provide the additional support and encouragement which make such programmes fully effective, reinforcing the learning which has taken place away from the workplace through the active experience at work. Despite all of the formal training provision available, much of what is learned derives from experience and from practice in the workplace or at site level.

The techniques of coaching and mentoring rely on the establishment of a close working relationship between the manager and the person for whose development or support he or she is responsible.

Coaching offers an informal opportunity for support between a developing person and a coach, who may be the immediate line manager, and who is experienced in the skills which are to be developed. The manager who takes on the role of coach needs to reflect on the existing competencies of the person being coached, with a view to ensuring that opportunities can be provided to practise and to extend them. Time should be allowed for shared reflection on the tasks undertaken and the experience acquired. With planning, the coach can ensure that there is scope for new challenges, whether through deputising during periods of absence, through membership of working parties, or though external activities undertaken under the aegis of professional bodies. An incremental approach is required to the extension of responsibilities, recognising that confidence in facing up to new tasks may be as important as part of the learning experience as the acquisition of new knowledge and skills.

A mentor is likely to be a more senior line manager within a similar functional specialism, although the line manager can take on the role of mentor. The mentor takes on a rather wider role than that which is provided by the coach – being concerned not so much with the acquisition or practice of particular skills as with the process of building a firm foundation for longer-term success. The mentor may provide background information and advice on the way in which the company works and on its culture and values, opening up new opportunities and contacts. This can help to encourage both confidence and a sense of competence which can aid career planning for newer entrants to the industry. In the face of workload fluctuations which may undermine a feeling of job security, mentoring has a special role to play for people coming into construction, but it can provide particular support for women or for black or Asian entrants who are underrepresented at more senior levels in British industry.

Both coaching and mentoring can provide an opportunity for more effective communication, but at their best they do rather more than this. They enable a trainee or a member of the team whose development is under consideration to discuss problems, and to receive counselling, information and feedback from a more senior manager. Not the least of the benefits is to the senior manager involved, who may develop a closer understanding of how it feels to be coming into the industry in the current insecure climate.

Team briefings

Team briefings can be a useful mechanism for communication in a face-to-face setting, involving no more than about 20 people for perhaps 30 minutes. It is probably the most common method of communication for the transmission of information, allowing the advantages of two-way communication. The skill of the person who delivers the briefing is important for effective communication. Not everyone is naturally equipped for this role, and training is a benefit for those who take on such a responsibility. It is important that the activity is not undertaken in a perfunctory or routine way, because that can be counterproductive, undermining rather than supporting the message which is intended. Team briefings can be useful for such purposes as updating an understanding of techniques or working methods, for encouraging employee involvement and understanding of the work process or project, or for refreshing awareness of health and safety issues. In general it seems that team briefings are more likely to be effective if they are undertaken on a regular basis and not confined simply to periods of crisis.

Team briefing can be used as a management tool from the top

of the organisation too, usually in the form of objective-setting cascades, which ensure that corporate objectives are communicated clearly to everyone in the organisation. The aim is to ensure that organisational objectives are taken on board at the level of divisions and sub-divisions. This is a practice which has had limited application in construction companies, but Tarmac plc provide an example of the practice with Tarmac Target 2000 (see the case study at the end of this chapter). The cascading process can involve a variety of forms of communication to reinforce the message and keep people talking about the ideas.

Figure 8   Cascading corporate objectives through the organisation

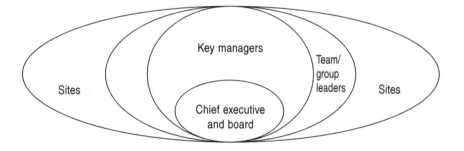

Teambuilding

One of the most challenging features of management within the construction industry is that of building the project team. Creating a team does not in itself guarantee that it will operate effectively, particularly where the team must be created and must operate effectively within a relatively short time-span. Teambuilding involves attention to the nature of the group and the characteristics of its members, the nature of the task which it is to undertake, and the environment or context within which the work is located.

Teambuilding requires skills of communication, as well as thought and attention to practices such as coaching and mentoring.

Problems can arise at a number of levels. A team member who is determined to dominate the group, or a conflict in personalities between two individuals within the project, may undermine the cohesion of the group and inhibit progress. A project will require a team with particular professional skills. The task of building mutual understanding between them is not always straightforward.

Reconciling departmental or professional loyalties within cross-functional project teams is central to the problem of effective performance. Functional management may lie outside the boundaries of the immediate project or working group. A surveyor may be more likely to perceive the managing surveyor as the 'line manager' rather than the project or contracts manager. At its best this arrangement can lead to clear professional standards from the different disciplines engaged within the project, but, if there is any confusion regarding roles or objectives, there can be a conflict of identity. At the individual level, motivation and performance rely on professional standards, on a clear understanding of corporate objectives, and on the capacity of the 'team leader' to bring together a group of people whose perceptions and priorities may differ, and to get the best from them. There must be agreed objectives and established ways of working, including ways of reconciling differences and resolving conflict.

The picture is complicated because most organisations have been reduced in size in recent years and the configuration of departments has changed. Sometimes established teams have been dismantled as a consequence, and it is important to recognise that informal practices – who is used to working with whom – may be one of the keys to effective performance. Conversely it may be necessary to break up teams with a strong performance profile in order to disseminate the benefits of their experience more widely. In many cases teams are created or recreated in response to project requirements. The individuals concerned must be encouraged to work together quickly, and to communicate clearly and regularly.

All of these points require a degree of familiarity of team members with each other; team effectiveness may be reduced if there is one team member who seeks to dominate (Torrington *et al*, 1991).

Groups have been seen as growing through four key stages:

> **Four stages of group development**
>
> *Forming:* There is no real group in being and each individual is looking for a role.
>
> *Storming:* Roles are being established and personal agendas are being set out, so that conflict may be apparent.
>
> *Norming:* Group norms and practices begin to work.
>
> *Performing:* There is a more effective focus on the task in hand.

Source: Handy, 1985: 170–171

However this is not an invariable pattern. If the task is sufficiently important, the group may move rapidly to its mature or 'performing' stage, but some of the questions which might have been raised with a more protracted opportunity for familiarisation may be left unresolved. This is a serious problem for contracts or project managers, who have to operate within a strict time scale. It can mean that some of the 'storming' which would be expected as part of group development may continue at an individual level, some group members pursuing hidden agendas while in theory at least they are fully committed to 'performing'.

The cost of developing a group to maturity may be too high for many of the shorter-term projects in the construction industry, although as an investment it may be an important contribution to success in initiatives with a longer time scale. For the individual who is left with a responsibility for the shorter-term project, some thoughts about the role and the problems of conflict management may be helpful. Guirdham (1990) suggests that managers should consider the objectives and interests of the different parties with the intention of identifying alternative solutions to the differences which may emerge, for example, in meeting situations.

Handy (1985) groups the leader's responsibilities under two broad headings: task functions and maintenance functions (1985: 177). Although the leader is not expected to undertake all of these roles, she or he is expected to see that they are fulfilled.

Task functions are concerned with initiating, information-seeking, diagnosing, opinion-seeking, evaluating, and decision-managing – in that order. Where problems are tackled systematically, and where potential solutions are identified and evaluated, the quality of decision-taking will be more effective.

Maintenance functions are intended to provide support mechanisms for group members and facilitate inter-personal relations within the group. Maintenance functions may include encouragement, peace-keeping, facilitating compromise, clarifying, and standard-setting.

Grievance-handling

It is a characteristic of the employment relationship that individuals on occasions feel dissatisfied or unhappy about some aspect of their work situation. These points of dissatisfaction may be resolved or forgotten in the course of time without requiring any further action. Alternatively, they may be accepted by the employee as a necessary though unsatisfactory feature of the job situation.

Line managers are likely to be aware of some of these problem areas, and from time to time may receive complaints or appeals for help in order to resolve them. This may be realistic in some circumstances – for example, where the complaint concerns conditions of work which can be amended or improved in some way. In themselves, these complaints may not constitute a formal grievance. The term 'grievance' is used here specifically to mean a complaint which has been formally lodged with a manager or a trade union representative.

Grievances of this sort are fairly unusual in practice, probably because the majority of employees are reluctant to take the risk of being identified as troublemakers and may believe in any case that they will make no progress through the formal expression of their concerns (Torrington and Hall, 1995: 531). This may be the case where dissatisfaction relates to the style and practices of the immediate line manager.

Early attention to problems and dissatisfaction may be a more effective solution than formal procedures, but where it cannot or has not been given, the employee has rights, within a framework of organisational justice, to use the grievance procedure. This provides for equity of treatment, for representation for the individual, and for different stages at which the problem may receive consideration.

In the first instance the grievance is raised with the individual line manager, with a view to finding a solution. Where the problem cannot be resolved at this level, representation can be made to a more senior level of management. If no satisfaction is received at this stage, reference can be made to the next or final stage within the procedure. Resolution of the issue should be sought at the earliest possible point within the procedure, and it is inherent in this type of arrangement that consideration of the issue should not become protracted.

Managers need to be aware of organisational procedures. Typically, the procedure is:

Stage 1: The employee takes the matter up with his or her immediate line manager.

Stage 2: Failing a settlement, the matter may be taken to a more senior manager such as the departmental head. There may be a time limit – for example, five working days.

Stage 3: If there is no settlement at Stage 2 within the specified time, the matter may proceed to a higher level of management – possibly an appropriate director, who will consult and seek a settlement.

Stage 4: If there is no settlement at Stage 3 within the specified time, there may be provision for a final stage in the procedure – for example, offering consideration at board level by a director who has no direct managerial accountability for the department in which the employee is employed.

Remember that complaints of discrimination on grounds of race or sex may be taken to the Commission for Racial Equality or the Equal Opportunities Commission, from whom advice can be sought (see address list).

Other procedures which may be applied are set out in collective agreements which relate to the conditions of employment of operatives. In essence these are similar to the organisational procedures outlined above, except that they provide for trade union representation, initially through a shop steward and later through a full-time official of the union. They may also apply in some cases (for example, under the building industry working rule agreement) to operatives who are designated self-employed. The other distinctive feature of the national collective agreements is the recognition which is reflected in them that an individual grievance can quickly escalate into a collective dispute. For this reason there is a tendency to treat these two issues – grievances and disputes – alongside each other, with reference to the conciliation mechanisms set up within the industry.

Individual managers may deal only rarely with formal complaints or grievances, but they handle problems, resolve disagreement, and endeavour to minimise conflict as part of their day-to-day activities. In doing so they use the organisational rules as a benchmark.

Organisational rules

Every work organisation has its own rules and the procedures through which they are implemented. At the most basic level, this is to ensure that employees do not bring the organisation into contravention of statutory obligations – for example, on health and safety at work, or on questions of sex or race equality. However, the framework of rules goes further in requiring employees to observe standards of behaviour and of output which conform to organisational objectives. Although they may rarely be referred to, the rules provide a method of controlling the individual and individual behaviour within the organisation.

Organisational rules are normally set out in written form in a staff handbook or in site rules which are distributed to new employees on appointment.

Site rules may cover issues such as:

❏ clocking in and out
❏ timekeeping
❏ absenteeism and absence through sickness or injury
❏ arrangements for overtime working
❏ drug and alcohol abuse
❏ site security
❏ damage to property
❏ safety helmets
❏ site safety arrangements
❏ quality assurance
❏ responsibility to the local community and the environment.

One of the functions of managers, at every level of the organisation, is a responsibility to ensure that rules are observed. In practice rules may rarely be referred to, for most people absorb the culture and the values of an organisation, and informal methods of communication may be as important as the formal written statements with respect to the framework of rules.

Induction training is a method of ensuring that rules are understood – describing the background and the reason for each rule so that a new recruit understands why it should be observed. Because rules are reviewed and periodically updated, personnel practitioners – or those who take responsibility for personnel matters within the organisation – will also be concerned to communicate with established employees as well as with new recruits, to ensure that rules are understood through the organisation as a whole.

Disciplinary procedures and practice

Ensuring that rules are observed is a routine management responsibility and one which requires some formal attention. Managers need to find the right balance between being authoritarian and being insufficiently clear about what is required. Disciplinary procedures require that an employee's attention is drawn to a performance which is below the standard expected or to behaviour which is unacceptable. On a day-to-day basis, caution or counselling for unsatisfactory performance may be a sufficient response to a disciplinary problem. However, because the ultimate sanction for breach of the rules is dismissal, managers need to be aware that employees have rights in law to pursue a claim for unfair dismissal, and may have recourse to an industrial tribunal to present their case. Managers should therefore be familiar with the disciplinary procedures of their own organisation and with the interviewing and record-keeping which may be required.

Disciplinary procedures should not be viewed primarily as a means of imposing sanctions. They should conversely be designed to emphasise and encourage improvements in individual conduct.

The Advisory, Conciliation and Arbitration Service (ACAS) has issued a model procedure and a code of practice, as well as guidance on the conduct of disciplinary issues.

ACAS says (ACAS *Code of Practice 1. Disciplinary Practice and Procedures in Employment*) that disciplinary procedures should:

❑ be in writing
❑ specify to whom they apply
❑ provide for matters to be dealt with quickly
❑ indicate the disciplinary actions which may be taken

- specify the levels of management which have the authority to take the various forms of disciplinary action, ensuring that immediate superiors do not normally have the power to dismiss without reference to senior management
- provide for individuals to be informed of the complaints against them and to be given an opportunity to state their case before decisions are reached
- give individuals the right to be accompanied by a trade union representative or by a fellow employee of their choice
- ensure that, except for gross misconduct, no employees are dismissed for a first breach of discipline
- ensure that disciplinary action is not taken until the case has been carefully investigated
- ensure that individuals are given an explanation for any penalty imposed
- provide a right of appeal and specify the procedure to be followed.

One reason for the existence of procedures within organisations is to ensure equity of treatment. If most members of a work group are customarily ten minutes late in commencing work, a manager will be failing to manage effectively if one individual is singled out for this misdemeanour. Rules are intended to be applied evenhandedly and without discrimination between individuals. It is important to bear in mind that issues which are perceived by a manager as disciplinary in nature may not necessarily derive from incompetence or ill-will by the individual concerned, and that it may be possible to find a more effective solution through discussion rather than through disciplinary action. It is also essential that there is no action until it is clear that there has been an offence which warrants it.

The key areas of responsibility for line managers are:

- ensuring that acceptable standards of conduct and performance are established
- being consistent about the application of these standards (unless there is some very good reason for variation)
- dealing with unacceptable performance or behaviour without delay and without over-reaction
- investigating more serious problems and handling them in

accordance with the established procedures of the organisation.

The identification of problems should, in the first instance, be handled through discussion and counselling with a view to an improvement in the individual's performance. It is not a question of initiating the disciplinary procedure at this stage – rather it is a matter of ensuring that the employee understands that there is a problem and that improvement is required.

Should this approach not resolve the difficulty, the matter should proceed to more formal disciplinary arrangements. At each stage there is a responsibility to investigate and to confirm the failure in performance or misdemeanour before any action is taken. The system of warnings which is a feature of formal disciplinary procedures must be clearly understood and carefully recorded, because it is one aspect of the arrangements expected of an employer as a part of the requirements of unfair dismissal legislation. Organisations have their own procedures, but the collective agreements for operatives mentioned in Chapter 8 below also include disciplinary procedures which apply to operatives.

In order for an employer to demonstrate fairness of treatment, there must be distinct stages in the procedure – for example:

❑ oral warning
❑ written warning (detailing the nature of the offence and the likely outcome if it is repeated)
❑ final written warning with an indication that suspension or dismissal may follow if there is any repetition of the offence.

In some cases there may be fewer stages – for example, the civil engineering working rule agreement provides only for an oral warning and then for a final written warning. Written warnings must be dated, signed, and kept on record for the period specified in the procedure.

The procedures must be clear about who does and who does not have the right to take disciplinary action and to dismiss an employee. Managers do not usually have the right to dismiss those working for them without reference to a more senior level of management. At each stage of procedure the employee has the right to present his or her case within a disciplinary interview, and the outcome of the interview should not be assumed in advance. The employee has the right to representation, and there should be provision for an appeal. Personnel departments within the larger organisations, including the public sector, normally take an advisory role, to support line managers through the procedure. ACAS conciliation officers may also be able to assist with advice.

Summary dismissal is allowed only in the event of gross misconduct – which may be defined within the rules or the relevant collective agreement. This may include theft, assault or threatening behaviour, wilful or reckless damage to property, the introduction, possession or use of drugs or alcohol on site, non-compliance with safety regulations or legislation, and sexual or racial harassment.

Unfair dismissal

Employees who have been in continuous employment with an employer for a minimum two-year period have the right not to be unfairly dismissed. Careful thought must be given to the meaning of the term 'employee' in this situation, because there is a growing volume of case-law concerned with the position of self-employed workers which provides that many of them could be deemed to be employees for the purposes of entitlements under employment law. Many organisations which have been using the services of self-employed workers on a continuous basis over a period of years are vulnerable to claims of unfair dismissal or unfair selection for redundancy. As we have seen in Chapter 2, 'self-employed' status is not guaranteed by holding a 714 tax certificate or by paying tax on an SC60 basis; and this must be taken into account in dismissal and redundancy situations.

A former employee with the requisite service can pursue a case of unfair dismissal to an industrial tribunal within a three-month time limit from the date of dismissal, and the employer is bound to respond. Redress can be sought either through reinstatement, re-engagement or (most commonly) through compensation. Dismissal is fair if fair grounds can be shown for it. Fair grounds for dismissal include lack of capability or qualifications, misconduct, redundancy, or some other substantial reason – normally a substantial business reason.

Complaints alleging unfair dismissal are made to the Central Office of Industrial Tribunals on a form which is obtainable from offices of the Employment Service. This is then passed on to ACAS with a view to conciliation – so that there is an attempt to assist the parties in settling the complaint without the need for a tribunal hearing. Conciliation is a voluntary process – if either of the parties disagrees, it cannot proceed. The role of the conciliation officer is intended to be neutral and independent: the conciliation officer does not act as a representative for either side. When a case cannot be settled through conciliation and has not been withdrawn, it proceeds to an industrial tribunal.

Industrial tribunals are made up of three members – a representative from employers' organisations, a representative from employees' associations (most often trade unions) and a chairperson who is legally qualified. They together ensure that the law is upheld with regard to employment, and their concern is with fairness in employment as a whole – not with the specific concerns of an organisation (Torrington and Hall, 1995). Tribunal proceedings can be lengthy, and the consequences of a decision in favour of the employee can be damaging not only for the employer but also for the manager involved. In certain cases – for example, in discrimination – the limits to the level of compensation have been lifted and employers are finding that the consequences in these areas are far more costly than they have been in the past. In the case of unfair dismissal claims, the limits to compensation payments still apply – but this does not mean that the prospect of tribunal procedures should be treated lightly. They may involve considerable preparation and can absorb substantial amounts of management time. This may be the case even if a claim is settled without a tribunal hearing. Organisations risk damaging their reputation in the wider community if they emerge with the tag of 'poor employer' because of an unfair dismissal claim. Smaller organisations can be particularly affected by the time and energy which is taken up by a tribunal, for senior managers may well have to give up valuable time and lose business opportunities in order to attend. The best defence against this is to ensure that any action which is taken is fair and reasonable in the circumstances.

Torrington and Hall (1995) point out that *the following dismissals are automatically unfair*:

❏ on the grounds of pregnancy

❏ because of trade union membership or trade union activity

❏ because an individual refuses to join a trade union

❏ as a direct result of a transfer in ownership of the organisation

- without a reason being given
- apparently inequitable selection for redundancy
- because of a criminal conviction which is spent under the terms of the Rehabilitation of Offenders Act.

The Electrical Contracting Joint Industry Board (JIB) received an exemption order from the Secretary of State, Department of Employment, in 1979, providing that the industry's Disputes Committee can hear complaints of unfair dismissal instead of such complaints being dealt with by industrial tribunals. There is provision for reference from the Disputes Committee to the National Appeals Committee. In this respect the Electrical Contracting JIB is unique, although the machinery is used only very rarely. No other industry has such an exemption. In unfair dismissal cases, appeals against decisions of the National Appeals Committee are referred to a legally qualified arbitrator.

Redundancy

The most common cause of dismissal in the construction industry in the 1990s has been because of redundancy. Employees with more than two years' service with their employer are entitled to compensation in the event of redundancy, based on their age, the length of their service and the level of their pay. Employees are also protected against unfair selection for redundancy, and have an entitlement to compensation in this event. The 1996 Employment Rights Act says that

> An employee who is dismissed shall be taken to be dismissed by reason of redundancy if the dismissal is wholly or mainly attributable to:
>
> a) the fact that the employer has ceased, or intends to cease, (i) to carry on the business for the purposes of which the employee was employed by him, or (ii) to carry on that business in the place where the employee was so employed; or
>
> b) the fact that the requirements of that business (i) for employees to carry out work of a particular kind, or (ii) for employees to carry out work of a particular kind in the place where the employee was so employed, have ceased or diminished or are expected to cease or diminish.

Employers must be able to demonstrate that there was a redundancy situation as defined above, that the criteria for selecting employees for redundancy were fair, and that they were fairly applied.

The process of selecting individuals for redundancy is not an easy one. Each organisation has its own standards and criteria, and individual managers involved in this process need to be clear about the criteria which exist within the organisation and which are to be applied. Voluntary severance is almost always preferable to enforced redundancies, but in many organisations the capacity for voluntary severance has been exhausted. It used to be the case that, when faced with the inevitability of cut-backs, employers operated what was known as the LIFO rule – that is, 'Last In, First Out' – but after the stringent reductions in staffing of recent years, this standard has ceased to be very useful and employers increasingly look at other factors such as attendance, skill, and competence.

Employers have an obligation to consult individual employees about redundancy or transfer of undertakings, and where more than 20 redundancies are proposed at one establishment within a 90-day period, to consult 'all appropriate representatives' of employees. The Collective Redundancies and Transfer of Undertakings (Protection of Employment) (Amendment) Regulations 1995, which came into force from 1 March 1996, gave new rights to employee representatives which formerly had been confined to representatives of a workforce which was represented by a trade union. This is a significant change in the construction industry because it necessitates consultation with representatives of administrative, professional, technical and clerical staffs who may be affected by redundancy as well as with representatives of the operative workforce, who formerly may have been covered by trade union representation. The professional and administrative grades were excluded from previous consultation rights because, for the most part, they were not members of a recognised trade union.

The appropriate representatives of employees are identified as employee representatives elected by the workforce for that purpose. They may be elected as and when the need arises (ie when redundancies are pending) or on a standing basis. If the employees are represented by an independent trade union, the 'appropriate representative' may be a trade union representative. Where employees both elect employee representatives and are in a group for which a trade union is recognised, the employer may choose whether to consult the elected employee representative or the trade union representative. The employee representatives must be employed by the employer at the time of their election. The 'appropriate representatives' must have access to employees who may be dismissed, and must have facilities to fulfil their representative function. Employee representatives have the right not to be subject to any penalty by the employer because of their role; they have the right to complain of unfair dismissal; and they have an entitlement to paid time off during working hours in order to perform their functions.

Employers must disclose information in writing to the appropriate representatives on the reasons for the redundancy proposal; the numbers and descriptions of those who it is proposed will be made redundant, and the total numbers of employees in that category; the proposed method of selection; the method of carrying out the redundancies; and the proposed method of calculating redundancy payments for individuals (Industrial Relations Services: *Industrial Relations Law Bulletin*, 1996: 7).

The following checklist sets out the issues for consideration in the event of redundancies:

❑ Can redundancies be avoided? Is there a more acceptable method of reducing workforce size (eg natural wastage, voluntary severance, retraining and redeployment, reduction or elimination of overtime, short-time working or temporary lay-off, early retirement, termination of short-term contracts)?

❑ Establish fair procedures for selection for redundancy (eg based on length of service, skills and experience, ability and performance. It is important that selection is not made on grounds which could constitute direct or indirect discrimination – eg a female employee on maternity leave selected for this reason).

❑ Check arrangements to ensure that they will be fairly applied (eg check if some sections of the workforce are more affected).

❑ All redundancies must be the subject of consultation with individuals affected.

❑ More than 20 redundancies in a 90-day period require consultation with 'appropriate representatives'. They will include representatives of the professional and administrative workforce. They will also include representatives of the operative workforce, who may be trade union representatives where a union is recognised.

❑ Where more than 100 dismissals are proposed within 90 days, consultation must begin at least 90 days before the first dismissals.

❑ Otherwise consultation must begin at least 30 days before the first of the dismissals.

❑ The employer must consult with 'a view to reaching agreement' with the appropriate representatives.

❑ Provide time-off with pay for redundant employees for the purposes of job-seeking or making training arrangements.

Employers also have a statutory duty to notify the local Department of Trade and Industry office in the event of redundancies.

Employees have an entitlement to statutory redundancy pay once they are over the age of 18 and have more than two years' service. The term 'employee' here can be construed to include some self-employed workers where they fulfil the legal definition of the term 'employee'. There is a maximum of 20 years' entitlement to statutory redundancy pay, and the levels are set according to age, length of service and wage level, in accordance with upper limits on the rate of earnings.

Further details of employer responsibilities and employee entitlements on redundancy are available from the Department of Trade and Industry.

CASE STUDY – **Communicating for change: Tarmac's Target 2000**

Promote an open management style that encourages ideas and initiatives from every level of the organisation and commit ourselves to the best available training.

(Tarmac, 1996)

Tarmac Plc is a leading construction services and heavy building materials group in the UK. With a turnover of approximately £2.5 billion in 1995, it has, like other major contractors, experienced the pressures of recession. Strategy has been concerned with ways of finding some stability and predictability in volatile markets. As a consequence, Tarmac began a radical restructuring programme in 1992, culminating in 1995 with a more focused group incorporating two business streams.

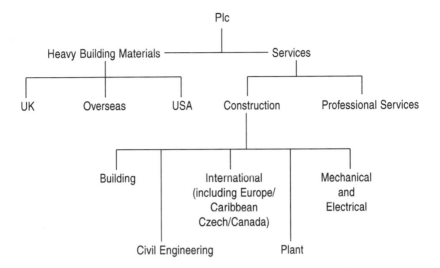

The group has shed more than 10,000 employees over the period 1990–95, and in looking to the future the company identified customer partnerships, innovative solutions and employee development as keys to success. A continuous performance improvement programme was initiated – and to give a more tangible base the programme was christened 'Target 2000'.

Target 2000
Target 2000 was created as a group programme to communicate the strategy and the vision for the future. Given the size, the complexity and the diversity of the company, communication was never going to be easy. Launched in 1994, Target 2000 focused on the new direction the company was to take, particularly on the concept of partnership with the client. As an internal communications process it cascaded information down from the chief executive to senior managers, and from this level through to sites and to depots in all of the various divisions within the company.

Tarmac focus for Target 2000	
Past	*Future*
British	World class
Company focus	Customer focus
Image linked to construction	Two streams of business
Inward-looking	Outward-looking
Profit-driven	Profitable
Quantity (process)	Quality (service)
Traditional	Innovation
Divisions	Companies
Fragmentation	Single group

The refocusing of the Tarmac portfolio in 1996 involved an exchange of businesses with George Wimpey plc. Tarmac 'sold' its housing division and took in Wimpey construction and minerals activities.

The company had a well established newspaper, distributed at depots and sites. This could not in itself resolve the problems of communicating the complex changes which were under way. The new campaign offered an opportunity to improve direct communications and to develop understanding of the problems faced by the Group.

The integration of new employees brought into the company from Wimpey in 1996 was coincidental with a renewal of the Target 2000 initiative. In itself the integration process was a major task. This was not simply because of the differences in terms and conditions of employment. It was also a question of ensuring the understanding and winning the allegiance of line managers in the various divisions, as well as ensuring that all employees down to site level were informed about all of the changes which were taking place.

Employee communication programmes are not commonplace in the construction industry. It is fairly unusual for a chief executive in this sector to sit down and talk to senior managers about cultural issues, including the process of change and management style. The Tarmac chief executive, Neville Simms, initiated this process by meeting 250 of the company's top managers, reaffirming corporate commitment to Target 2000, with a focus on customer partnership, quality, innovation and continuous performance improvement. The meeting provided the opportunity to discuss the change in the company's image and to outline information which should be cascaded throughout the organisation. It also offered the opportunity for cross-fertilisation of discussion and ideas between the different parts of the company – something which would not normally take place.

The client focus reflected the changing nature of the group's business, the customer needs and the improvement of products and services featuring high on the agenda. However, Target 2000 went further in reaffirming the commitment to health and safety and to improving the environmental impact of the company's activities. Better training and personal development opportunities, working to full potential and effective teamworking, recognition of achievements, and learning from mistakes, were all identified as part of the process, and awards were proposed to recognise particular contributions at divisional level.

Team 2000

Each Tarmac business has a degree of autonomy in developing aims and in deciding on the ways in which the process of change could best be implemented, recognition coming through a group-wide competitive award process. Within Tarmac Construction the process of continuous performance improvement was encouraged through the creation of Team 2000.

Interestingly, there was a move to look outside the construction industry for benchmark companies who had worked through similar changes. The initiative was followed through by 'change agents' – individuals who were appointed to instigate new ways of doing things at local level.

Tarmac Construction appointed 12 people, drawn from different areas of the company, whose sole task for a period of 12 months, was to act as facilitators for change. Responsible to a director, the team's activities exemplified the new Tarmac Group approach. Over the first 12 months they were to support best practice and facilitate problem-solving in over 100 projects – some of them small-scale and specific, others more openended. At the end of the 12 months, the team were returned to other responsibilities and were replaced with newcomers from other parts of the company.

The focus, perhaps inevitably, has been on 'people issues'. There has been an interest in the creation of effective work teams and teambuilding, with a growing emphasis not simply on who is put into a team but on how people can be brought together effectively – how people find out about one another and develop more effective working relationships. Sub-contractors are brought into the process, with a view to reducing the adversarial nature of relationships and to building trust.

On one successful project, Team 2000 were involved in facilitating risk analysis by seeking to identify the top ten potential construction problems involved in a particular project. The initiative involved work with the senior site group and client representatives, and (separately) with a more junior site group and planning team. The outcomes related not simply to resolution of technical problems, or actions to be taken in the event of systems failure, but to the importance of the interplay between the human actors as a means for effective anticipation of technical problems. The recruitment and continuity of skilled labour, for example, was one of the key issues identified with the client as being important to project success.

The Tarmac/Wimpey asset exchange is, perhaps inevitably, a focus for Team 2000 initiatives. Team members have been working with the Midlands building operations to identify key issues involved in the integration of the two businesses and to manage a successful initial transition in ownership into the company. In facilitating contacts between the two groups, Team 2000 set an agenda for change which focused on individual perceptions and concerns, and allowed brainstorming and discussion about the implications of change in terms of longer-term implications – for strategy and image, for customer focus and office systems, as well as for managers and for employees. The process involved pairing individuals from the different organisations, exchanging information on appraisal and particularly the move to competence-based appraisal – as well as discussion about information requirements on terms and conditions of employment.

Team 2000 have an on-going role in facilitating communications at a fundamental level. The uneven development of information systems inhibited communication between divisions and with sites. Early initiatives were concerned with cost controls, but the advent of e-mail promises a wider and more open pattern of communication within the organisation.

Effective communications and the use of employee commitment campaigns obviously cannot resolve all of the problems which derive from operating in uncertain markets – either for senior managers or for individual employees. The emphasis is on incremental and, where appropriate, radical improvement. A strong communication programme is seen as a way of preparing people for the changes taking place and enabling individuals to understand and contribute to the processes under way. There is an organisational concern to avoid 'initiative overload', but a realisation that by the end of the 1990s the shape, structure and method of operation of the company will be very different from the pattern evident only ten years previously.

With thanks to Jane Lord of Tarmac Plc, Frank Duggan of Tarmac Construction Personnel, and employees of Team 2000 for their assistance.

CHAPTER 8

EMPLOYEE RELATIONS IN THE BRITISH CONSTRUCTION INDUSTRY

This chapter is concerned with collective bargaining and with the ways in which it supports the management of the employment relationship. It looks at the collective bargaining structures and at the parties to collective bargaining in relation to a number of construction agreements. It considers the benefits of membership of employers' associations and of trade unions and assesses the impact of the various agreements, highlighting their implications at the level of the enterprise and on site. In doing this it contrasts the formal procedures for employee relations at national level with the less formalised arrangements which often exist at site level. Discussion within this chapter relates primarily to operatives because, with only a few notable exceptions, salaried staffs tend not to be covered by such agreements.

Collective agreements

Collective bargaining in the UK is a voluntary process in which employee representatives meet employers or their representatives with the aim of reaching agreements to regulate terms and conditions of employment within the various sectors of the industry. National collective agreements have a long history within construction: their origins lie in the 19th century. Despite the move away from national bargaining in some other sectors during the 1980s – most notably in the engineering industry – national bargaining still survives within the construction sector. However, some of these collective agreements have been significantly undermined because of the proliferation of labour-only sub-contracting and self-employment which has fragmented employment relationships and has undermined the voluntary framework of employment regulation.

It might seem that in any industry with so many small firms there is no real need for collective bargaining, since within a small firm everybody knows everyone else. The proprietor in the smaller firm knows how well people work and what they are worth, in terms of pay levels. To some extent this is what happens in practice, for labour markets and personal contact play an important part in determining actual rates of pay within a particular sector and a particular area. However, collective bargaining has contributed to the notion of a 'going rate' for particular trades or groups of operatives, and many employers in smaller firms find it useful to be able to refer to collectively agreed rates of pay and national standards for working conditions. This is important in an industry where labour is often required to be mobile – not just from job to job but from employer to employer. Industry-level agreements (in building sometimes referred to as 'the working rule agreement') provide for arrangements for holiday pay, sickness pay and pension arrangements – issues which require long-term commitment and co-ordination of practices between employers if employees are to derive any real benefit.

Collectively agreed rates are important too because they constitute a benchmark which is publicly recognisable. Given the many unpredictable features of the industry – the diversity of the product, the varying geographical location, the unpredictability of conditions – there are some advantages to rates of pay and working conditions which are nationally recognised.

Clients may expect contractors and their sub-contractors to seek out the lowest possible labour price, but employers usually recognise that this will not allow them to attract and to retain operatives with the appropriate skills or commitment to the work. In some areas employers feel that they need a benchmark figure below which pay is not allowed to fall. In other cases the agreement may come closer to setting actual pay rates rather than setting minimum standards (under the engineering construction industry agreement, for example). In either case there is a need to ensure that, in the words of one construction manager, 'Everyone's tendering against the same set of rules.'

Collective bargaining can enhance industry's performance by providing a national forum for the consideration of major issues which are of shared concern. This can be particularly important on a longer-term project, ensuring that costs – and particularly variations to labour costs – can be planned, and that performance is assured. Variations to pay – for example, through an annual pay increase – can be anticipated through a commitment in the client contract to making adjustments in line with amendments to the appropriate collective agreement.

Table 5   National collective agreements in the construction industry

Agreement	Signatory employers	Signatory trade unions	Employees in scope (approx.)
Building	Building Employers Confederation	UCATT; T&GWU; GMB	250,000
Civil Engineering	Fed. of Civil Engineering Contractors	T&GWU; GMB; UCATT	90,000
Engineering Construction	Engineering Construction Industry Association; Thermal Insulation Contractors' Association; Electrical Contractors' Association of Scotland	AEEU; GMB; MSF & T&GWU	18,000
Electrical Contracting Joint Industry Board (England, Wales and Northern Ireland)	Electrical Contractors' Association (ECA)	AEEU	43,000
Heating, Ventilating, Air Conditioning, Piping and Domestic Engineering	Heating and Ventilating Contractors' Association (HVCA)	MSF	20,000
Environmental Engineering	ECA; ECA (Scotland); HVCA, Plumbing, Heating and Mechanical Services; Scottish Plumbing and Mechanical Service Employers	AEEU (EESA)	12,000

Each of the agreements identified in Table 5 sets out the terms and conditions of employment, including such features as wages, shift and overtime pay, hours of work, holiday pay and all associated arrangements, including details of additional payments and special allowances. Such aspects of the agreement are normally subject to annual, or at the least to biennial, amendment.

In principle, national collective agreements allow employers and employees to avoid a free-for-all in terms of the price of labour. Each agreement provides a reward 'package' for the different grades recognised under the agreement, allowing for the many variations in circumstances and providing for the particular features of each sub-sector of the industry. In essence, the arrangements support the notion of fair and consistent application of human resource policies, involving the principle of equality of treatment of the different work groups – principles which could easily be forgotten if they were not formalised. Because labour is relatively mobile, the establishment of a collectively agreed rate would seem to avoid the problems of leapfrogging in the rate of pay. However, there is a significant difference between the formal system of collective bargaining and the arrangements which actually apply at site level under some of the agreements – most notably for building. We will consider in turn the significance of national arrangements, of arrangements at enterprise level, and of arrangements at site level.

National bargaining: the formal structures

Collective agreements in the UK are not, in themselves, legally binding. They have legal significance only where the terms and conditions established by a collective agreement are incorporated into the individual's contract of employment. Employers have no obligation to recognise trade unions, and participation in the collective bargaining process has to be understood as a voluntary activity which results from management decision-taking – an outcome of management choice on the way in which employment relationships should be managed. Such decisions reflect the material interests and the environmental pressures in operation, but they also reflect historical tradition or custom – and formal structures may evolve more slowly than changing attitudes and values.

As we noted above, the construction industry is unusual in

the retention of a formal commitment to national collective bargaining and the continued operation of employers' associations which continue to carry significant responsibilities for multi-employer arrangements.

Employers' associations

Employers' associations exist to represent the interests of employers within their sector. They can often claim a history which is as long as that of the trade unions – and, like the trade unions, they have been under some pressure in recent years, with a tendency for membership to decline. Nonetheless they play an important part in setting standards within the industry because they regulate the relations between employers and their employees or employee representatives.

Bargaining within a multi-employer framework, through employers' associations, may minimise the role of trade unions and shop stewards at the organisational level. This may explain the importance of such arrangements in the construction industry, where some employers prefer to deal with trade unions at arms' length – or not at all.

Employers' associations provide members with:

❏ standards on employment which are industry-wide

❏ advice on problem areas relating to employment, health and safety at work

❏ support in handling problems – for example, dismissals or strikes

❏ trade representation

❏ support in public affairs – for example, on economic or taxation issues.

Most employers' associations in construction comprise a mix of large and small firms, and there is a sensitive political balance between the distinctive interests of the different types of member. In general it is the larger firms which have a stronger controlling influence on policy and on the negotiation process because the larger groups are better able to afford the luxury of time for an individual from their company to represent them on a regular basis. Smaller firms sometimes encounter difficulties in playing an active role because there is always a risk that the business will suffer if key personnel are withdrawn even for a short period. Despite this there are many small companies which make a strong contribution to their employers' association, especially at regional level, and employers' organisations can survive only to the extent that their members continue to believe that they are receiving value for money in terms of the financial cost of membership. They try to ensure the visible representation of their smaller members and their interests.

Membership of the largest employers' associations in construction has declined in recent years, as some former members have gone out of business while others have reconsidered membership for other reasons. We highlight the position of four of the most prominent organisations.

The Building Employers' Confederation (BEC), which is over 100 years old, is one of the largest of the employers' associations, registering 5,000 members in the mid-1990s – down from a figure of 10,000 ten years previously. The BEC is made up of five semi-autonomous sections. The smallest, but by no means the least significant, is the National Contractors' Group, which has only 40 member firms, who are among the largest players in the industry. The bulk of the BEC's membership is made up of the National Federation of Builders, which includes 4,000 members, many of which are quite small companies. The Housebuilders' Federation has 800 member firms. Next in line is the Federation of Building Specialist Contractors, an umbrella group which brings together the scaffolders, painters and the traditional building trades. The British Woodworking Federation, which also operates within the BEC, has some 300 member companies, ranging from national contractors through to small joinery shops. The BEC had a significant political voice in the 1980s, individual construction companies having links, through financial donations, to the Conservative Party. Membership activities focus particularly on the Regions, which provide a contact point for member activities.

The Federation of Civil Engineering Contractors (FCEC) is much smaller than the BEC in terms of the number of member companies – it has something approaching 300 member firms. Its members are larger construction companies which undertake civil engineering works, all of the big firms within the sector retaining membership.

The Electrical Contractors' Association (ECA) is the employers' side of the Electrical Contracting Joint Industry Board in

England, Wales, Northern Ireland and the Republic of Ireland. It has about 1,900 member firms, ranging in size from small firms to multi-nationals. There is a separate Electrical Contractors' Association of Scotland.

The newest employers' association in the industry was established in 1994, when the Oil and Chemical Plant Constructors' Association reached agreement with the National Engineering Construction Employers' Association to form the Engineering Construction Industry Association. This body has 350 member firms, ranging in size from those with fewer than five employees to those with more than 1,000. Its member firms are engaged on engineering construction projects, including power generation, steelwork erection and steel bridge construction. It is a specialist employers' body dealing specifically with these areas of construction activity. The National Agreement for the Engineering Construction Industry is unusual in the extent of its influence. Membership of the employers' association means that engineering construction companies can access its support in avoiding industrial disputes.

Other employers' groups operate along similar lines to those described above. The Heating and Ventilating Contractors' Association (HVCA) provide broadly the same range of services to their members, with advice and support on good employment practice. It underpins the employers' side of the Heating and Ventilating Contracting Agreement and also the Environmental Engineering Agreement. The Federation of Master Builders (FMB), which has 17,000 member firms, recruits only among the smaller companies and has no large firms in membership. It is party to a small firms' agreement with the Transport & General Workers Union which is known as the Building and Allied Trades Joint Industrial Council.

In practice there were specific issues which drew the members of these employers' associations together. Initially, they were motivated by the desire to control the price of labour and to withstand the influence of organised labour within their particular sector. In recent years they have set standards on employment practice, advising member firms and offering support to those who are in dispute or who are facing claims at industrial tribunals.

None of the organisations concerned would be opposed to self-employment in itself, but representatives say that self-employment has gone 'too far', and particularly that damage is being done to the institutions which regulate the industry because of the fragmentary effects of self-employment. There is anxiety at the prospect of Inland Revenue's intervention within this situation, and a growing awareness that the discrepancies in the position of the self-employed may give rise to a legal challenge. The Construction Industry Employers' Council draws together the different groups to enable them to make joint representation to the Inland Revenue and to the government about the nature and the process of change.

Membership of an employers' association thus gives employers a voice on developments within their industry. It allows for ready access to information and advice on management of the employment relationship, and provides support in the event of difficulties.

Trade unions

People join trade unions because they feel the need for protection at work, in terms of their job security, their rates of pay and their working conditions. This may not always be welcome to managers, who might argue that trade union members are misguided, or that the long term interest of employees are served only if managers are allowed the freedom to do what they think necessary to make a profit. However, within the prevailing insecure climate in the construction industry, it is unrealistic to expect workers at any level to place their trust unequivocally in management. Differences in view are inevitable. The benefits which can accrue for managers through the recognition of trade unions derive from the advantages of improved communications and better understanding of different points of view. It is possible then to take account of such differences and to discuss issues with site or job representatives with the objective of reaching a negotiated solution. Trade union recognition means managers can sustain longer-term relationships with trade union officers, which can be useful where there are problems that could be jointly resolved.

Trade unions represent their members over a range of issues, but the most important issues in which they are involved in the construction industry are:

❏ negotiating on wages and conditions
❏ involvement and consultation in health and safety procedures and systems

❑ pursuing legal claims on behalf of members
❑ handling grievances, disputes and disciplinary cases.

Given the range of their activities, it is useful to know something about the different trade unions which operate within the construction industry.

The logic of trade union membership in the UK can be explained only through their historical development. It was the craft trade unions which were the first to organise. The unions with a craft tradition – notably the forerunners of the Union of Construction Allied Trades & Technicians (UCATT) and the Amalgamated Engineering and Electrical Union (AEEU) were formed in the mid-nineteenth century. The 'general' unions were created a quarter of a century later, and consolidated their position only after 1919, but changes in industrial structure and in the labour process have adjusted the boundaries of each of these organisations, and nowadays recruitment is more open and often competitive between the different unions.

Trade union membership is difficult to sustain in the private sector of the industry, where the absence of job security leads individuals to drop out of membership when they cease to be employed in a unionised workplace. This means that unions recruit members over and over again – indeed, the major preoccupation of construction trade unionism is simply to sustain some real semblance of organisation – and in this they are not helped by employers who are rather less enthusiastic about trade union involvement within the enterprise or on site than they are at national level. Trade unions tend to recruit along general lines, including all categories of employees, and there is fierce competition for members. Trade union membership in the construction industry is scattered through a number of trade unions, all of whom have seen severe membership loss over the last decade. There is very little membership among professional, administrative, technical or clerical occupations within the private sector (Druker and White, 1995).

The density of union organisation in the private-sector construction industry is lower than in other parts of private-sector industry. There is a more significant trade union presence in some parts of the industry – notably in engineering construction, in electrical contracting, and in local authorities. Trade union organisation within all parts of construction has suffered immeasurably since the rise in self-employment from the beginning of the 1980s.

The major trade unions recruiting in the construction industry are:

- Union of Construction Allied Trades and Technicians (UCATT)
- Transport and General Workers Union (T&GWU)
- General Municipal Boilermakers and Allied Trades Union (GMB)
- Amalgamated Engineering and Electrical Union (AEEU)
- Manufacturing Science and Finance (MSF)

UCATT

UCATT was formed from an amalgamation of the craft trade unions in the building industry in 1972 and has been, traditionally, the major trade union recruiting within the private sector of the building industry and among local authority building workers. It has just over 100,000 members (at end 1995), of whom around 50,000 are employed in the private sector. The remainder are employed in the public sector – in local authorities, in the health service, or in parts of manufacturing industry.

UCATT has suffered substantial membership loss but there has been resistance to the notion of merger with any other trade union. By the end of 1995, the union's General Secretary, George Brumwell, claimed that UCATT was in financial surplus and had the capacity to survive.

Transport and General Workers Union (T&GWU)

The T&GWU is, as its name suggests, a general union, which, historically, attracted lesser-skilled workers, although it has had a skilled membership base in the construction industry since the absorption of the National Association of Operative Plasterers some 30 years ago. Its full membership in 1996 was 857,000, and it is one of the largest trade unions in the UK. The T&GWU is divided into trade groups including a trade group for the construction industry which claims 23,000 members (Summer 1996).

The T&GWU is represented in most of the major agreements for the industry.

The GMB

The GMB is another of the general trade unions derived historically from the recruitment of lesser-skilled and women workers. It has only a small membership within the private sector of construction, but a rather larger claim to representation in building materials and in the furniture sector since it took over the Furniture, Timber and Allied Trades Union. In 1996 it had 740,349 members, the Construction, Furniture, Timber and Allied section encompassing about 10 per cent of this figure.

The GMB is signatory to the Building and Civil Engineering Industry Agreements and to the Engineering Construction Agreement. It also has membership under a number of company level agreements and in furniture and woodworking machine shops.

The Amalgamated Engineering and Electrical Union (AEEU)

The AEEU was traditionally the union for skilled workers in the engineering industry, but took in engineering construction workers from the 1960s. It has expanded its activities in the field of construction having absorbed the controversial Electrical, Electronic Telecommunications and Plumbing Trades Union (EETPU) in 1992, and is the key negotiator on behalf of employees in electrical contracting and plumbing. It had 725,000 members in December 1995, including membership in engineering, in electrical contracting and plumbing, in manufacturing, and a small minority of members in construction. It was a signatory to the Engineering Construction Industry Agreement from its inception in the early 1980s. The tiny Construction Building Group does not have recognition under the Building and Civil Engineering Industry national agreements, although some individual firms have conceded recognition for AEEU members.

Manufacturing Science and Finance (MSF)

MSF is a large general union which, historically, had its membership base among supervisory and white-collar staffs. It has 415,000 members (1996), but only a small minority are in the construction industry. Within this sector MSF is signatory only to the Engineering Construction Agreement and the Heating and Ventilating Agreement.

Trade Union activities

Effective organisation and communication at site level can avoid or regulate some of the traditional conflicts at site level, and trade unions can play a positive part in this process. Although there are no legal rights to trade union representation in the UK, a decision to work with trade unions can contribute to more positive interaction between the different groups of people on site, and provides recourse to a balancing external influence in the event of site problems. The evidence rests in the approach taken in engineering construction, which was particularly strike-prone in the 1960s and 1970s. The creation of a new agreement for engineering construction, supported both by employers and by trade unions, has contributed to more peaceful industrial relations since 1981.

Support for collective bargaining is a matter of corporate policy: individual managers need to be clear about the position of their own company. Employers' associations normally expect their member firms to uphold agreements to which the association is a signatory. Where the company is a member of an employers' association, full-time trade union officials from the trade union (or unions) party to that agreement will expect, after advance arrangement with the employer's senior representative, to have access to a site, in order to see that the agreement is being adhered to. They will want to ensure that the people on site are trade union members – whoever they are working for. They will also want to establish relations with site management and to be sure that agreements are being upheld. They are likely to seek an agreement to ensure that members' trade union subscriptions are deducted from pay and passed directly to the union – a system known as 'check-off'. They will want to see that conditions of work are at least at the standard specified by the agreement and by the body of legislation which is concerned with site conditions. This is especially important in the area of health and safety and, given the risks within the industry, it is to the employer's advantage that accredited safety representatives are involved in such discussions.

Trade unions are organised according to rules which must conform to certain legal requirements and to the democratic principles of their own organisation. Most expect trade union members to belong to a branch that has the right to nominate representatives to national conference or similar events. Trade union officials are likely to operate with a regional or district focus – an arrangement which allows effective relations to be sustained at project and regional level. All of the trade unions involved in collective bargaining in the construction industry are affiliated to the Labour Party, but trade union influence in Labour activities has been reduced in recent years. The majority of union members are unlikely to be political activists.

The appointment of trade union representatives (shop stewards) is the responsibility of the individual trade unions. When an operative has been employed by the employer for a minimum period (eg four weeks for the building industry, three months for heating and ventilating), and where the operative has been properly appointed by his union as a steward, the union must notify the employer in writing for formal recognition, which may not be withheld unreasonably. The duties and functions of shop stewards are normally specified within trade union rules. In general terms they are expected to represent members of the union or trade employed on the site or job.

Where there is more than one steward, the site unions may appoint one of the stewards as a 'convenor steward' or 'senior steward'. The convenor steward may represent operatives on matters affecting more than one trade or union. Alternatively, a senior steward may represent the interests of operatives in the whole company or in a company region.

Where a trade union is recognised by the employer and a shop or convenor steward is appointed, that person has certain statutory rights to be given paid time off work for carrying out trade union duties and for training in respect of those duties. An employer is required to grant such time as is reasonable in the circumstances – leaving scope for negotiation over the industrial relations duties in question.

The ACAS code of practice on this issue says that account should be taken of operational requirements, production processes, and health and safety implications of time-off arrangements.

The advantages for the project or contracts manager in having a steward or convenor on site derive from the added benefits of direct communication with a workforce representative. An effective trade union representative is likely to know what is going on and where the potential problems or aggravation points may lie. On the basis that pre-empting problems may be more effective than resolving them, this is a valuable contribution to smoothing the progress of the project and avoiding unnecessary delays. There is always a danger that relationships at workforce level can become unnecessarily complex or difficult. Issues which require site-level consultation or negotiation can be discussed with the trade union representative, and even if solutions are not easy, there is, after agreement, a shared responsibility for communication and implementation.

Enterprise-level

Companies which are members of an employers' association are normally expected to apply the agreement to which that association is a signatory. National bargaining is sustained by the dual commitment of employers and trade unions, and this means that affiliated companies must implement agreements. Despite organisational problems particularly resulting from self-employment – and the Building Industry Agreement in particular is not always regularly applied – there has to date been no fundamental attempt to move away from prevailing national multi-employer arrangements. Employers' associations – for example in civil engineering – report a continued commitment from their members to the institutions of national bargaining for directly employed people, particularly in terms of the grading structures which are set by the agreements. Bonuses and take-home pay may be higher than the figures negotiated nationally, but the terms of the agreement provide a reference point for many employers.

Yet there is another side to the management of employee relations in construction. The survival of formal collective agreements suggests a 'proceduralism' which does not really exist in practice. Trade unions are not well organised at site or at enterprise level. Larger contractors have remained committed in principle to the notion of national collective agreements, but neither in the larger enterprise nor in the smaller firms is the day-to-day organisation of employee relations fully related to national bargaining.

In reality, the balance in employment in many larger firms has shifted fundamentally, so that professional, managerial and administrative staffs now form the greater number of employees within the organisation. These groups, for the most part, have no collective representation. Where manual employees are retained, they are fewer in number, so that national agreements may provide a useful benchmark for the company in setting pay rates and working conditions.

In most companies, however, there is some flexibility in inter-pretation: agreements may be only partly observed. The Building Industry Agreement sets wage rates which are far removed from actual payments made, and the diminishing attention to the agreement is reflected in the decreasing sale of holiday stamps from the Building and Civil Engineering Holidays with Pay Company. Employers sometimes choose to top up pay rates to local labour market levels, or to apply only specific aspects of the agreement (for example, working hours or travel arrangements). Although the Electrical Contracting Joint Industry Board agreement and the National Agreement for the Engineering Construction Industry are more regularly observed, the Building Agreement in particular has been seri-ously affected in the extent of its application by the effects of self-employment.

Handling industrial conflict

Despite these limitations, one of the key advantages for employ-ers in the support for national bargaining is that collective agreements provide conciliation procedures to resolve conflict and to prevent strikes or other forms of industrial action.

The risk of industrial action never disappears, even though it has been comparatively rare in the 1990s. Industrial action, as an overt expression of conflict between management and labour, may seem to be little more than a folk memory in an industry which saw its last national dispute a quarter of a century ago. Only three stoppages were recorded in the 12 months to March 1994, involving just 200 workers and fewer than 500 strike days (*Employment Gazette*, June 1994). This compares with 20 stoppages involving 4,900 workers with 22,000 strike days five years earlier (*Employment Gazette*, June 1989). Yet the temporary alliance of interests of the construc-tion project can be easily disrupted by industrial action, and there is no reason to assume that the current low level of strikes can be assured indefinitely. Higher levels of activity within the industry are often accompanied by more assertive behaviour from the workforce.

Although it is true that attitudes have changed with the growth in self-employment, construction managers at a senior level retain a cautious awareness that collective resistance from quite a small number of operatives can mean substantial delays and significant financial losses on projects which are working to very tight margins. Even groups of 'self-employed' workers have been known to take industrial action in the 1990s!

Conciliation or disputes procedures were set up to deal with the problems generated by disputes and to provide a mechanism whereby they can be resolved within a framework of rules. They normally serve to delay official industrial action, in that the parties to the collective agreement undertake to exhaust conciliation procedures before a withdrawal of labour. Typically, a procedure provides for full discussion and consideration of a problem at local level, with the scope for a reference to national level (via a regional panel in some cases). The sequence of the procedure is set out in Figure 9 below. One benefit of the formal bargaining structures is the availability of expert 'external' advice and representation which is tapped when disputes cannot be resolved internally. Of course the services of ACAS are open to employers and trade unions in the event of an industrial dispute, but the industry procedures are set within the context of established arrangements for the industry and supported by people who have a specialist understanding of the difficulties to be faced. Given the immediacy of some of the problems which can arise at site level, there is often provision for the local stages of the procedure to be bypassed, with provision for an early hearing at national level if the parties to the agreement find this acceptable.

In some companies a commitment is made to an industrial relations function outside the personnel department, who has a 'roving' brief and a responsibility to support site management in dealing with industrial conflict. The key skills of this old-style industrial relations officer in the construction industry lie in the capacity to avert or to resolve disputes or potential disputes with the manual workforce, within the framework of the conciliation procedures set out under the national agreement. Nowadays these skills are less likely to be provided by a specialist. Increasingly, it is the project or contracts manager who takes this responsibility and, at the minimum, this may involve personal contact with trade union officers, a knowledge of procedures, and an ability to find an informal way through the adversarial relationships at site level as an essential feature of the job.

To some extent employers may rely on the support of the law to inhibit the spread of problems since the 1982 Employment Act limited a 'lawful' dispute to action by employees against

Figure 9   Disputes procedures – the principles set by national collective agreements

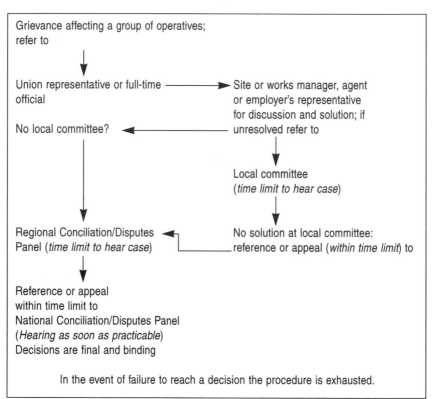

their employer. Trade unions are required by the 1992 Trade Union and Labour Relations (Consolidation) Act to ballot their members before industrial action. However, recourse to the law is very much a response after the event. It does nothing to develop more positive relations. A more pro-active and thoughtful approach to the management of relationships could provide for more positive outcomes.

Site agreements/large sites

Effective organisation of employee relations at site level involves planning and negotiation about the rules and the procedures which are to apply. This is particularly important on larger sites, which are likely to be longer-lasting and more complex. Site agreements (for example, on the new Severn crossing) provide the basis for developing a shared under-standing of the rules of conduct and a commitment to them. They can also ensure that problems are resolved quickly and effectively.

Client attitudes are important in setting the framework for discussion about site arrangements, and an experienced client who understands the potential contribution of human resource management to productivity and to quality may wish to ensure that standards are set in an appropriate way. From the client's perspective there will be advantages in ensuring the effective management of people on site – both those who are directly employed and those who are employed via sub-contractors. Clients who are regularly involved in contracting have more information against which they can develop relationships with contractors and improve practices at site level on the basis of partnership and good practice.

Large sites agreements remain important in the 1990s, despite the alleged diminution in the importance of employee relations, because of the need to provide stability within the temporary project arrangements and in order to minimise risk in the unpredictable arena of people management.

Arrangements vary to some extent, according to sector. The Building Industry Working Rule Agreement provides that such agreements may be made

> on jobs where by reason of the size of the project, its location or other special circumstances, it is jointly agreed between the company, the BEC and the operatives' side of the Council to be desirable.

The Engineering Construction Agreement provides for project 'nomination' to be agreed between the NJC and the client. This process requires the establishment of a Project Joint Council and in effect establishes a project agreement supplementary to the national agreement and organised in accordance with the specific needs of the client and the locality.

Sub-contracting and the management of the employment relationship

Although formal rules and procedures are long established, relations with the site workforce may sometimes lie beyond the scope of such rules. Thirty years ago the Royal Commission on Trade Unions and Employers Association (the Donovan

Commission) drew the distinction between formal structures of industrial relations and the informal arrangements (whereby formal arrangements would be varied for local circumstances). Within the construction industry arrangements may often in reality be unformalised – that is, they may be on the margins of the employment relationship, mediated through sub-contractors who take the day-to-day responsibility for resolving management problems and for dealing with workers who may claim for tax purposes that they are self-employed.

There are both advantages and disadvantages to these arrangements in a number of respects – and some of these are discussed in Chapter 2. The use of sub-contractors may relieve site management of some of the responsibilities associated with task allocation and work organisation at site level, as well as removing some of the immediate pressures which give rise to the employee relations procedures outlined above.

Where the management role is devolved to sub-contractors, many workers will come on site with a sub-contractor, either individually, or as part of a gang. This may remove the need for the construction manager or main contractor to sustain a direct involvement in the management of the employment relationship – for example, through the need to plan the way in which a directly employed workforce is deployed and redeployed between sites. However, the use of sub-contractors does not magically resolve all of the questions of employee resourcing, communications, or discipline on site. It merely means that some of these issues must be dealt with at arms' length rather than through direct involvement and planning. Instead of being directly responsible for the management of labour, the project manager finds that there is a responsibility instead to ensure that the commercial contract is established only with those sub-contractors who are reliable in terms of their performance and delivery.

The following is a quality checklist for sub-contract labour:

❑ Will the sub-contractors recruit, train and reward their workforce?

❑ Will the sub-contract workforce be employed or self-employed?

❑ Are the sub-contract workforce known and used regularly by the sub-contractor?

❑ Does the work involve vetting security for individual workers? Are you confident that you can comply if using sub-contract labour?

❑ Will the sub-contract workforce have the knowledge and skills required to do an effective job? (For example, is their position confirmed by inclusion on the skills register?)

Specialist sub-contractors may have a greater opportunity to develop the expertise of those who work with them by concentrating on particular skills or parcels of work. Some smaller firms may use only workers who are known to them personally, and who are acknowledged to be reliable. These are real advantages which need to be given greater recognition. Conversely, the emphasis on achieving the lowest tender price may mean that less attention is given to employment practices than should really be the case, because the arrangements for employment – or for self-employment – can impact on the overall contract performance. In some cases – for example, on major repair and maintenance contracts – the sub-contractor will be working on the client's premises, alongside the client's own workforce. This situation can pose security problems, and some attention should be given to ensuring that only bona fide operatives are brought onto the site. Some companies put pressure on their sub-contractors to ensure that if they are bringing people on site they are either direct employees or they are 'regular' self-employed people – ie part of the key or core staff regularly engaged with that contractor The use of operatives whose name is included on the skills register (see Chapter 5) provides some protection both for the contractor and for the client.

Although contractors will know which sub-contractors they have on site, there are occasions when work is sub-let informally. Situations of this type provide a range of problems alternative to those presented by direct employment, and they are by no means more easily resolved. Sub-contractors often suffer from cash-flow problems, and one recurrent 'employee relations' difficulty is the situation which arises when the sub-contractor defaults on payments to the workforce, leaving the main contractor or construction manager to deal with the resulting difficulties.

On a day-to-day basis there is a need for the contractor and the sub-contractor to ensure that the correct level of supervision is available. One of the advantages of sub-contract gangs is said to be the continuity in work relations and the benefits of familiarity and good communications within a small work group. If there is not sufficient support for the people who are actually doing the work, they may not be equipped to deal with problems – and work can slow down or actually stop as a consequence. The 'typical' problems which arise are where one trade contractor or sub-contractor interferes with, or causes a delay to, the work of another contractor or sub-contractor. In this sort of situation there are all sorts of claims and counter-claims which need to be resolved before the problem becomes more serious.

Sub-contracting does not, then, bring easy answers to the problems of managing the employment relationship on site, and the advantages must be balanced against the different types of disadvantage which can emerge. The adversarial nature of contracting relationships was a theme which ran through the Latham Report (Latham, 1994). Site managers are dependent on the relationship with sub-contractors to deliver high productivity and quality, but they are managing people at one remove. It is no solution to say that poor workmanship is spotted and that the sub-contractor can be dealt with through normal commercial processes. This only provides redress after problems have occurred – the aim is to avoid the problems in the first place. Sub-contractors face the same difficulties, in terms of the recruitment and retention of skilled workers, as those which have beset the larger contractors. Some project managers and sub-contractors find their own way through these problems by means of their informal networks of contacts within the industry. It can be difficult, within this framework, to ensure that the people who are brought on site by sub-contractors are given the support they need to do an effective job.

There is nothing easy about the question of employee relations in the construction industry. Formal rules and procedures are balanced by loose networks and personal contacts. Employment regulation is accompanied by the benefits of informality and an almost infinite flexibility in site practices. For anyone who is making their living in the construction industry it is worth reviewing the way in which things work. How far should formal voluntary regulation be encouraged? How can it be made to serve a useful purpose within the industry? How can contractors and sub-contractors work together to ensure the most effective and productive delivery for clients of the industry? There are no fixed or easy answers to these questions – but consideration at every stage needs to take account of the full implications of the arrangements which are selected, for the particular project, for the organisations involved, and for the people who make a living within the industry.

CHAPTER 9

MANAGING HEALTH AND SAFETY AT WORK

The effective management of health and safety at work is one of the most important issues which people in the construction industry have to contend with. It is a key responsibility for everyone who works within the industry – for contractors and their clients, for sub-contractors and site managers, for employees and their representatives, and for the self-employed. This chapter provides an update on recent legislation and looks briefly at the changes which are being initiated. It begins by outlining the scale of the problems facing the industry. It identifies legal responsibilities with particular attention to the Health and Safety at Work Act (HASAWA) 1974, the Construction (Design and Management) (CDM) Regulations 1994 and the Construction (Health, Safety and Welfare) Regulations (CHSW) 1996. Health and safety is an issue which everyone agrees is important in principle – but in practice the implementation of improved safety standards costs money and requires planning. Health and safety planning must be an integral part of the responsibilities involved in the management of people. This means that health and safety issues should be incorporated into management system procedures, thereby supporting a consistent approach throughout every organisation.

The construction industry has an unenviable safety record. The high number of fatalities and the significant scale of serious accidents or near misses has been the subject of concern for many years. The industry has the highest fatal injury rate by industrial sector over the period 1986–94. Although the death toll has diminished in the 1990s, there is no room for complacency. The fatal accident incident rate (that is, the number of fatalities in relation to the numbers working in the industry) actually increased in 1993–94, as did the incidence of non-fatal major injuries to the self-employed in the same period (HSC, 1995: 8, 27). Accident levels are unacceptably high.

Figure 10   Fatal accidents in construction

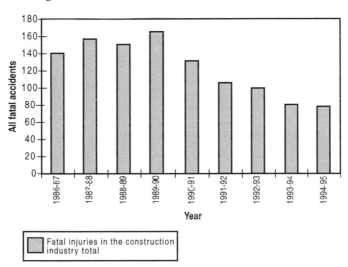

The three most common causes of accidental death and injury (according to the Health and Safety Executive, 1995a) are:

❑ falls – because of problems of access and failure to ensure that the working place is safe when people are working at heights

❑ falling materials – when people are hit by objects or loads which fall while being lifted or which drop from working platforms

❑ mobile plant and site vehicles.

As the web of contracting and sub-contracting activity in the industry becomes more intricate, as the pace of activity speeds up, and as technology becomes more sophisticated, so the task of safety management becomes more complex and requires greater attention. The fragmented nature of the industry and the high number of sub-contractors magnify the problems generated by a mobile, often self-employed workforce, many of whom lack

LEEDS COLLEGE OF BUILDING

training. The traditional culture of the industry, with its predominantly male workforce on site, does not encourage safe working practices. Apparently small improvements – for example, ensuring that hard hats are actually worn – have required extensive commitment from different sections of the industry.

There are continuing problems in terms of occupational health. The construction workforce experiences a high incidence of respiratory problems deriving from exposure to dusts and chemicals – for example, the incidence of mesothelioma and lung cancer. Chemicals can be inhaled. Small particles of dust or fibres can be breathed in, doing long-term damage in some cases. Aerosols, fumes, vapours and gases can all cause problems too and may also be absorbed into the bloodstream. Exposure to asbestos should now be controlled, but the incidence of asbestos-related problems continues to be high, partly because of the time-lag in manifestation (HSC, 1995). Manual handling is one of the major causes of strain and injury, and back problems resulting from manual handling are a high risk.

More common occupational health problems can be irritating rather than life-threatening. Dermatitis, a skin inflammation caused by 'irritants' or 'sensitisors', often affects the hands or arms of people who work with woods, plastics, dyes, adhesives or insecticides.

Other hazards can lead to long-term physical damage which, although it may not threaten life, may undermine its quality. Hearing loss resulting from exposure to prolonged and excessive noise at work is just one example.

Accidents and ill-health have a high cost for the victims and their families. Individual workers who suffer work accidents and work-related ill-health have been estimated to lose around £1 billion a year in reduced incomes (at 1990 prices: HSE, undated). There is a high cost for industry too, with a cost to employers of personal injury work accidents and work-related ill-health estimated at £1.5 billion each year (HSE, undated).

Health and safety law

Legislation represents a minimum standard in health and safety management. The aim should not merely be concerned with compliance. Rather it should be to improve on safety practice and to integrate an awareness of safety into all aspects of construction management.

There is a history of legislation which relates specifically to the construction industry – for example, construction regulations which were introduced in the 1960s set legal standards on a number of specific issues. Some regulations such as the Construction (Lifting operations) Regulations, 1961, are still in force, but other regulations have been incorporated into the Construction (Health, Safety and Welfare) Regulations, 1996, which came into force in September 1996, and are discussed below.

Some of the most important legislation is general in its scope. The Health and Safety at Work Act, 1974, provides a framework for the consideration of health and safety issues by all employers, by suppliers, by employees, and by the self-employed.

The Health and Safety at Work etc. Act (HASAWA), 1974

The Health and Safety at Work etc. Act, 1974, together with the Management of Health and Safety at Work Regulations, 1992, and other health and safety legislation applies to all employers, to employees and to the self-employed, regardless of the industry or whether a project falls within the scope of the CDM regulations.

Under HASAWA 1974, employers have a responsibility to ensure the health, safety and welfare of employees. They must

❑ provide and maintain safe plant and systems of work

❑ make arrangements for safe use, handling, storage, and transport of articles and substances

❑ provide health and safety information, instruction, training and supervision

❑ maintain the place of work, including the entrance and exit, so that it is safe and without risks to health

❑ provide and maintain a safe working environment and adequate welfare facilities

❑ prepare a written safety policy (for employers with more than five employees)

❑ consult safety representatives and, where requested by two or more safety representatives, set up a safety committee

❑ make no charge for safety equipment where the employer has a legal responsibility for providing such equipment

❑ not expose people who are not their employees to any risk to health and safety

❑ maintain premises, plant and machinery without risk to health and safety.

Designers, manufacturers, importers and suppliers must ensure that the design and construction of articles and substances is safe and without risk (Section 6). Employees must take reasonable care for themselves and for other people at work, and not interfere with anything provided in the interests of health and safety (Sections 7–8).

Health and Safety Executive (HSE)

The 1974 Act established the Health and Safety Executive, whose inspectors (HSE Inspectors) have the job of policing industry, to provide advice on health and safety standards and to ensure that laws are upheld. There are different types of inspectors to deal with factories, agriculture, mines, quarries, nuclear installations and explosives. Part of the inspectorate is devoted specifically to the construction industry, and there are currently around 130 inspectors with specialist knowledge in this area, including 20 with a particular focus on the recent CDM regulations. Local authorities also have environmental health departments, whose officers – Environmental Health Officers, or EHOs – have particular responsibilities in dealing with offices, shops and warehouses.

As at July 1996, the HSE inspectors can

❑ enter premises, inspect and investigate
❑ take measurements, samples or photographs
❑ seize and destroy dangerous items
❑ obtain information and statements
❑ issue Improvement Notices which require certain specified improvements to be made within a prescribed time limit
❑ prohibit the continuation of work through Prohibition Notices until specified improvements are made.

Breaking the Health and Safety at Work Act is a criminal offence.

If all other attempts to improve a situation have no success, the Inspector has the power to prosecute an employer. Prosecution can be initiated for failure to comply with an improvement notice or a prohibition notice, for obstructing inspectors in the course of their duties, for failure to carry out any of the general duties of the Health and Safety at Work Act, for breaching any Health and Safety Regulations, and for making a false statement or entry in a document or register which is required by law to be kept.

In the case of a breach of one of the laws on health and safety at work on the part of a 'body corporate' – that is, a limited company or local authority – when the offence has been committed with the consent or connivance of any director, manager or officer of that organisation, or can be attributable to neglect on his or her part, the director, manager or officer involved may be found guilty and punished accordingly.

A company or local authority or a board of directors can be prosecuted. Where an individual functional director or executive of a local authority is guilty of an offence, he or she can be prosecuted too. A company or local authority can also be prosecuted and held liable for an offence that derives from an act or omission of a junior officer or official.

The CDM Regulations, 1994

More recently, the Single European Act, 1987, established that member states of the European Union (EU) should pay particular attention to encouraging improvements, especially in the working environment, in relation to the health and safety of workers. The UK is committed to supporting health and safety initiatives which come from the EU. Among the resulting European legislation is the Temporary or Mobile Worksites Directive, 1992, which set the framework for renewed attention to health and safety within the UK in the form of the Construction (Design and Management) Regulations (referred to hereafter as the CDM Regulations), 1994.

The CDM Regulations require a major change in the way in which the industry tackles safety issues. In the past, the focus of responsibility has been on individual employers. The CDM Regulations are essentially concerned with planning, with teamwork and with co-ordination in the preparation and management of health and safety. The regulations recognise the complexity of working arrangements in construction, where project teams are made up of people from different organisations who are working together on a temporary basis. The aim of the CDM Regulations is to ensure that health and safety is systematically built into each project from the beginning, incorporating clear lines of accountability for the process within the professional team. The regulations are also intended to ensure that proper resources are allocated for health and safety. Communication on health and safety issues is essential, and there is an intention of ensuring that health and safety is given due importance and features high on the agenda at planning and project meetings at all stages of the planning and the construction process.

All of those who are involved in planning and the construction process share the responsibility for health and safety management.

The CDM Regulations place specific responsibilities on duty holders, particularly

❏ the client (who is responsible for the appointment of a planning supervisor)
❏ the planning supervisor
❏ designers
❏ the principal contractor and contractors.

All of these groups have particular responsibilities for safety and for the minimisation of risks to health and safety at all stages of the project.

When do the CDM Regulations apply?
The CDM Regulations apply to building, civil engineering and engineering construction work, including new build construction. This can include the alteration, renovation and maintenance of a structure, site clearance, the demolition and dismantling of a structure, and temporary works where the work is of a sufficient scale. The Health and Safety Executive is the only enforcing authority for CDM (HSC/Coniac, 1995: 3).

The CDM Regulations apply if the work is to last for 30 days or more and involves more than four people on site at any one time. The local authority can be the enforcing authority for construction health and safety purposes where the work is carried out in offices, shops, and similar premises without interrupting normal activities in the premises and without separating construction from other activities, and where the work is not notifiable. The maintenance or removal of insulation on pipes, boilers, or other parts of heating or water systems is also excluded.

Where the construction work is expected to take longer than

30 days, or where it involves more than 500 person-days of construction work, there is a requirement that the HSE should be notified in writing. A person-day is defined as a day in which a normal full shift is worked by one person.

Client responsibilities for health and safety

It is the client's responsibility to plan for health and safety from the inception of the project, and to decide if it falls within the scope of responsibility of the CDM Regulations. Whereas the client may have been rather remote from the project in the past, the CDM Regulations allocate legal responsibilities to the client.

The 'client' is anyone for whom a construction project is carried out. Once a decision has been taken by the client that a project should proceed, it is the client's responsibility to implement the regulations. As a fail-safe against ignorance of the Regulations on the part of the client, the designer has a responsibility to ensure that the client is aware of the duties to which he or she is subject. Clients may decide to appoint an agent to act on their behalf and to fulfil their responsibilities under the regulations. Where there are several clients associated with a project, they may nominate one of their number to act as agent. The details of the agent, who must be competent to take on these duties, should be notified to the HSE.

The client must also appoint a planning supervisor whose role is to co-ordinate health and safety. This must take place as soon as practicable once the client is committed to proceeding with the project. Planning is the key to operational effectiveness. The planning supervisor is a new role which may draw on expertise from a variety of different areas and professions – architects, engineers, surveyors and safety specialists. The role of planning supervisor may be undertaken by the client, by the lead designer, by a contractor, or by a specialist organisation. The choice will be made in accordance with project needs. It seems likely that, where the principal contractor is primarily concerned with management of both the design and construction process (for example, in management fee contracting or design and build), the role may be merged with that of planning supervisor. Alternatively, the client is not precluded from taking on the role (Joyce, 1995).

Appointment of the planning supervisor should be undertaken with care, for it is essential that the appointee is competent for the task in question. The appointment may be offered – after due consideration, to a company, a partnership or an individual, provided that the planning supervisor appointed allocates adequate resources to perform the role. The 'adequacy' of resources can be determined in accordance with the nature and size of the project, looking at such issues as the management systems, the technical facilities and the quality assurance principles which will be in place (Joyce, 1995: 89).

The client must provide the planning supervisor with information relevant to health and safety. Such information must include information about the site and about premises, as well as information about work processes and activities. Information may take the form of drawings, plans or previous surveys. If information is not readily available, the client must make such arrangements as are necessary to ensure that it is provided. This will enable the planning supervisor to meet responsibilities to ensure that a health and safety plan is prepared and to establish a health and safety file (Joyce, 1995).

The planning supervisor must advise on the competence of any designer and the adequacy of the designer's provision for health and safety, and ensure that designers comply with their duties under the Regulations.

The client has a responsibility to ensure that any designer who is appointed to the project is competent in respect of provision for health and safety. The client may seek the advice of the planning supervisor on this matter, and the planning supervisor has a legal duty to provide this advice if requested (HSC/Coniac, 1995: 10).

The client is also responsible for the appointment of the principal contractor, who must be competent for the role.

The planning supervisor

The planning supervisor, who is appointed by the client, receives from him or her any information relevant to the question of health and safety. It is important that the client and planning supervisor have an early understanding of what information should be available from the client, and when it will be available – for example, when particular packages of work are to commence and when they are to be delivered. It is also important for the client to be clear about the storage medium – for example, about what form of information technology should be applied: whether CD-ROMs or optical disks should be used.

The planning supervisor is then responsible for notification of the project to the HSE (local office) if appropriate. This notification should be sent as soon as practicable after the appointment of the planning supervisor. It should not be delayed until the principal contractor is appointed. If the planning supervisor believes that notification of the project is unnecessary, it is good practice for the reasons to be recorded in writing.

If so requested by the client, the planning supervisor must advise on the competence of the designers and the adequacy of their provision for health and safety. The planning supervisor is not required to participate in decisions about design. The role is concerned solely with ensuring that decisions about design have been taken in accordance with the regulations and to see that designers comply with their duties.

The planning supervisor must take reasonable steps to ensure co-operation between designers and to establish, as far as is reasonably practicable, that they comply with their duties so that proper care is given to the co-ordination of the health and safety aspects of design. In particular the planning supervisor must ensure that information flows freely between the different designers, that proper account of health and safety is taken by the designers, and that there is co-ordination between different designers to see how the different aspects of design may affect health and safety.

The planning supervisor must ensure that designers comply with their CDM duties. This may involve a review of designers' procedures, to consider how they have analysed and assessed health and safety risks and tried to minimise risks. This means that temporary works which are incorporated into the final structure fall within the remit of the planning supervisor.

The planning supervisor is responsible for ensuring that **a health and safety file** is prepared. This commences during the early stages of the project with information on design. Additional information is provided by the principal contractor to the planning supervisor during the construction phase of the project. The file must be updated to include any changes made as the project progresses – for example, because of the design input of specialist sub-contractors or following variations to the original design. Such information is passed up to the principal contractor by sub-contractors and thence to the planning supervisor. It will include information supplied by the client and any other information gathered by the planning supervisor in the process of preparation of **the health and safety plan**. The planning supervisor will need to put procedures into place to ensure that the principal contractor is duly notifying any changes to design information or any other information relevant to the project.

The planning supervisor holds and controls access to the health and safety file until the conclusion of the construction phase. At this point, responsibility passes back to the client.

As we have seen, it is the planning supervisor who is also responsible for ensuring that the health and safety plan is produced. This should begin at the earliest stages of project design and be completed so that it can be made available with the tender documents. This information is then available to those tendering for the position of principal contractor who can be expected to indicate how they would manage any hazards or risks which may be involved in the project. Their approach to safety management can then be taken into account by the client.

To summarise: once appointed, the planning supervisor must

☐ notify the HSE of the project, if appropriate

☐ establish clear avenues of communication with the client

☐ allocate adequate resources to the project

☐ be in a position to advise clients and contractors on designers and their provision for health and safety

☐ ensure that a health and safety plan is available at the commencement of the tendering stage.

Designers

Designers can play an important part in ensuring that health and safety is taken into account from the earliest stages of the project, ensuring that designs do not necessitate unnecessary risks to workers in the construction process. In order to fulfil these obligations, the designer(s) must understand how risks may arise in the construction process and also in the repair and maintenance of the structures which they design. If they do not have the knowledge or information necessary in order to do this, they must consult appropriate specialists to ensure that it is taken into account.

Early on in the project, designers have a responsibility to make the client aware of his or her duties with respect to health and safety, to identify health and safety hazards and the risks of any design work, to follow the hierarchy of risk control, and to provide adequate information on health and safety to those who need it. The hierarchy of risk control (in descending order) is:

- ❏ altering the design to avoid the risk
- ❏ combating the risk at source
- ❏ giving priority to measures which will protect people.

The designer must co-operate with the planning supervisor and with any other designers involved in the project. As the project progresses, the same responsibilities extend to those who undertake the more detailed design specifications – for example, mechanical and electrical sub-contractors who carry out design responsibilities.

Where the designers specify particular materials, plant, substances or equipment, they have an obligation to identify the risks which may arise from their use, and to take steps to minimise such risks. They have an obligation to co-operate with the planning supervisor and other designers.

Principal contractor and contractors

The principal contractor has the responsibility for co-ordinating health and safety management on site. Essentially the principal contractor must take account of the initial information from the planning supervisor and incorporate it into a management strategy for the project. Information which is conveyed in the pre-tender stage health and safety plan will tell prospective contractors about the risks involved in the project and any major requirements for health and safety management. At a general level, companies will already have established safety policies, but they will need to identify the resources which may be required to give effective implementation to the management of health and safety within the particular project. They will also need to demonstrate competence to carry out the work in a way which meets health and safety requirements.

Once appointed, the principal contractor holds a particular responsibility for health and safety management. This includes the development and the implementation of the health and safety plan already commenced by the planning supervisor. The principal contractor must develop a health and safety plan for the construction phase, ensuring that it sets out clearly the arrangements which ensure the health and safety of all those involved in the construction process, and all those who could be affected by it.

The client should not allow the construction phase to commence until the principal contractor has a suitable safety plan. In reality this means that arrangements must have been set up from the early stages of the project, including a framework for managing the organisation, and procedures for dealing with emergencies, for communications and for welfare. The procedures for health and safety planning must also be incorporated into the construction planning process. It means that the principal contractor will discuss and agree the processes of co-ordination and communication of information and the way in which health and safety should be handled.

The principal contractor is responsible, then, for obtaining and checking safety and method statements from contractors, for assessing training and information needs, and for ensuring the co-ordination and co-operation of contractors who are on the project. Responsibilities include ensuring that information and training for health and safety has been provided. The principal contractor may specify particular standards of competence or particular qualifications which should apply at a more general level – for example, for fork-lift-truck drivers or for scaffolders – where their competence may affect the overall level of safety on site.

The planning supervisor is responsible for advising the client, if requested, on the suitability of the principal contractor's health and safety plan.

To summarise: the principal contractor is responsible for

❑ establishing communication arrangements between contractors concerning health and safety

❑ ensuring information and consultation arrangements on health and safety for those on site

❑ monitoring health and safety

❑ passing information on to the planning supervisor for inclusion in the health and safety file

❑ ensuring that only authorised personnel are allowed on site.

Principal contractors have the main influence on the communications strategy for the project. Information about the health and safety aspects of the project must be included where the principal contractor is putting together information for contracting or sub-contracting packages on site. This should include arrangements for health and safety management of the work, references to recognised codes of practice which are relevant to the risks, monitoring arrangements, site rules and procedures (eg on training), and any rules concerning further sub-contracting.

The principal contractor must assess the hazards and risks at every phase of construction. Safety method statements may be required from contractors or sub-contractors on site if the work involves particular risks to health and safety. Principal contractors have an important role in ensuring that sub-contractors are competent to undertake the work in question. In practice this means some assessment of the sub-contractor in relation to the activity and the method proposed. In each case the contractor is expected to pay particular attention to risks to his or her own employees and to those of others. The principal contractor must ensure at this stage that the method statements are adequate and consistent with the health and safety plan.

The principal contractor must give additional consideration to the interface between the work of one contractor and that of another to ensure that there is no creation of a combined risk. An important feature of the role of the principal contractor is to ensure that there is an integrated approach to health and safety issues and that areas of concern which are project-wide are reviewed at site meetings. This includes emergency arrangements (for example, for dealing with fire, or first aid), the provision of plant and equipment which is used by more than one contractor, and the communication of health and safety information. The principal contractor is responsible for monitoring, and must also ensure that the health and safety plan is amended and updated to take into account method statements and any significant changes that affect the plan as the project progresses.

In practice, the health and safety plan for the project should specify clearly the frequency of site meetings; health and safety should feature significantly on the agenda. There is a high level of interdependence in many projects, and careful attention at project and site meetings is required to define communication procedures about health and safety.

Construction (Health, Safety and Welfare) (CHSW) Regulations, 1996

The 1996 Construction (Health, Safety and Welfare) Regulations were proposed in order to rationalise and to update earlier regulations from the 1960s. They are intended to protect the health, safety and welfare of everyone in the industry, and they lay down duties for employers, for the self-employed, and for those who control the way in which construction work is carried out.

The regulations laid before Parliament in June 1996 set a general duty to ensure a safe place of work and a safe means of access to and from the place of work – whether the work is to be undertaken on the ground or at height. They require employers to take precautions to prevent falls from heights. Scaffolding, access equipment, harnesses and nets must be put up only under the supervision of a 'competent person'. People who are at work and those who are in the vicinity must be protected from injury by falling materials or objects. There must be attention to the risks of structural collapse, and to the hazards of dismantling and demolition activities. Particular attention is given in the Regulations to special areas of risk – such as the use of explosive charges, the possible collapse of ground around excavations, and the danger of drowning.

The Regulations, which came into force in September 1996, also deal with the management of traffic routes on site and the prevention and control of emergencies (HSE, 1996). Contractors, sub-contractors, managers and safety representatives within the industry need to plan for implementation of the regulations. Anyone who is engaged in construction work has a responsibility to co-operate with others on matters of health and safety. Employees have an additional duty – to carry out their own work in a safe way.

Welfare provision on site

The same Regulations require those who are in control of a site to provide decent toilets and showers, as well as changing rooms for people to remove and store their site clothing. The Construction (Health, Safety and Welfare) Regulations, 1996, also specify that sites should have arrangements for rest rooms and for areas where workers can prepare and eat food (HSE, 1996). These issues may be less pressing than the more urgent safety requirements which relate to the accident levels within the construction sector, yet at the same time the question of welfare provision should be more easily resolved.

Attitudes to individual workers are communicated by the level of welfare provision at site level. Inadequate provision for the physical needs of the workforce sends a clear message about the value which is put on their contribution and skill. The construction industry has been slow to develop the standards which are taken for granted in other sectors. Changing attitudes and the new professionalism within the industry require a reconsideration of some of these traditional values. The provision of toilets, drinking water and washrooms on site should automatically have been provided in line with regulations which were passed some 30 years ago. Yet in the mid-1990s prosecutions still take place for failure to comply with such basic provision.

As in all areas of health and safety management, there is scope for further discussion of what constitutes good practice and appropriate provision, over and above minimum legal requirements, in the context of an industry which is so dependent on the people on site.

Safety management on site

Effective health and safety management must begin within the individual firm, so that there is an organisational commitment and expertise which is transferred from project to project. The commitment to health and safety is one component in the commitment to quality. Professionals, managers, supervisors, and those who are running their own business need an opportunity to undergo training, to discuss and to plan for health and safety, and to update their knowledge on a regular basis as a part of the commitment to managing in a changing environment. Continuous professional development involves an appreciation of innovation and changing techniques, but it also necessitates an understanding of the safest and most effective processes through which they can be implemented.

The impact of two major sets of regulations relating to construction (the CDM Regulations, 1994, and the Construction [Health, Safety and Welfare] Regulations, 1996, both discussed above) has given a new profile to health and safety management. The new rules have necessitated a major rethink in many areas as to how safety is built into the construction process. People who in the past may have felt that safety was not an issue for which they had responsibility in their professional capacity, now have to be aware of the safety implications of their decisions. Construction professionals – for example, estimators, planners and people in marketing – need to become aware of the regulations and to review the ways in which their decisions might, indirectly if not directly, impact on their effective implementation.

Principal contractors are required to take a new interest in the competence of sub-contractors, and this may mean more careful monitoring and evaluation of the performance of sub-contractors on safety issues in the future. Sub-contractors and smaller firms must review their approach to safety issues to ensure that their record is a positive one.

Major contractors who retain a specialist health and safety function are able to respond to the regulations through publicity and training, through reviewing and modifying management systems, through safety documentation and bulletins, and through encouraging attention to safety in face-to-face contact on site.

Contracts and site managers are at the sharp end of safety management – balancing the pressures of conflicting demands and facing the consequences in human terms if something does go wrong. The nature of the problems they have to contend with will vary significantly and there is no one 'standard' response to the new regulatory framework for construction safety. Safety management must be established in relation to each particular project, and to the construction and maintenance processes it requires. Training should be appropriate in relation to the nature, size and risk of the typical project which organisations or individuals are involved in.

Attention to health and safety practice is an integral part of site management, which requires daily (or even twice-daily) management inspections. Each individual who takes on such responsibility must think carefully about the approach to be used in the context of the particular project and the risks it may pose. At this level the identification of problems requires prompt attention to remedy any defects in safety practice with attention to specific hazards (eg scaffolding, trenches) and in order to identify and to resolve issues before they become serious.

Employee safety representatives can play a part in site safety inspections, and can contribute to the safety monitoring

Kvaerner Construction Ltd

Kvaerner Construction Ltd (formerly Trafalgar House Construction Ltd) began their response to the CDM Regulations with a publicity 'roadshow' to inform clients and sub-contractors of the implications.

They had already reviewed the potential impact of the regulations on the industry as well as on their own business at the point when they were brought into effect, and estimated that 70 per cent of their workforce needed CDM-related advice. They established a three-tier training programme, including site supervisors, managers and those who were to be involved in the new 'planning supervisor' activities which arose from the Regulations. Participants now learn what CDM is about and consider how they have to change their practices in order to conform to the regulations.

Through monthly safety meetings on site, and through quarterly meetings at regional level, safety advisors are able to provide additional information and support for contracts and site managers (over and above the discussions at weekly site meetings). They also discuss the changes in documentation for the safety management system which were necessitated by the new responsibilities of principal contractors. These changes were fed back into the quality assurance process in accordance with the commitments of the organisation under ISO9001.

[With thanks to Adrian Sprague, Divisional Technical Services Director, Kvaerner Construction Ltd.]

process. The low density of trade union organisation and the fragmentation of the workforce means that it is unusual to find safety representatives formally appointed by trade union members, as they are entitled to do. The entitlement to appoint safety representatives has been extended to those who are not trade union members, but there is little evidence to date that this will increase the number of workforce-appointed safety representatives. In their absence some contractors, and occasionally some sub-contractors, may appoint their own safety representatives to support site managers and to assist in anticipating problems and contributing to their solution.

More formal site inspections provide an essential mechanism for an external check by principal contractors on developments at site level. Visits to the site by a safety officer or safety advisor provide a record of problems and the opportunity for a review of progress at the next inspection. The frequency of formal inspections depends on the size and the context of the operations, and should take account of progress in the work. In excavations (including shafts and tunnels), for example, inspections are necessary at the beginning of every shift.

A safety audit, possibly conducted by an external consultant, may provide an additional check on what management are actually doing on site – to see that the documentation is correctly used and that procedures are being implemented. An audit of safety practice can lead to further training or other activities to overcome any weaknesses.

Safety communication with site workers

Given the complexity of operations on many sites, good practice in health and safety – like a commitment to quality – comes from the establishment of effective management systems and good communications between the key players on site. Companies must appoint a competent health and safety officer to assist them if they employ five or more employees, although this may not necessarily be a full-time appointment. In larger companies, this may be a specialist advisory role, the post-holders having professional training and specialist knowledge in the field of health and safety. This offers the advantage of high-level expertise and up-to-date understanding of new developments. An individual who holds an advisory role has the responsibility of communicating widely and effectively within his or her organisation, facilitating improvements in understanding at a general level, particularly among line managers within the organisation, and providing opportunities for additional training or for the circulation of information.

In smaller organisations, an individual who has the role of health and safety officer may bear a number of other responsibilities, and need not be exclusively allocated to responsibility for health and safety. Although this may mean improved understanding of the pressures on line management, it can also mean an element of role conflict, making it more difficult to concentrate on health and safety issues.

Successful health and safety management depends on the attitudes of the people involved as much as on what the law may say. Policies have little impact if they are not effectively communicated to those who are expected to put them into practice. It is not simply a matter of setting up procedures – it is also a question of ensuring that they are taken seriously and implemented with commitment by line managers and by those who are in a position of responsibility. Employers can sometimes take advantage of funding support from the Construction Industry Training Board for training (see Chapter 5). Smaller firms may find that they can buy in to courses or safety programmes which are run by larger firms in their area or by contractors with whom they work regularly.

In communicating about health and safety, much depends not just on what is said but on how it is said. Although individual firms may be conscientious in their approach, the legacy of individual experience often contributes to complacency or a lack of care. People are quick to understand if there is a coded message which downplays the importance of health and safety – and with an emphasis on task management and completion to deadlines, the industry culture can work against the effectiveness of communications about health and safety. Payment systems – particularly payment by the task – can contribute to safety's being downplayed. This issue is as important in the smaller business as it is for the larger contractors, for small firms may rely on individuals to manage their own work, with a considerable degree of control over the way in which it is organised and little supervision in practice. Similarly, there may be problems if health and safety standards are set in a 'visionary' way which does not lead to practical implementation. Health and safety responsibilities must be clear, and their relevance to the project must be readily apparent to everyone involved.

At the project level, the opportunities for clear communication are available in any of seven ways.

☐ *Induction training* offers the opportunity to set out a clear and unambiguous commitment to good practice on health and safety at the commencement of work on a project. This should include information on the main hazards, on organisation on site, on health and safety management (who is responsible and what to do if there is a problem), on emergency and evacuation procedures, and on site rules.

☐ *Written communications* are essential – for example, through a site handbook or site rules which can include a section on health and safety, spelling out the expectations of the principal contractor. Regular, focused communication may be more helpful than voluminous documentation provided at the commencement of a project.

❏ *Site notices* can include those which are statutorily required and canteen notices which update information.

❏ *Toolbox talks* or *task-focused health and safety talks.* Verbal communication and reminders from supervisors can play an important part in creating a safety culture and in setting standards at the level of the individual workgroup which reinforce the safety message. The use of toolbox talks with time set aside for communication can emphasise the importance of the message. To be effective the technique needs to be clear, focused and relevant to the actual issues on site. If an organisation is identifying risk and producing risk assessment, it should lead to a clearly formulated method statement. This can be actioned through direct communication via a toolbox talk. The message can be given added weight if more senior managers as well as supervisors are involved. This type of communication is probably more beneficial if carried out at regular intervals, but not for too long. It may include sub-contractors and their employees as well as directly employed operatives.

❏ *Site health and safety representatives*: the site workforce can discuss safety issues and offer advice. On large sites, trade unions may have appointed safety representatives who can make a contribution to site safety by undertaking inspections and reporting problems. Safety representatives can play an important part in liaison with the site workforce to take up safety problems and to ensure that safety is taken seriously.

❏ *Site safety committees* can be established on a site-wide basis as a forum for discussion of the views of the different groups on site. If a safety committee is set up which is not site-wide, the principal contractor will have to find a mechanism for eliciting the views of those who are not covered by it. A safety committee provides an important and useful mechanism for consultation and for monitoring arrangements.

❏ *Refresher training.* On long-term contracts – for example, those which last for more than a year – there will be a need for updated information and refresher training. This could be provided on a quarterly basis, with information appropriate to the project or the tasks involved.

The management of health, safety and welfare provides a benchmark against which other claims about quality and productivity can be set. The Construction (Design and Management) Regulations, 1994, put a new premium on planning and organisation for safety, particularly as an aspect of the pre-construction phase. The principal contractor retains key responsibilities within the construction phase, but co-ordination between all of the parties to the construction process is an important dimension within safety management. So too is involvement and communication with the site workforce, and workforce safety representatives have an important part to play in identifying problems and proposing solutions.

Health and safety is not an issue which can be separated from other aspects of site management. It is closely integrated with the management of quality and productivity, with resource allocation and effective human resource management. Within this chapter we have been able to offer only an overview of current areas of concern. Those who wish to improve their knowledge and understanding in this area can benefit from the wide range of specialist literature from professional and safety organisations such as the Royal Society for the Prevention of Accidents (RoSPA) and the Health and Safety Executive itself.

The following is a checklist of relevant legislation:

Factories Act, 1961
Construction (Lifting Operations) Regulations, 1961
Health and Safety at Work etc. Act, 1974
Management of Health and Safety at Work Regulations, 1992
Workplace (Health, Safety and Welfare) Regulations, 1992
Provision and Use of Work Equipment Regulations, 1992
Personal Protective Equipment at Work Regulations, 1992
Manual Handling of Loads Regulations, 1992
Work with Display Screen Equipment Regulations, 1990
Control of Substances Hazardous to Health Regulations, 1994
Noise at Work Regulations, 1989
Construction (Head Protection) Regulations, 1989
Construction (Design and Management) Regulations, 1994
Construction (Health, Safety and Welfare) Regulations, 1996

CHAPTER 10

WORKING OVERSEAS

Construction is an international industry. The major British contractors are multi-national companies which have for many years been involved in contracts overseas, particularly in the countries of the Commonwealth. Smaller and medium-sized firms are also able to benefit from opportunities outside the UK. The potential for international work is constantly shifting, and this chapter looks at the personnel corollaries of such arrangements, with particular attention to the position of the expatriate employee. It considers the nature of overseas work and the implications for staffing and people management. Questions of pay and conditions are particularly important – and this chapter identifies the sort of 'package' which someone transferred overseas for a project might expect.

Multi-national contractors

The largest British contractors are themselves multi-nationals, or part of multi-national organisations, and overseas operations provide an important alternative to the British market, particularly in periods of recession. There are few parts of the world which have not been visited by British contractors who respond to market opportunities, whether they are in the Americas, the Middle East, the Far East, Africa, eastern Europe, or elsewhere. In terms of the value of the contracts obtained, North America continues to be the most significant location, although the Far East and the Middle East are also important markets. The countries of Europe have traditionally seen less activity by British contractors than the more distant countries of the Commonwealth, but, since the fall of the Berlin wall, opportunities in Europe – particularly in the countries of the European

Union – are of increasing interest to British construction firms.

Product or geographical divisions of such companies, both within and outside the UK, are likely to have a degree of autonomy and to take a devolved responsibility for the profitability of their own self-standing operation, subject to financial controls from corporate head office. This means that they will deal with marketing, operational and personnel management largely independently of the parent company.

Mergers and acquisitions have been an important part of the process of globalisation in that they provide one mechanism by which enterprises can enter a new market or reinforce their market position either by purchasing a competitor company or by strengthening their base through the purchase of a smaller organisation.

The other mechanism for accessing markets is through joint ventures or partnerships with other companies. Where contractors have not yet established a permanent base within another country, they may choose to retain an office, either independently or in conjunction with a local partner. Such partnerships provide an opportunity to retain a presence and to benefit from local know-how without the unnecessary cost of retaining a permanent base.

Local partnerships may be a requirement for contractors in some markets – for example, in parts of the Middle East. International firms have a choice in resourcing contracts by using parent-country nationals, host-country nationals, or through the employment of people from other countries.

Although companies themselves may be global, projects are locally-based. Local knowledge of markets and the capacity to network with foreign governments and overseas clients are necessary attributes as a lever for competitive advantage. Inevitably, it is the larger projects which attract major contractors, who may operate within partnerships or as part of a consortium. Contractors may be affected by the globalisation of business where key clients cross frontiers. Clients then face a choice of working with local contractors or continuing established relationships – and some British contractors have found that new opportunities have been opened up in Europe because of the Europeanisation of client activities. Equally, there are contractors from the mainland of Europe and from Japan who are now established within the UK for the same reasons. European rules on procurement require that access to tender lists for public sector contracts is open, but locally-based contractors have the advantage of knowledge and experience of local building practices and requirements.

Although companies may have a division focused exclusively on international or overseas work, international companies are likely to encourage overseas initiatives and other divisions will probably also be involved in bidding for overseas work. Transfer to an overseas projects is not therefore limited to employees within an international division of such a company. This means that contractors may be awarded contracts in circumstances where they tendered, or were given significant support, from the UK.

'Overseas' work is most likely to be construed to mean work outside the countries of the European Union. Although there are clear differences in the cultural, climatic and living conditions between different European states, these differences are less marked than those between the UK and the countries in the Middle or Far East, Asia, Africa or Latin America. In all cases it is important to identify and to manage the employment relationship so as to take account of the differences which exist, but these are likely to be less significant and to require different solutions within the European context in comparison with other parts of the world.

Planning, recruitment and projects overseas

The increased value of overseas contracts suggests that the amount of overseas working required within the construction sector must have increased. Yet it is not clear that this is in fact the case. The development of overseas subsidiaries and the extension of the range of overseas networks may contribute to reducing the scale of long-term working overseas, but there is no clear evidence at present that expatriate working is more important than it was, say, ten years ago. Brewster (1991), commenting on multi-national behaviour, notes that in sectors such as banking, petroleum and engineering, some major British employers are reducing their use of expatriates.

There is a fundamental contrast between businesses which are deemed to be global in orientation and those in which subsidiaries are allowed to determine their own actions. Global businesses are seen as those in which markets may be integrated – but a distinction is made between companies in which corporate headquarters has a directive role and those which are truly global.

Probably the most widely cited typology of management in multi-national enterprises (MNEs) is that offered by Perlmutter (1974). In terms of its policies on resourcing, an organisation can use one of four policies, or a combination of them. They are:

☐ *Ethnocentric* – filling top management positions in overseas operations with HQ transferees who are parent-company nationals (PCNs). Host-country nationals (HCNs) are not equally transferred to the parent country. Correspondingly, home-country practices and values are assumed as the norm, with minimal adaptation to other cultures.

☐ *Polycentric* – filling top management positions with HCNs. The polycentric operation is likely to devolve considerable management responsibility, although financial and corporate controls may not be relinquished.

☐ *Regiocentric* – filling top management positions in defined 'regions' with nationals of the country within the region (where a 'region' corresponds to a continent within global industries). This policy is likely to reflect (or to correspond to) the international product division within the global management structure.

☐ *Geocentric* – filling top management positions on the basis of merit regardless of nationality, so adopting global policies which downplay the significance of the country of origin and which reflect the global markets and interests of the enterprise in question.

The ethnocentric and the polycentric models are currently more common as reference points within the construction industry, mainly because overseas operations may often be restricted in time to the duration of a particular project or to specific market opportunities. Where such operations are short-term, the scope for the more complex interaction suggested by the regiocentric or geocentric approaches may not be practicable. Many of the shorter-term projects or subsidiary activities may rely on localised knowledge, coupled with corporate support and control.

Planning is vital because effective staffing is essential to the operation of an international project but there are significant costs to be taken into account when people are transferred overseas. Much of the literature concerned with international management is concerned with the advantages and disadvantages of using parent-company nationals. Expatriates are expensive and, where practicable, a company may for cost reasons therefore prefer to recruit locally. There may be resentment of expatriate managers, particularly if there is an absence of cultural sensitivity on their part. Conversely, research focused on managers in Europe suggests that foreign clients and sometimes foreign governments have a preference for parent-company nationals (Scullion, 1992).

There is a political issue to be taken into account too, for major projects of the type which attract the interest of overseas contractors may be government-funded or may attract government interest. Infrastructural work is likely to have the potential for job creation, with possible benefits for the local economy. Emerging countries have their own trades and professional people. Whereas in the past it was common for craftsmen as well as managers to be transferred overseas, companies are increasingly likely to rely on local labour markets for the recruitment of operatives and foremen, and to transfer in only the more senior or professional people who have experience of the company and its ways of working – professional and technical staffs, including civil engineers, other engineers, project managers and management consultants. The actual balance in terms of people imported for the duration of the contract and those who are recruited in the host country, is likely to depend on the location and the nature of the project, client preference, and the type of expertise required.

Yet the capacity to bring in experienced professionals may be the key to success in winning the contract. Technical expertise is an essential prerequisite for overseas posts, ranked most highly by multi-national companies across industry sectors (Brewster, 1991: 51). Inevitably, though, rather more is required than this. The expatriate management team may be concerned with marketing and corporate representation as well as with specific project-based issues. Expatriates engaged on construction projects are probably more likely than expatriates in general to be opening up new locations for the company – rather than moving in to established plants or offices. It also seems more likely that they will be required to relocate quickly – without the benefit of a 'lead-in' time which may be offered in some other sectors. Research concerned with the competencies required for international success recognise the disparities between different areas of functional specialisation and the geographical area of assignment. However, the same research points to four dimensions which are of importance regardless of these factors (Baumgarten, 1995). These are: leadership skills, initiative, emotional stability, and motivation – competencies that might provide a particular focus for the selection or development of international staff.

During the estimating and tendering stages of a project, decisions must be taken on the balance of resourcing – from the host country and from the parent country – and on the costs involved. Contractors will themselves maintain extensive information but may also access the services of specialist consultancies so that if a project director is considering sending someone overseas, such information can be readily available. It is important that calculations do not minimise the costs involved, and that full account is taken of the costs of social security or National Insurance payments and taxation in the host country.

Decisions on the recruitment of personnel to be transferred will probably be made by the project manager, or possibly by the projects director, supported by personnel. The role of the personnel department will probably be concerned with the amendments to the employment contract. Personnel may be required to take on a 'care and concern' role, supporting the individual in relation to personal problems or worries, or handling crisis situations, both overseas and of family at home (Brewster, 1991: 36).

Willingness to work overseas may well be a condition of the contract – written in to the terms and conditions of all professional and managerial staff on appointment. However, the choice of people for an overseas assignment requires particular care. The opportunity to work overseas may be important in providing unique opportunities for career development and the challenge of working on projects which may attract international recognition. Yet there may be factors which inhibit the enthusiasm of suitable candidates, particularly in relation to their personal circumstances.

The majority of expatriates are men, many of them with families, and expatriate work may not always fit together with family responsibilities or expectations. The opportunity to work overseas has to be reconciled with the demands of a family. This may effectively preclude many women from taking up such a challenge; equally, male candidates for overseas projects may feel that a wife's career and children's educational opportunities should take priority. Women candidates may be overlooked because their companies have failed to confront traditional gender stereotyping, but equally some women may prefer not to take up the challenge of some of the tougher assignments. Ironically, there is evidence that women are better able to handle cultural change and to work as part of culturally mixed project teams (Barham and Devine, 1991: 24, cited in Scullion, 1992).

Family understanding and support is essential for a successful expatriate posting – and this factor has to be built into organisational planning and employee selection for such opportunities.

A decision to use one or more employees from the UK presupposes that they are best able to deliver on commitments to the client. An expatriate will have the benefit of greater familiarity with the organisation, its culture and systems, as well as being of proven technical expertise. The selection of someone to work overseas will depend on the location to which he or she is to be sent, and it is important that there is as much information available as possible. Major construction projects overseas are often in remote places, difficult of access and with little in the way of leisure pastimes outside working hours. Often they are to be found in areas which have been hit by natural disasters or where the infrastructure has been destroyed by war. From time to time we read of employees of multi-national companies who are stranded in distant places because of political problems or natural disasters. Those taking decisions on sending people abroad for a significant period need to take account of the precise nature of the location and the circumstances of the project. So too do those accepting such opportunities.

Torrington (1994: 21) suggests four major criteria for consideration:

❑ *Culture:* What is the relationship between the British and the government and people of the foreign country? What is the visa situation? What is the religion and culture of the country? Is this a politically stable environment or is there evidence of political instability? What is the position of women? What are the crime levels? Can personal security be guaranteed?

❑ *Economic development:* How well developed is the economy

of the host country? What sort of accommodation is available? What is the cost of living and what does it mean for local living standards? Are there local or international schools which will be acceptable?

❏ *Geographical location:* What is the precise location of the project? Is this a remote location with difficult access? What is the climate like? Will there be language difficulties? Is there an expatriate community? If the spouse goes too, will there be any prospect of employment? How good are the medical services and how quickly can people be got out in the event of an emergency?

❏ *The job:* Who is the client and what is the project? Who will be employed and how much support can be expected? How does the project differ from the work which is undertaken in the home environment? To what extent will it involve management of local nationals?

All these points are of vital importance to employees and to their families, and many of them will be common to expatriates in other industries. However, in the construction industry people are rarely moving to manage an established situation or workplace. More often they are relocating in order to initiate a project, sometimes in very difficult circumstances, so careful attention to the selection of staff to take on such responsibilities is required. It is essential that there is a realistic picture of the circumstances in which the project is to be undertaken, and that this is conveyed to job candidates. It follows that someone may be suitable for, and successful in, one environment and not another, and that the choice that is made is critical to the success of the project and, potentially to the career and development of the individual too.

The 'average' stay abroad may be about a year, but this clearly disguises wide variation in the length of an overseas commitment. Some projects will be of a much longer duration. The costs of returning someone to the UK before the conclusion of the project are high, particularly if the individual is a senior person on the project. This is most likely to occur if the details about the nature and circumstances of the project are not fully clarified in advance. Expatriate staff need to be particularly flexible and adaptable in their approach because the requirements of their work may be less predictable than in the UK. There may be less support than in the home circumstances, and the vagaries of local politics or the absence of an effective infra-structure may cause problems in progressing work according to plan.

There are obvious benefits where companies are able to deploy someone with a knowledge of the language and under-standing of the local culture. The English have been slow to recognise the importance of language acquisition, particularly because English is seen as the language of international busi-ness and markets are most often found in the countries of the Commonwealth. Yet expatriate managers will be operating in culturally mixed project teams, often supervising employees who are host-country nationals. The ability to communicate and to understand local values can be an important aid to team-building and to the success of a project. In the absence of language skills, managers should be encouraged to develop greater cultural awareness and sensitivity, particularly with regard to religious practices and social taboos. Some companies are able to take advantage of the diversity of their UK workforce as they develop their contacts and contracts overseas. This does require effective record-keeping in the personnel area in order to identify the people who may have special knowledge or skills which could be helpful to the project.

Although managers in other sectors may be permitted the luxury of several months of preparation and adjustment prior to an overseas assignment, this is unlikely to be the case for project managers or construction professionals, whose work circumstances are less predictable so that employees must respond to project opportunities as and when they occur. During the pre-departure stage, the personnel department and/or senior managers in the contracting organisation may provide briefing and background information on the project location and cultural issues, as well as on the technical aspects of the project itself. Further information and guidance may be available, either through the scheduled briefings, or via customised programmes, which can be arranged by the Centre for International Briefing (in Farnham, Surrey: see address list).

Pay and conditions for overseas staff

In most cases, the challenges of an overseas posting are accom-panied by the possibility of higher pay and greater tax advantages. Indeed, the financial benefits may be an important part of the incentive when considering career opportunities outside the home country, so it is important to be clear from the outset about all aspects of the remuneration package. There is evidence in European research of a growing reluctance among senior UK managers to work overseas as expatriates (Scullion, 1992), though this may be as much do to with problems of re-patriation as with the compensation package during the period abroad.

Key issues for the expatriate are:

❑ How long is the contract for? How often can he or she return home, and for how long?

❑ What will be paid? What will this represent in real terms?

❑ Where will payment be made?

❑ If an element of the payment is in the local currency, what outgoings will be involved?

❑ What local taxes, social security or welfare payments must be made, and who will take responsibility for them?

❑ Who will be responsible for additional family costs – in particular for education?

❑ What are the arrangements for medical insurance and care?

❑ What other insurance arrangements will be made?

How long is the contract for?

A commitment to work overseas may be fixed-term – that is, for the duration of a particular contract. In this case the place of employment will be the named area or such other location as may be mutually agreeable. Alternatively, it may be an open-ended commitment to overseas working. Some companies prefer an open-ended contract because it offers flexibility in an uncertain contracting climate. There may be tax advantages too, in that an open-ended commitment to work overseas may be more likely to attract immediate tax concessions in the UK.

Arrangements for visits home should be clearly specified in terms of the frequency, cost, and other implications. Some companies have a penalty clause if an employee chooses to return to the UK before completion of the project or within a specified period.

Adjustments to pay and expenses

In principle, expatriate employees expect a higher salary while overseas, partly in response to the longer hours likely to be worked, but also as a recompense for particular factors relating to the location. These may include

☐ adjustment for the hardship or circumstances in the host country
☐ adjustment for the cost of living
☐ adjustment for tax and social security costs.

Where companies have a substantial number of overseas managers, they may have their own library of pay information, but many organisations seek support from specialist consultants such as Employment Conditions Abroad.

Hardship allowances range from around 30 per cent of salary to zero, depending on the location of the project. Hardship factors are decided on the basis of climate, health risk and socio-political factors. It is the areas which have been subjected to particular problems which are most likely to be in need of infrastructural development – in Kuwait, in Beirut and in Bosnia, construction activity has followed periods of armed conflict and construction personnel have been among the first in to these countries following such problems. Where the climate is uncomfortable, where there are significant health hazards because of poor sanitation, epidemics or disease, or where there are conditions of current or recent civil war or risk to personal security, the hardship allowance is likely to be more highly rated. Other factors which may be taken into account include the extent to which there is an imposed isolation because of limited communication, poor transport facilities and the absence of social and recreational facilities. It follows that there is little likelihood of a hardship payment for a project in western Europe, Australasia or North America.

Adjustment to living costs poses an additional and complex problem because account must be taken of the possibility that the expatriate employee must maintain two homes – one in the UK and one overseas. Much will depend on arrangements for the employee's family. In general the intention is to ensure that expatriates are not out of pocket while working overseas, and that if an employee is located outside the UK without family, accommodation may be provided or found for the duration, together with arrangements or support for other living costs – there may be canteen provision, laundry arrangements, and so on. Where someone is going to one of the tougher locations, he or she is less likely to take the family, and in this situation there may be some particular compensation.

The majority of expatriate managers are men, and – in suitable circumstances – most companies encourage them to take wives and families, recognising the value and importance of this support mechanism, for if family arrangements are satisfactorily resolved, the employee is more likely to settle comfortably to the role that is required. Many organisations acknowledge that concern for family well-being may be the single most important factor governing the individual's adaptation to the new role, and that this concern may most readily be accommodated where the individual is accompanied by the family and suitable arrangements made for them. The costs of the children's accompanying their parents may be borne by the company, and account will be taken of any additional costs for schools, either in the host country or at home if the children do not accompany their parents.

In this case, the employee and family may be expected to make their own accommodation arrangements and an advance visit may be arranged and funded by the company to enable them to do this. Alternatively, there may be a period in temporary accommodation until a more permanent base can be found. In those circumstances the company will usually find the cost of rental, together with support for the payment of utilities – gas, water and electricity. Accommodation costs are notoriously high in some parts of the world – in Hong Kong for example – and there may be an upper limit on the accommodation allowance which might be provided. Yet in general, companies say that they will look at each case on its merits, recognising that there can be sharp variations in costs over time as well as between locations.

Where there is a family home in the UK, there will be the option of selling or renting it during the absence, but the tax liability on any rental income will be the responsibility of the employee.

Other variations in living costs may be met by some part of the salary's being transferred into the local currency, but the employee also has to recognise that, in a few locations, it may not be possible to bring money out of the country at the end of the time there. Medical expenses will be covered for the overseas location, both for the employee and for his or her family, although there may be some exclusions for optical, dental and maternity costs, or for medical attention required because of alchohol or drug abuse.

Taxation and National Insurance

Questions of taxation and National Insurance are complex and require detailed attention. Tax payments must be built into the planning for the remuneration package for the expatriate, who could otherwise find himself or herself with a responsibility for tax in two locations. A UK employee may be liable to tax in the UK until he or she has been working outside the country for at least a year, and will also be liable to tax in the host country.

National Insurance contributions must also be accounted for, particularly since these are lower in Britain than in almost any other part of Europe.

Companies are likely to seek policies of tax equalisation, to offset the costs which would have been incurred in the home country against costs which will be incurred in the overseas environment. A positive step involves arranging for independent financial advice too. For example, one major organisation which has a significant volume of overseas work arranges for its expatriate employees to meet an independent financial advisor before their departure in order to assess their tax liabilities and investment opportunities.

Evaluating performance overseas

Appraisal systems which operate in the home context are, in theory at least, equally applicable to employees who are working overseas. Yet rigorous performance appraisal systems are far from universal among the expatriate workforce (Brewster, 1991: 78). Although personnel practitioners in construction say that performance management is conducted for overseas employees on the same basis as for other employees, there is also a view that the implementation of formal appraisal interviews for expatriates may be less systematic than for home employees. Because expatriates may be operating in an isolated environment with few personal supports, there are also concerns that feedback and comments should be structured in a way which is helpful, which recognises the complexities of the work situation, and which can be assimilated and implemented in that particular location.

Communication and maintaining confidence

Communications systems are particularly important for the overseas employee who may be working in an isolated environment, in particular need of support. Firstly, it is important that the expatriate does not feel forgotten and that he or she is kept in touch with developments in the company – particularly if these are of direct relevance to his or her circumstances. E-mail and Internet communication have not yet resolved this problem, although they may be of increasing use and relevance in the future. Newsletters and circulars may be helpful, as are contacts with visitors who 'parachute in' from time to time. The personnel department in the parent company may take on the responsibility of providing a communication route, offering some reassurance that listening and support will be there if needed.

Secondly, it is essential that there are emergency systems in place, operating around the clock to support expatriates in the event of major disasters, or serious illness of the employee or of a family member either in the host country or at home. In extreme cases, expatriates may need support with medical arrangements or with travel arrangements out of the country because of a serious accident or poor health. Crises or natural disasters in the host country may be a source of anxiety to family at home, and the employing company has a responsibility both to employees and to their families in situations of this type. Where organisations have given thought to these problems, they provide a direct personal contact with a telephone number, or they ensure that telephone lines are manned around the clock, so that there is always a point of contact when needed.

Repatriation

Concerns about repatriation have been identified as among the most important in inhibiting managers from accepting overseas assignments. When considered for an overseas posting, managers tend to ask about their job prospects and pay prospects at the end of the project. Technical and engineering staff want to know that the skills and expertise they are honing while they are away will have some value for the company when they return, that they will not be forgotten, and that their career prospects will be enhanced rather than jeopardised because of their time away.

This problem is compounded because of the insecurities within the UK construction industry and the fact that it is difficult to offer guarantees for the years ahead. Certainly it is important to be able to reassure candidates for an overseas post that they will be better placed, rather than worse off, whatever the wider circumstances of the company. Although larger contractors may offer a commitment that an expatriate will be re-assimilated into the former department or division, it can be difficult in practice to absorb people back into the company, particularly if they have spent a lengthy time overseas. The process of re-assimilation requires a degree of care and sensitivity on the part of home-based project directors if the benefit of the overseas experience is not to be lost.

Approaches on repatriation identified by Brewster (1991: 95) include:

☐ *debriefing*: meetings with the individual prior to the end of the assignment to consider career prospects
☐ *project responsibilities*: involvement with other work projects to maintain external links
☐ *support networks*: through travel, newsletters, family networks and clubs
☐ *systematic management reviews*: with appropriate senior executives
☐ *mentoring*: with a more senior individual in the parent country
☐ *careful career planning*: as one aspect of human resource planning within the company as a whole.

Differences in Europe

In some ways Europe is not perceived as an overseas work location – yet further consideration may be needed to take account of the challenge which is posed by operations on the mainland of Europe. Because the value of European contracts is growing, there are increasing contacts with other European countries, but these may be more likely to take the form of work through host-country subsidiaries and liaison through regular reciprocal visits, rather than through the establishment of an expatriate-led management team in another country.

For the individual who is required to take up residence in Europe, there are a range of considerations to take into account.

On the one hand, there are many similarities between Britain and other countries of the European Union – in terms of living standards, infrastructure and expectations of the working population. Yet in other respects there may be a considerable culture shock for the individual who leaves Britain to take up residence in Paris, Rome or Berlin, despite the many similarities. There is, however, an increasing accumulation of experience in preparation for this eventuality as undergraduates and post-graduates coming in to the industry are today more likely than in the past to have acquired some language skills or to consider European practices and policies in their professional area as part of their training and professional development.

Major enterprises are less likely to make special provision for managers or other employees working in EU countries than for those in other parts of the world. European staff may be treated in the same way as local employees, with salary adjustments to bring them in line with the equivalent position within the country of operation. People are then subject to local tax and National Insurance payments, although it is also likely that there will be some additional accommodation allowance. In Europe, as in other parts of the world, expatriates may be encouraged to take their families with them, but of course the cost and the relative ease of travel may encourage a preference for more regular visits home rather than disruption of family arrangements.

Questions of language and culture are important. Although the British may share some aspects of the culture of other European countries, Europe has its own linguistic diversity and may be less likely than Commonwealth countries to use English as a day-to-day working language, at least outside northern Europe. Secondly, the question of national culture may be significant, despite the apparent geographic proximity of other countries of western Europe. In a classic study, Hofstede highlighted the importance of national cultural differences, which provide sharp contrasts in thinking, behaviour and expectations – in the 'software of the mind' as Hofstede calls it – within Europe as well as in other parts of the world (Hofstede,1980). Thirdly, there are significant variations in the way in which, say, German or French organisations train people, organise their businesses, pay employees, set up career structures, and so on. Fourthly, the areas of growing interest for many contractors may be the newly emerging markets in the more distant parts of central and eastern Europe. Russia is a country which has huge potential for expansion in workload, but investment carries with it concerns about contractual payments and political stability. Business practice and competitive contracting is less embedded in recent experience in eastern Europe, and this may pose particular problems for expatriate British employees.

The framework for employment and employment rights differs significantly in western Europe from practices in the UK. Countries on the mainland of Europe share some common features despite the wide diversity in national practices. Employment tends to be regulated, employees having rights in law which have a real impact on employer behaviour in the workplace. There has been a relatively high level of unionisation (ie relative to many other parts of the world) and an acknowledged role for the 'social partners', emerging as aspects of post-war political and economic settlements. State intervention has tended to support collective bargaining, formalising the role and contribution of trade unions and employers' associations. It has also set the framework for employee consultation through various forms of works councils or workers' councils. The historical experience and the socio-political framework for industrial relations vary significantly from country to country, but within the mainland countries of the EU there are common themes and approaches to employment and to industrial relations practice.

The UK is a notable exception to the European approach. The absence of explicit rights on employment issues differentiates the UK from much of the mainland. Successive governments from 1979 have actively pursued policies of deregulation and resisted European regulatory initiatives. This is particularly visible within the construction sector, where self-employment in the UK takes a form which would not be permissible in countries such as Germany or Belgium. The arrival of self-employed British construction workers on sites in Germany during the post-unification boom years in the early 1990s was not in itself a reflection of increased involvement by British contractors there. These self-employed workers were operating outside the collective agreements and legal framework of the German industry. Their presence contributed to complaints and, subsequently, to legislation to reinforce the regulated working conditions which have been traditional in Germany in the post-war years.

It is important that when senior managers are exploring the

possibility of contracts on the mainland of Europe, they are clear about the legal framework and the employment responsibilities with which they would be expected to operate. Organisations such as Incomes Data Services (IDS) provide a country-by-country analysis of these issues, which can be useful in setting such a context (see for example IDS, 1996b). It is also essential that managers who are being posted to an alternative location within Europe are conversant with the main principles within which they will be expected to operate – both with regard to the commercial contract and with respect to the employment contract of employees in the host country.

This is important with respect to European legislation, as well as in relation to laws of the individual member states. The decision by the British government to 'opt out' of European social policy commitments has meant that organisations which operate in Britain may have been unaffected by some European Directives. However, once an organisation establishes a base on the mainland of Europe, it is expected to comply with European standards and with all aspects of EU social policy. The European Directive on Consultation and Information for Employees, which was approved in 1994, for example, applies only to companies with 1,000 employees in Europe and 150 employees in two member states, excluding the UK. To date, no British construction firms have been affected, but a decision to expand employment on the European mainland (or a change of policy by the British government in favour of an 'opt in' to social policy commitments) could generate new responsibilities to comply.

One important initiative focuses particularly on the 'posted' worker – that is a worker who is required by his or her employer to relocate from one country to another. The free movement of labour is a fundamental principle of the European Union (EU), and workers have the right to move around in search of employment. Given the commitment of many governments as well as of employers and trade unions in Europe to the maintenance and observation of collective agreements or of national minimum standards on wages and working conditions, employers who cross frontiers must expect to observe the collective agreements as well as the laws of the countries in which they operate. This is a particularly sensitive issue in Germany because of the impact of migrant labour from Britain, as well as from central and eastern Europe.

The Posted Workers' Directive was introduced in the early

1990s in order to confront such problems. It seemed for some time that this initiative was doomed never to progress, and that legislation would be confined to the national level. In 1996 the Posted Workers' Directive was revived. It provides that employers who second or sub-contract their workers to work in another country, or labour agencies which send people to work in another member state, would be bound to observe the law of the host country in relation to pay and working conditions. This will include provision on wage rates and allowances, on hours of work, on annual leave entitlement, and on health and safety protection. It will also cover discrimination and protection of vulnerable groups, and temporary work.

Some of the difficulties in agreeing the terms of this Directive related to whether such terms should be applicable from the first day of a worker's employment in another country. There was discussion about exceptions where employees are engaged in a country for less than a month, or where employees were working on the installation of equipment supplied by their employer during the first eight days. An exception which is permitted for member states is where there are collective bargaining agreements which set minimum pay standards.

It will take time before the Directive is implemented in the national law of the EU member states, but it seems probable that it will be given effect before the end of the century.

In conclusion it must be said that this chapter only touches on some of the very important questions relating to the behaviour of construction organisations which work across international frontiers and the management of employees overseas. There is some evidence of change in practices within British-based firms, with movement away from traditional ethnocentric approaches in former British colonies towards arrangements which explore new markets on the basis of polycentrism, with scope for localised knowledge and experience to be brought into play. Planning and organisation are a prerequisite for overseas intervention. Cultural sensitivity and an informed appreciation of the diversity of national sociopolitical frameworks are also essential. There is an emergent literature in this area, but there remains a need for more focused research on the behaviour of British-based multi-national enterprises where these include construction as a significant part of their portfolio, both in terms of their strategy and in relation to people management.

LIST OF ABBREVIATIONS

ACAS	Advisory, Conciliation and Arbitration Service
AEEU	Amalgamated Engineering and Electrical Union
APC	Assessment of Professional Competence
APTC	Administrative, Professional, Technical and Clerical
BATJIC	Building and Allied Trades Joint Industrial Council
BEC	Building Employers' Confederation
BTEC	Business and Technology Education Council
CBI	Confederation of British Industry
CDM	Construction (Design and Management) Regulations, 1994
CECCB	Civil Engineering Construction Conciliation Board
CHSW	Construction (Health, Safety and Welfare) Regulations, 1996
CIB	Construction Industry Board
CIGLI	City and Guilds London Institute
CIOB	Chartered Institute of Building
CISC	Construction Industry Standing Conference
CITB	Construction Industry Training Board
CPD	Continuous Professional Development
CRE	Commission for Racial Equality
CSCS	Construction Skills Certification Scheme
DfEE	Department for Education and Employment
DOE	Department of the Environment
ECA	Electrical Contractors' Association
ECA(Scot)	Electrical Contractors' Association Scotland
ECIA	Engineering Construction Industry Association

EOC	Equal Opportunities Commission
FCEC	Federation of Civil Engineering Contractors
FMB	Federation of Master Builders
GMB	General, Municipal and Boilermakers Trade Union
GNVQ	General National Vocational Qualification
GSVQ	General Scottish Vocational Qualification
HASAWA	Health and Safety at Work Act
HRP	Human Resource Planning
HSE	Health and Safety Executive
HVCA	Heating and Ventilating Contractors' Association
IAM	Institute of Administrative Management
ICE	Institution of Civil Engineers
IDS	Incomes Data Services
IIP	Investors in People
IPD	Institute of Personnel and Development
JIB	Joint Industry Board
LEC	Local Enterprise Council
LFS	Labour Force Survey
LIFO	Last In, First Out
LOSC	Labour Only Sub-contractor(s)
MBO	Management By Objectives
MSF	Manufacturing, Science and Finance Union
NJCBI	National Joint Council for the Building Industry
NVQ	National Vocational Qualification
PAYE	Pay As You Earn
PFI	Private Finance Initiative
PBR	Payment By Results
PRP	Profit-Related Pay
RIBA	Royal Institute of British Architects
RICS	Royal Institution of Chartered Surveyors
RoSPA	Royal Society for the Prevention of Accidents
SAYE	Save As You Earn
SCOTVEC	Scottish Vocational Education Council
SVQ	Scottish Vocational Qualification
TEC	Training and Enterprise Council
TICA	Thermal Insulation Contractors' Association
TGWU	Transport and General Workers Union
UCATT	Union of Construction Allied Trades & Technicians
WAMT	Women and Manual Trades
WRA	Working Rule Agreement

REFERENCES

ADAMS J. S. (1965) 'Injustice in social exchange.' In Berkowitz (ed.), *Advances in Experimental Social Psychology.* Vol 2, New York, Academic Press.

ALDERFER C. P. (1972) *Existence, Relatedness and Growth.* London, Collier-Macmillan Ltd.

AGAPIOU A., PRICE A. AND MCCAFFER R. (1995a) 'Forecasting the supply of construction skills in the UK.' *Construction Management and Economics*, 13, 353–364.

AGAPIOU, A., PRICE, A.D.F., AND MCCAFFER, R. (1995b) 'Planning future construction skill requirements: understanding labour resource issues.' *Construction Management and Economics*, 13, 149–161.

ARMSTRONG M. AND MURLIS II. (1994) *Reward Management. A Handbook of Remuneration Strategy and Practice.* 3rd Ed. London, Kogan Page.

BALL, M. (1988) *Rebuilding construction.* London, Routledge.

BAUMGARTEN, K. 'Training and development of international staff.' In HARZING, A. AND RUYSSEVELDT, J.V. (eds) (1995) *International Human Resource Management.* London, Sage.

BEARDSWORTH, A.D., KEIL, E.T., BRESNAN, A. AND BRYMAN, A. (1988) 'Management, transcience and sub-contracting: the case of the construction site.' *Journal of Management Studies* 25 (6) November, 603–625.

BRESNAN M., WRAY K., BRYMAN A., BEARDSWORTH A., FORD, J. AND KEIL E. (1985) 'The flexibility of recruitment in the construction industry: formalisation or re-casualisation?' *Sociology*, Vol. 19, 108–124.

BREWSTER, C. (1991) *The Management of Expatriates.* Cranfield School of Management, monograph No. 5. London, Kogan Page.

CHILD J. (1984) *Organization. A Guide to Problems and Practice.* 2nd Ed. London, Harper & Row.

CITB (1994) *Proposals for The Construction Industry Training Scheme for Craft and Operative New Entrants.* Joint Action Group on New Entrant Training. Bircham Newton, CITB.

CLARKE L. AND WALL C. (1995) *Skills and the Construction Process. A comparative study of vocational training and quality in social housebuilding.* Bristol, The Policy Press.

COMMISSION FOR RACIAL EQUALITY (1995) *Building Equality. Report of a formal investigation into the Construction Industry Training Board,* 1995. London, Commission for Racial Equality.

CONSTRUCTION INDUSTRY BOARD (1995) *Equal Opportunities in the Construction Industry.* Interim report. Construction Industry Board Working group 8. London, Building Employers' Confederation.

CSCS (1995) Construction Skills Certification Scheme Booklet. May 1995. 2nd Ed.

DEPARTMENT OF EMPLOYMENT (1989 and 1994) *Employment Gazette.*

DEPARTMENT OF THE ENVIRONMENT (1995) Digest of data for the construction industry. 2nd Ed. London, HMSO.

DEPARTMENT OF THE ENVIRONMENT (1996) *Housing and Construction Statistics, 1984–94.* London, HMSO.

DRUCKER P. (1989) *The Practice of Management.* Heinemann.

DRUKER, J. AND MACALLAN, H. (1996) 'Work status and self-employment in the UK construction industry.' Small Business Research Trust monograph. Milton Keynes.

DRUKER, J. AND WHITE, G. (1995) 'Misunderstood and undervalued; personnel management in construction.' *Human Resource Management Journal*, 5 (3) (Spring), 77–91.

DRUKER, J., WHITE, G., HEGEWISCH, A. AND MAYNE, L. (1996) 'Between hard and soft human resource management.' *Construction Management and Economics*, 15 September.

DRUKER J. AND WHITE G. (1996) *Survey of Reward Practices in the Construction Industry.* London, University of Greenwich Business School.

EIU (1978) *Public ownership in the construction industries.* Economist Intelligence Unit.

EUROPEAN COMMISSION (c. 1993) *Strategies for the European construction sector.* Ch. 8.

FORD J., JEPSON M., BRYMAN A., KEIL T., BRESNEN M. AND BEARDSWORTH A. (1982) 'Management of recruitment in the construction industry.' *International Journal of Project Management*, 1 (2), 76–82.

FRYER B. (1990) *The Practice of Construction Management*. 2nd Ed. Oxford, BSP Professional Books.

GREED C. (1991) *Surveying Sisters. Women in a Traditional Male Profession*. London, Routledge.

GUEST, D. (1989) 'Personnel and human resource management: can you tell the difference?' *Personnel Management*, 21 (1) 48–51.

GUEST, D. (1987) 'Human resource management and industrial relations.' *Journal of Management Studies*, 24 (5) September, 503–521.

GUEST, D. (1990) 'HRM and the American Dream.' *Journal of Management Studies*, 27 (4) July, 377–397.

GUIRDHAM, M. (1990) *Interpersonal Skills at Work*. London, Prentice Hall.

HANDY, C. (1985) *Understanding Organisations*. 3rd Ed. London, Penguin Books.

HARRISON R. (1992a) *Employee Development*. London, IPD.

HARRISON R. (1992b) 'Employee Development at Barratt.' In WINSTANLEY D. AND WOODALL J. *Case Studies in Personnel*. London, IPD.

HATCHETT M. (1992) *Construction Craft Supervision*. London, Batsford (in association with the CIOB).

HEALTH AND SAFETY COMMISSION (1995) *Health and Safety Statistics 1994/5*. London, HMSO.

HEALTH AND SAFETY COMMISSION/CONSTRUCTION INDUSTRY ADVISORY COMMITTEE (1995). *A Guide to Managing Health and Safety in Construction*. London, HMSO.

HEALTH AND SAFETY EXECUTIVE (HSE) (1995a) *Health and Safety for Small Construction Sites*. Sudbury, Suffolk, HSE Books.

HEALTH AND SAFETY EXECUTIVE (1996) *A Guide to the Construction (Health, Safety and Welfare) Regulations, 1996*. London, HSE.

HEALTH AND SAFETY EXECUTIVE (undated) *The Costs to the British Economy of Work Accidents and Work-related Ill Health*. London, HMSO.

HENDRY, C. (1995) *Human Resource Management: A strategic approach to employment*. London, Butterworth Heinemann.

HERZBERG F. *et al* (1959) *The Motivation to Work*. New York, John Wiley.

HILLEBRANDT, P. M. AND CANNON, J. (1990) *The Modern Construction Firm*. London, Macmillan.

245

HOFSTEDE, G. (1980) *Culture's Consequences*. London, Sage.

INCOMES DATA SSERVICES (IDS) (1993) *Investors In People*. IDS Study No 530, May.

INCOMES DATA SERVICES (IDS) (1995) *Profit Sharing and Share Options*. IDS Study 583, August 1995.

INCOMES DATA SERVICES (IDS) (1996) *Profit Related Pay*. IDS Study 603, June 1996.

INCOMES DATA SERVICES (1996b) *Pay and Conditions in Germany*. London, IDS International Documents.

INDUSTRIAL RELATIONS LAW REPORTS 1995: 493. Lane v. Shire Roofing Company (Oxford) Ltd.

INDUSTRIAL RELATIONS SERVICES (1996) *Industrial Relations Law Bulletin: Consultation on redundancies and business transfers*. February. 2–13.

INDUSTRIAL SOCIETY (1985) *Survey of Training Costs*. London, The Industrial Society.

JOYCE, R. (1995) *The CDM Regulations Explained*. London, Thomas Telford publications.

KENNEY, J. AND REID, M. (1988) Training Interventions. 2nd Ed. IPM, London; 5th Ed. (1996), by REID M. AND BARRINGTON H. London, IPD. Labour Market Trends, 1996.

LANGFORD D., HANCOCK M. R., FELLOWS R. AND GALE A. W. (1995) *Human Resources Management in Construction*. Longman.

LANGFORD D. AND NEWCOMBE R. (1992) 'Management Development in Construction.' In *Management Education and Development*, 18 (3), 223–243.

LATHAM, M. (1994) *Constructing the Team; Joint review of procurement and contractual arrangements in the UK construction industry*. Department of the Environment. London, HMSO.

LAWLER E. E. (1990) Strategic Pay. San Francisco, Jossey Bass.

LEWIS P. (1992) *Practical Employment Law*. Oxford, Blackwell.

LOCKE E. A. (1968) 'Towards a Theory of Task Motivation and Incentives'. *Organizational Behaviour and Human Performance*, Vol. 3, 157–89.

LORD A. (1992) 'Career development and matrix management at Joiner Construction.' In WINSTANLEY D. AND WOODALL J., *Case Studies in Personnel*. London, IPD.

MASLOW A. H. (1954) *Motivation and Personality*. New York, Harper and Row.

MACGREGOR D. (1960) *The Human Side of Enterprise*. New York, McGraw-Hill.

MPHAKE J. (1989) 'Management Development in Construction.' In *Management Education and Development*, 18 (3), 223–243.

PERLMUTTER, H.V. AND HEENAn, D.A. (1974) 'How multinational should your top managers be?' *Harvard Business Review*, November/December, 52, 121–132.

PETERS, T. AND AUSTIN, N. (1985) *A Passion for Excellence: The leadership difference*. Glasgow, William Collins.

PETERS, T. AND WATERMAN, R. (1982) *In Search of Excellence: Lessons from America's best-run companies*. New York, Harper and Row.

PHELPS BROWN, E.H. (1968) *Report of the Committee of Inquiry into certain matters concerning labour in building and civil engineering*. Cmnd 3714. London, HMSO.

PORTER I. W. AND LAWLER E. E. (1968) *Managerial Attitudes and Performance*. Irwin.

SCULLION, H. (1992) 'Strategic recruitment and development of the "international manager": some European considerations.' *Human Resource Management Journal*, 3 (1) Autumn 1992, 57–69.

SCHUSTER J. R. AND ZINGHEIM P. K. (1992) *The New Pay. Linking employee and organizational performance*. New York, Lexington Books.

STOREY, J. AND SISSON, K. (1990) 'Limits to transformation. Human resource management in the British context. *Industrial Relations Journal*, 21 (1), 60–65.

STOREY, J. (1992) *Developments in the Management of Human Resources*. Oxford, Blackwell.

TORRINGTON, D. (1994) *International Human Resource Management: Think globally, act locally*. Hemel Hempstead, Prentice Hall.

TORRINGTON, D; HALL, L.; HAYLOR, I. AND MYERS, J. (1991) 'Employee Resourcing.' *Management Studies* No. 2. London, Institute of Personnel Management.

TORRINGTON, D. AND HALL, L. (1995) *Personnel Management: HRM in Action*. London, Prentice Hall.

VROOM V. (1964) *Work and Motivation*. New York, John Wiley.

WILLIAMS, A., DOBSON, P. AND WALTERS, M. (1989) *Changing Culture*. London, IPM.

WINCH, G. (1994) 'The search for flexibility: the case of the construction industry.' *Work, Employment and Society*, Vol. 8 (4) December, 593–606.

WOMEN AND MANUAL TRADES (1995) LYLE, I. Submission to working group 8, Latham Review Implementation Forum. London, WAMT.

YOUNG B. (1990) 'An integrated approach to career development in the construction industry.' Occasional Paper No.41. Chartered Institute of Building.

YOUNG, B., (1991) 'Reasons for changing jobs within a career structure.' *Leadership and Organisation Development Journal*, 12 (1), 12–16.

USEFUL ADDRESSES

Advisory, Conciliation and Arbitration Service (ACAS)
Head Office
180 Borough High Street
London SE9 1LW

Amalgamated Engineering and Electrical Union
110 Peckham Road
London SE15 5EL

Building Employers Confederation
82 New Cavendish Street
London W1M 8AD

The Centre for International Briefing
The Castle
Farnham
Surrey GU9 OAG

Chartered Institute of Building
Englemere
Kings Ride
Ascot
Berks. SL5 7TB

Commission for Racial Equality
Elliott House
10/12 Allington Street
London SW1E 5EH

Construction Group of Personnel Managers
c/o Secretary, Lea Rig

Hitcham Road
Burnham
Bucks. SL1 7DX

Construction Industry Training Board
Head Office
Bircham Newton Training Centre
Bircham Newton
Nr Kings Lynn
Norfolk PE31 6RH

Construction Industry Training Board
Administrative Offices
Hillgate House
8th Floor
26 Old Bailey
London EC4M 7QA

Electrical Contractors' Association
34 Palace Court
London W2 4HY

Employment Conditions Abroad
Anchor House
15 Britten Street
London SW3 3TY

Engineering Construction Industry Association
17 Dartmouth Street
London SW1H 9BL
Tel: 0171 799 2000

Engineering Construction Industry National Joint Council
Walmar House
6th Floor, 296 Regent Street
London W1R 5HB
Tel: 0171 636 6291; Fax 0171 323 3402

Equal Opportunities Commission
Overseas House
Quay Street
Manchester M3 3HN
Tel: 0161 833 9244

European Federation of Building and Woodworkers
Rue Royale 45
1000 Brussels
Belgium

Federation of Civil Engineering Contractors
Cowdray House
6 Portugal Street
London WC2A 2HJ
Tel: 0171 404 4020

Federation of Master Builders
Gordon Fisher House
14/15 Great James Street
London WC1N 3DP

FIEC (European Construction Employers' Federation)
Fédération de l'Industrie
Avenue Louise 66
1050 Bruxelles
Belgium

GMB (General and Municipal Union)
22–24 Worple Road
London SW19 4DD

Health and Safety Executive
1 Long Lane
London SE1 4PG

Heating and Ventilating Contractors' Association
Esca House
34 Palace Court
Bayswater
London W2 4JG

Incomes Data Services
193 St John Street
London EC1V 4LS

Institute of Personnel and Development
IPD House
35 Camp Road
Wimbledon SW19 4UX

Institution of Civil Engineers,
9 Great George Street
London SW1P 3AA

Manufacturing Science and Finance
33–37 Moreland Street
London EC1V 8BB

National Joint Council for the Engineering Construction Industry
Walmar House
6th Floor, 296 Regent Street
London W1R 5HB

RIBA (Royal Institute of British Architects)
66 Portland Place
London W1N 4AD

RICS (Royal Institution of Chartered Surveyors)
12 Great George Street
London SW1P 3AD

RoSPA (Royal Society for the Prevention of Accidents)
Head Office
Edgbaston Park
353 Bristol Road
Birmingham
B5 7ST

Transport and General Workers Union
16 Palace Street
Victoria
London SW1E 5JD

UCATT,
177 Abbeville road
London SW4 9RL

Women and Manual Trades
52/54 Featherstone Street
London EC1Y 8RT

INDEX

INDEX

labour needs analysis 46
labour-only sub-contractors (LOSC)
10, 33, 52
    involvement in training 111
labour supply forecasting 28
labour turnover 24, 26, 33, 45
Laing Engineering 138
Lane v. *Shire Roofing Company
(1995)* 39–40
language skills, expatriates 230, 237
leadership, of groups 160–61
learning organisations 114–15
letters of appointment 60
levies for training 97, 100
LIFO rule 170
local authorities
    construction activities 12
    direct labour organisations 3, 12,
    96
    health and safety enforcement
    204, 206
'lump' labour *see* self-employed
labour

management by objectives (MBO) 73
management development 116,
133–5, 139
    at Shepherd Construction 144
management of change *see* change
management
managerial workforce, human
    resource planning 24–7
manpower planning *see* human
resource planning
Mansell 9
manual workers
    benefits 68–9, 90–91, 92–3
    earnings 69, 87
    grading systems 76
    job evaluation 76
    motivation 72
    pay systems 64, 65, 66, 67, 68,
    69, 81–2, 86
    recruitment and selection 44–6,
    52
    testing 57–8
    training 95–112
    see also craft workers; operative
    workers
Manufacturing Science and Finance

(MSF) 180, 188
Maslow, A.H. 71, 72
maternity pay 91, 92
mentoring 156–7
mergers 8, 223
misconduct *see* disciplinary
    procedures; gross misconduct
mobility
    manual workers 29, 31–2, 33
    professional staff 26, 27
Modern Apprenticeships 23, 104,
110
motivation 7, 65, 70–75
Mowlem Training (case-study) 112
multi-national contractors 222–4
multi-national enterprises, resourc-
    ing policies 225

national collective agreements 61,
65, 68, 69, 178–81, 191–2
    disciplinary procedures 166
    grievance procedures 162
national collective bargaining 64, 68,
86, 181–8
national cultural differences 228,
230, 237
National Federation of Builders 183
National Insurance payments 34, 39,
61
    expatriates 234
National Vocational Qualifications
76, 95, 99, 101–4
    see also standards for construc-
    tion
National Working Rules *see* national
    collective agreements
networking 32, 52
'New Pay' systems 67
non-manual staff
    benefits 91, 92–3
    earnings 69, 87
    grading systems 76, 79
    job evaluation 76
    pay systems 64, 65, 67, 70, 82,
    85, 86
    training and development 113–39

objectives, cascading of 158
    see also targets
occupational health problems 202

257